THE ROADS
TO TRUTH

THE ROADS

TO TRUTH

In Search of New Thought's Roots

Sherry Evans

Northern Lights Publications
Park City, Utah

Printed and bound in the United States of America

ISBN Number: 0-9763630-0-3
Library of Congress Control Number: 2004099009

ATTENTION UNIVERSITIES, COLLEGES, CHURCHES, AND PROFESSIONAL ORGANIZATIONS: Quantity discounts are available on bulk purchases of this book for educational, gift purposes, or as premiums for increasing magazine subscriptions or renewals. Special books or book excerpts can also be created to fit specific needs. For information please contact:

Northern Lights Publications
P.O. Box 682435
Park City, UT 84068
(435) 940-1646

www.NLPubls.com

*For all those whose thoughts, words and deeds
brought me to this moment in time*

ACKNOWLEDGMENTS

Inasmuch as this book is a work of fact, I have relied heavily on the historical, philosophical, scientific, and religious sources listed in the Bibliography for the facts and concepts presented herein.

This book likely would not exist if I had not attended the classes of Rev. Jill Carl. I credit her thought-provoking questions and passionate love of this philosophy with propelling me down this path.

I wish to thank those who so willingly offered their time to read and critique my manuscript: Linda Howard, Chris Evans, Edy Roberts, Sara Rose, Chris and Katie Sodermark, and Gayla Orton; the talented Stephanie Evans for the use of her fabulous photographs and Chris Evans for his splendid cover design.

I also wish to thank my friends and family who so patiently listened as I incessantly spoke about the research and writing of this book.

CONTENTS

INTRODUCTION

I first encountered New Thought, though I didn't know it by that term, almost twenty years ago during a particularly depressing period of my life. A friend gave me some audio tapes that were intended to pick up my spirits. I listened to them repeatedly during my daily walks to my university classes and gradually integrated into my psyche the ideas presented. Among many other things, the tapes taught me that the only limits are the ones I impose on myself and that my inner thoughts play an integral role in my outer experience. As it dawned on me that I alone was responsible for my moods, my despondency began to lift. In time, I became aware that my daily regimen was strengthening and healing both my soul and body.

At that point I had been on what I called *My Quest* for several years. Consumed with finding the truth about God, I enrolled in a philosophy class called "Faith and Reason," an exploration of the philosophical arguments for and against the existence of God. I had no inkling of the chaos this choice would produce in my soul.

Having difficulty early in the quarter with an assigned paper, I arranged to speak to my professor. To my comment concerning a belief in God he incredulously responded, "You still believe in God? Why?" I was not sure what to say. I went home and began to think. I had often questioned the truth of different religions but had never questioned the truth of God. Why? I suppose it was because I grew up with God. There was never a time that I wasn't exposed to the truth of the existence of God. I realized the importance of questioning this belief. In fact, it was imperative that I question where this belief came from and why I believed. At that point I made the philosophically-skeptical move of suspending all my beliefs about God.

I truly no longer knew if there was a God, but, as do all rigorous skeptics, I continued to question. I spent about a month in this skeptical place, searching my soul, my mind and my memory. I remembered incidents from the distant past—times when I felt I had received answers to my prayers and more recently, when I believed that God had carried me because I hadn't had strength of my own to sustain me. I decided that yes, there is a God, but I realized that I no longer had a belief as to exactly what God is. I could no longer accept a God who set up a narrow way that few are able to find, as the Bible says and as many religions teach, and then sentences to hell, purgatory or a lower kingdom of heaven those who do not find it. I could not accept a vengeful, angry God so easily hurt by his children's mistakes (sins) that he would punish them with everlasting damnation. I could, however, accept a loving God who cares about his children, and gently guides them, talks to them, listens to them, and provides for their needs. A God who would joyously welcome them back into its presence.

It was clear that this God was not the God taught in the various Christian churches I had attended. As I no longer felt connected to the people or the teachings of the church I had been attending, I was for the first time in my life without a church and a religion. But I did have God. I put church behind me and withdrew into my college studies.

I spent the next 18 months or so focusing on school, my social relationships, my children, and my psyche. As I processed what I believed about God and organized religion, I became increasingly convinced that somehow God and humanity are integrally connected. My Quest then became one of finding the truth about that connection.

During this time a college friend invited me to visit his church, and I accepted. I went with him a few times, but while I enjoyed the messages, the service as a whole lacked the spirit and life I had felt at the evangelical churches I had attended. During one service the guest speaker, a minister at our city's sole African-American Baptist church, invited the congregation to visit. My friend and I accepted that offer, and, along with my daughter, found ourselves the only white people in attendance. It was just like I had seen in the movies—lots of beautiful voices joyfully singing songs of praise to Jesus and audience participation by way of numerous shouts of "Amen brother!" Though I enjoyed the service, I felt like an outsider and could not see myself attending on a regular basis. I again felt a familiar disillusionment, and so once more I put church into the back of my mind. It wasn't long, though, before the song of the Eternal Voice that Ernest Holmes speaks of began echoing loudly through my being. My spiritual life again became my priority.

It was now 1990. I was completing a degree in philosophy and had a wide range of classes from which to pick. I have no memory of what prompted me to sign up for a class on Taoism. In retrospect, I credit inspiration, for the resonance I felt with this philosophy stimulated me to continue my Quest for God, eventually leading me to New Thought.

I began questioning again and was consumed with knowing the truth about God and about my relationship to God. Is there a God? If so, is God a He, a She, or an It? the Universe, an energy, or The Force of *Star Wars*? Is there more than one God? Is God personal or impersonal? What are the characteristics of God? Does God care about me, about the people of our world, about the world itself? If so, how can He/She/It allow such horrible things to take place? If God created everything that exists and God is Love, then how can evil exist? Who was I? How did I fit into the scheme of things? Was I a child of God, in the sense that God is my Father in Heaven? Was I just one of God's myriad creations, one of the ten thousand things, as taught in Taoism, or did I evolve from lower forms as Darwin thought?

Being without a church or support group for a couple of years had been acceptable, but sometime during the summer of 1990, I became aware that a listlessness had been building for some time and determined it was a symptom of an inner emptiness. There seemed to be a spiritual hole in me that badly needed filling. At times I missed the spirit and the atmosphere of my previous church, but as I no longer accepted their fundamentalist teachings, I knew that I would not feel comfortable attending.

So, I decided to go church shopping. Because of the radical changes I had made in my beliefs, I was certain that no traditional Christian church would fill my needs. I also was fairly certain I would not find a church that taught Taoism but hoped to find something I could resonate with in some way. I got out the Yellow Pages and began looking through the listings. I ran across the name of a church I had never heard of before—the Church of Religious Science—and called the number listed. I asked the man who answered if the church was a Christian church and what they believed. I became progressively excited as he answered my many questions, for he described exactly what I, through my many studies, had come to believe. I had again encountered New Thought.

Over the next twelve years I attended several different New Thought churches on a regular basis and read numerous books of a New Thought bent. After studying these numerous works and attending classes at one of the churches, I became increasingly interested in the origin of New Thought's various principles. To my mind, a church needs to be based on some sort of authority. The New Thought churches I attended were not Christian per se, though they talked about God and Jesus. But it was a different kind of God and a different Jesus than had been taught to me in the Bible-based churches I had attended in the past. Since the theology of New Thought, if it can be called such, was so different than that of these mainstream churches, I wondered on what authority they based their beliefs. It felt like truth. It felt good in my head and in my heart. Still, I needed to know from where and from whom these ideas came.

I could readily see that some of their teachings were of a Christian bent, and I recognized from my college years that many New Thought ideas parallel the views of various Western philosophers, both ancient and modern. Having written my Master's thesis on Taoism and Zen Buddhism, I also recognized that New Thought contains some Eastern ideas. The origins of some principles of New Thought were unknown to me, though, and after launching my search, I discovered them in various Western philosophies and in the one major Eastern philosophy I had not yet studied—Hinduism. I found some in the pioneering work of Phineas Parkhurst Quimby in the field of mental healing. Most surprising of all, I found that many were actually Bible-based.

Inasmuch as all of these philosophies are old—Hinduism being as old as twelve thousand years—New Thought definitely is not new. So why is it called *New* Thought? The search for the answer to that question took me to nineteenth century American history, specifically to the history of New England, and the beginnings of a movement known as Transcendentalism, the first American philosophy. While the term *Transcendentalism* is unfamiliar to most, many recognize the names of the two most famous transcendentalists—Ralph Waldo Emerson and Henry David Thoreau. Even if one doesn't know that it was Thoreau who said it, the notion of marching to the beat of a different drummer is likely a familiar one.

Transcendentalism played a huge role in the development of New Thought, especially the forms known as Unity and Religious Science, whose founders were profoundly influenced by Emerson. My years of research also turned up connections with Idealism, a philosophy espoused by such notable minds as Plato, Socrates, Pythagorus, Rene Descartes, and many others who are generally unknown outside of philosophical circles.

One of the first New Thought writers, Warren Felt Evans, refers to many other philosophers, mystics and esoteric philosophies in his writings. Ernest Holmes, founder of Religious Science, and Charles Fillmore, cofounder of Unity, the two largest New Thought groups in existence today, consider their philosophies to be syntheses of the many truths contained in the world's philosophies.

All the many minds of these various philosophies espouse what the German philosopher Gottfried Leibniz calls *philosophia perennis* —the perennial philosophy—which, according to Aldous Huxley, is immemorial and universal. He defines the perennial philosophy as

> the metaphysic that recognizes a divine Reality substantial to the world of things and lives and minds; the psychology that finds in the soul something similar to, or even identical with, divine Reality; the ethic that places man's final end in the knowledge of the immanent and transcendent Ground of all being. The Perennial Philosophy is primarily concerned with the one, divine Reality substantial to the manifold world of things and lives and minds. But the nature of this one Reality is such that it cannot be directly and immediately apprehended except by those who have chosen to fulfill certain conditions, making themselves loving, pure in heart, and poor in spirit.

The teachings of the many minds that make up the perennial philosophy, which I believe forms the basis of New Thought, are studied in depth in the chapters that follow.

Chapter two discusses what New Thought is, why it is considered to be scientific, whether or not it is Christian, and how it got its name. Chapter three discusses the founders of the three main New Thought groups, how these groups came to be formed, and what they believe. The reader who is familiar with New Thought philosophy may wish to read chapter one, which sets out historical, psychological and philosophical background to New Thought, and then skip to chapter four, which should be read before any of the later chapters. Each succeeding chapter follows one of the roads that the founders of the New Thought philosophy traveled in developing their philosophies. Chapter thirteen looks at the many laws that New Thought encompasses, and chapter fourteen discusses specifically the perennial philosophy and its connection with science and New Thought.

Inasmuch as many of the minds we visit on this journey taught the same or very similar concepts, these concepts are discussed in detail in the beginning but are touched on only briefly later in our journey. This is not because one mind is more important than another, but because I do not wish to bore the reader with repetitive themes.

The writing of this book entailed massive amounts of research. I undertook this endeavor for my own knowledge and interest, and have not followed the commonly-accepted practice of using endnotes, mainly because I find them extremely irritating. Instead, I have noted the author or work within the chapter text and provided a complete bibliography of source materials at the back of this book.

I.

A SHORT JAUNT
THROUGH HISTORY

History goes out of control almost as often as nature does.
Mason Cooley (b. 1927), U.S. aphorist

Before beginning our journey through New Thought, I feel it helpful to lay out some background information and to put into perspective the world to which New Thought was born. What follows is a brief summary of the tumultuous nineteenth century and the first three decades of the twentieth century, mainly as it affects America, as that is when and where New Thought was born.

At the close of New Thought's formative years, all of the current states had been admitted to the Union except Alaska and Hawaii. But at the beginning, there were only the original thirteen colonies plus Tennessee, Kentucky, and Vermont. In fact, at the beginning of the nineteenth century the United States had existed as an entity for only twenty-four years.

The social, political and economic climate of the nineteenth century can be expressed by one word—conflict. The progress made in science, technology and medicine brought tremendous changes to the Western world. Such massive change resulted in increased materialism, poverty, prostitution and crime. In spite of, or perhaps because of, scientific erosion of long-held religious beliefs, numerous movements and religions formed.

In Europe at the beginning of the century, Robespierre's reign of terror and the ensuing revolution in France had just ended. Napoleon ruled France and most of the German states. Upon his abdication in 1814, the Congress of Vienna divided his kingdom into thirty-nine independent states. England and Ireland united, forming the United Kingdom. The British began populating northern Ireland, leading to life-changing discontent among the Irish.

By the 1820s more than 100,000 Irish had immigrated to the United States. Ireland's potato crop failure in 1845 further stimulated immigration, and by the end of the century 1.5 million had left Ireland. Victoria became Queen of England in 1837, commencing the reign of the Windsors, who are still in power today. Mid-century, widespread crop failures and failed revolutions precipitated the immigration of more than one million Germans.

In America the focus turned from revolution to expansion, exploration and industrialization. It was the time of Manifest Destiny and Lewis and Clark's famous trip west to find a route to the Pacific Ocean. With the purchase of the Louisiana Territory and the acquisition of Florida and Texas, adventurous Easterners began migrating south and west. Wagon trains west reached their peak in the 1840s. The discovery of gold at Sutter's Mill in California and Pikes Peak in Colorado and of silver at Virginia City, Nevada in the 1850s further stimulated migration.

Small proprietors with their handmade goods were being edged out of the market by businesses with technologically-advanced machinery that mass-produced goods, often at a lower price than small proprietors could offer. The vast numbers of workers required by these large factories resulted in a rapid growth of urban cities and decreased rural farm populations.

The capitalism and materialism that rankled the transcendentalists, and later the socialists, escalated and with it the push for private ownership of property, a free market economy, resistence to government interference, and a focus on profit rather than worker safety and satisfaction.

During the first two decades of the century new modes of transportation developed. While the West utilized horse-drawn wagons, stagecoaches and horses, the East relied on horse-drawn carriages and steamboats. Railroads developed in the East during the 1820s, spreading gradually westward. In 1869 when the transatlantic railroad connecting the east coast to the west coast was completed, it became the dominant mode of transportation throughout the remainder of the century. Mid-century, cable cars began running in San Francisco and the first American bicycles were manufactured. The last two decades of the century brought electric trolley lines, elevated railways, subways, and for the affluent, electrically-powered and gasoline-powered cars.

New and improved means of communication emerged. Lead pencils and fountain and ballpoint pens were manufactured; improvements in the printing press resulted in mass-circulation daily newspapers; Morse code was developed for use with the newly completed telegraph. The second half of the century brought the transatlantic cable, typewriters, Dictaphones, and telephones. The Pony Express began mail delivery in 1860, running between St. Joseph, Missouri and Sacramento, California.

In the early decades of this century, Phineas Parkhurst Quimby performed his experiments with mesmerism and Transcendentalism moved through New England without benefit of telephones, light bulbs or vehicles. The telegraph was the only means of long-distance communication, railroads were in their infancy, and wagon trains moved adventurous souls out to the "Wild West." New religions formed as the Industrial Revolution radically changed society.

Philosophers switched focus from the rigidly intellectual to the passionately emotional. The rise of the Romantic movement in Europe put an end to the Enlightenment (also known as the Age of Reason) and to the Cartesian-Newtonian world view, which exulted the harmonious order of nature and the emotional and intellectual uniformity of people. The new romantic movement no longer viewed the world and its inhabitants as operating like machines. It stressed emotion, intuition and individual uniqueness over reason, logic and social conformity. A belief in humanity's ability to better itself developed from this shift in thought, producing many efforts at social reform.

An antislavery society had been formed in New England by the Quakers in the late 1700s, and when Romanticism came to America just as the slavery issue escalated, increasing numbers of people began taking up the abolitionists' position. A political party formed in opposition to slavery, and numerous abolitionist newspapers and speakers spread word of slavery's evils throughout the country. The American Colonization Society formed in order to buy slaves, free them and then send them to a colony on the west coast of Africa named Liberia, from the Latin word for "free," that had been purchased for this purpose.

Shipping the former slaves proved costly, but the Society managed to send several thousand before lack of finances forced them to disband.

Reformers lobbied for improved educational opportunities for African-American children and higher educational opportunities for all women. They insisted that schoolbooks be written in uniform common speech and founded colleges that accepted women. Schools for people with physical disabilities and hospitals for those with mental illnesses were organized. They established local public libraries and state boards of health, and saw that prison conditions were improved.

Because the use of alcohol was linked to crime, poverty and illness, a temperance organization was founded in 1826. Prohibition eventually became the law, though not until 1919 and only until 1933.

As part of the spirit of perfectionism a number of groups founded utopian communities between 1805 and 1864. Ranging from celibate to polygamous and secular to religious, the groups focused on community, shared goods and common ownership of property. Though none of these groups achieved long-term success, their influence is still felt today. The Shakers provide well-crafted furniture. The Oneida community's silver company still produces quality silverware. The Amana colonies continue to manufacture kitchen appliances. And the Mormon communal experiment evolved into one of today's fastest-growing churches.

Socialist philosophies advocated by Karl Marx and Friedrich Engels became popular, mainly in Europe. In 1848 they wrote the *Communist Manifesto* from which came socialism and communism. Both systems are similar, as both advocate elimination of private property and collectivization of goods. Theoretically, however, in socialism the government or state controls property and provides programs for collectivization while in communism there is no state or government, and all goods and property are distributed equally among the people. Ironically, the American religious communes mentioned in the previous paragraph operated similarly to the atheistic communism proposed by Marx and Engels.

In the mid-1800s while Quimby formed the ideas about mental healing that later became associated with New Thought, the government fought wars with the Native Americans over the appropriation of their lands and their removal to reservations. Harriet Tubman escaped slavery and began conducting other slaves to freedom with the help of the Underground Railroad. Harriet Beecher Stowe published her antislavery novel *Uncle Tom's Cabin*. With the exception of James Polk all of the presidents of the United States—William Henry Harrison, John Tyler, Zachary Taylor, and Millard Fillmore—were members of the Whig Party. The Supreme Court held that African-Americans are not citizens. The first American woman received a medical degree and subsequently opened the first hospital staffed solely by women. Industrialization dominated the workforce, and immigrants poured into the country. Samuel Colt invented the revolver. Charles Darwin published his theory of evolution. The Civil War raged. And water closets in private homes moved indoors, though they didn't warrant a separate room until late in the century.

By the time the founders of the earliest New Thought groups —Divine Science and Unity—began writing and teaching in the decades after the Civil War, the Fifteenth Amendment had been added to the Bill of Rights giving all men the right to vote. That right wasn't given to women for another 50 years, though the suffragist movement actively lobbied during the last decades of the century. America and Canada agreed to divide their countries into four time zones. The Indian wars ended with the massacre at Wounded Knee Creek in the Dakota Territory. Clara Barton formed the American Red Cross, Daniel Williams performed the world's first open-heart surgery, and researchers isolated the bacterium responsible for pneumonia. Montgomery Ward, the first mail-order company, began operating, and Thomas Edison, the Wizard of Menlo Park, had patented most of his one thousand inventions.

During the last few decades of the century inventors developed many products that made life a little easier and more pleasant. Among those products were steel plows (which were new to America but which had been in use in China for three thousand years), vulcanized rubber, sewing machines, passenger elevators, escalators, electric street lights, phonographs, incandescent electric lamps, Kodak's first photographic cameras, sound cameras, and movie projectors. Levi Straus began making sturdy denim clothing for the miners, which eventually made its way to the general public. The first successful computer—a punched-card tabulating machine—was developed toward the end of the century. And let's not forget chewing gum, the safety razor, and saccharine, the first sugar substitute.

Encouraged by Romanticism, brothers Jakob and Wilhelm Grimm collected stories and fairy tales and published them in three volumes in 1812, 1815 and 1822. Other influential artists, writers, and musician/composers of this time period include Claude Monet, Paul Gaugin, Vincent van Gogh, Washington Irving, Nathaniel Hawthorne, James Fenimore Cooper, John Greenleaf Whittier, Henry Wadsworth Longfellow, Herman Melville, Mark Twain, Edgar Allan Poe, Henry James, Ralph Waldo Emerson, Henry David Thoreau, Walt Whitman, Louisa May Alcott, Henri Ibsen, Emily Dickinson, Charles Dickens, Thomas Hardy, William Wordsworth, George Bernard Shaw, Samuel Taylor Coleridge, Thomas Carlyle, Gustav Flaubert, Anton Chekhov, Fyodor Dostoevsky, Stephen Foster, John Philip Sousa, Frederic Chopin, Peter Tchaikovsky, Claude Debussy, Johannes Brahms, Richard Wagner, and Johann Strauss.

The last founder of the major New Thought groups, Ernest Holmes, began writing and teaching at the end of the second decade of the twentieth century. Much had changed in the thirty years since the founding of the first groups. Holmes witnessed the mass production of automobiles, the development of airplanes and rocket motors, taxi service, motorized buses, and the first motorcycle—the Harley-Davidson; and radio, long-distance and overseas telephone and teletype communication. Only the affluent could afford long distance telephone service, for a three-minute call from Denver to New York City cost more than an average worker's weekly wage.

At the beginning of the twentieth century nine out of ten adults could read or write, though only six percent had graduated from high school. The average wage was 22 cents an hour, and the average worker earned $200 to $400 per year. Professionals such as accountants, dentists, veterinarians, and engineers earned between $1500 and $5,000 per year. Eighteen percent of all households employed at least one full-time servant or domestic.

The average American could expect to live 47 years. Tuberculosis, influenza, pneumonia, diarrhea, heart disease, and stroke were the leading causes of death. Most births took place at home. Ninety percent of all physicians had no college education. Instead, they attended medical schools, many of which were considered to be substandard. Marijuana, heroin and morphine were legal drugs and could be obtained without prescription at drugstores because they were considered helpful for the complexion, the mind, the stomach, and the bowels.

Most urban houses contained electric lights, and indoor plumbing had vastly improved. Fourteen percent of homes had a bathtub, though just eight percent contained a telephone. These conveniences, however, had yet to make it to many rural locales.

Moving pictures and cartoons appeared along with theaters in which to view them. Eight thousand cars traveled on but 144 miles of paved roads at a posted speed limit, in most cities, of 10 mph.

The Nineteenth Amendment finally gave women the right to vote. Child labor laws, along with compulsory education laws, eliminated the practice of working young children from sunrise to sunset.

But the areas of advancement that are of most importance to our journey are those in science, philosophy and psychology.

During the nineteenth century the focus of science in America had been on practical applications resulting in thousands of inventions. World War I changed that focus. Between 1910 and 1920 American physicists devoted themselves to attracting students to theoretical physics. In fact, some felt that it was of national security to do so. Their efforts paid off, and by 1930 degrees in physics nearly tripled. The leading physicists, who for the most part were European, began taking positions in American universities, partly because of the rising Nazi/Jew problems. Increases in astronomical capabilities produced proof that the universe is expanding, and the last and furthest planet, Pluto, was discovered.

With the help of Albert Einstein's theories of relativity and Max Planck's work concerning light particles, the laws of nature developed by Isaac Newton in the 1700s during the Scientific Revolution were gradually dismissed. Scientists discovered progressively smaller particles known as subatomic particles existing in an unpredictable and changeable environment. The quantum world revealed itself to be a world in which Newton's laws did not hold.

The Romanticism that emerged in reaction to the Scientific Revolution changed the view of matter. Humans no longer consisted of dead, mechanical matter. Rather, they contained a vital and purposive substance able to grow and improve with time. This was evolution but a form of evolution very different from that of Darwin's random selection.

Nineteenth century Romanticism provided several concepts important for psychology and for the study of New Thought. The aim of psychology, from its beginnings in the works of Plato to the present time, is epistemological—to discover how the human mind receives and formulates knowledge. Romanticists felt the proper use of the mind's analytic abilities was sentient. Since they viewed the unconscious (the subjective and passionate) as more important than the conscious (the objective and rational), they produced philosophy, literature and art intended to evoke emotional response.

Romanticism influenced three late-eighteenth century theories of psychology important to our study: 1) Jean-Baptiste Lamarck's naturalistic psychology—an evolutionary theory that states that organic and inorganic matter are fundamentally different; that organic, or living, matter possesses an innate drive to perfect itself; and that it strives to adapt itself to its surroundings, changing itself in the process; 2) Franz Anton Mesmer's mesmerism, now called hypnosis, with which he invoked cures of physiological illness that resulted from psychological causes; and 3) Jeremy Bentham's utilitarianism, which advocated making conscious choices that maximize personal pleasure or happiness and minimize pain—a psycho-philosophy that applied to government as well as individuals. Once we have begun our travels, the significance of these and the following psychological theories will become apparent.

During the first half of the nineteenth century a number of psychological theories developed that are important to our purposes. Johann Friedrich Herbart viewed psychology as applied metaphysics and proposed a theory of the conscious and the unconscious. The mind Herbart envisioned contained ideas of varying intensity, with the strong ones able to cross from unconsciousness into consciousness. John Stuart Mill proposed the theory that matter is not real of itself but is perceived as real by our fallible senses. This is very similar to the theory of Bishop George Berkeley, except that Berkeley includes God in his theory. Berkeley is very important to the study of New Thought, and his theories are discussed in later chapters. Auguste Comte proposed a positivist psychology, a theory that restricts human knowledge to what is immediately observable. Positivism is discussed in chapter two.

The latter half of the century brought Gustav Theodore Fechner's experimental psychology. He observed that the content of consciousness can be manipulated by controlling the stimuli to which a person is exposed, thus making possible experiments involving the mind. His psychophysics was, he believed, a response to the mind/body problem, which had been a plague to philosophy since the time of the ancient Greeks. He saw the mind and brain as two aspects of the same reality; thus functionally relating physical stimuli to the brain and subjective sensations of the mind.

It also saw the rise of Sigmund Freud, the Viennese physician and psychoanalyst, and his work with hypnosis and hysteria—the phenomenon of physical symptoms being caused by psychological disturbances. Freud also developed the familiar concept of the threefold mind consisting of id, ego and superego. The psychical research of Frederick Myers in the late nineteenth century carried forth Freud's work with hysteria and was an attempt to scientifically prove immortality. He carefully examined Freud's studies and determined that the phenomenon of hysteria demonstrates the power of the mind over the body. Myers's work in some ways parallels that of Quimby's, whose contributions to New Thought are discussed in depth in chapter five. Myers developed a theory of the unconscious that he called the *subliminal self*. Unlike Freud's unconscious—a mental place beyond our awareness where irrational and often frightening ideas can affect behavior—Myers's subliminal self, though still irrational, is not a place, but is an integral part of the self that is able to communicate with a transcendent spiritual world. Myers believes his theory shows that soul and body are separate and proves spiritual evolution; that is, the romantic notion of the ever-progressing and perfecting of the soul.

William James, the first American psychologist and philosopher, admired Myers and took Myers's work seriously. James is an important figure in the formulation of New Thought philosophy. His contributions are discussed in chapter eight.

Wilhelm Wundt, considered the founder of the science of psychology, held that all mental experiences result from unperceived mental processes. From his studies of individual consciousness he discovered an intimate connection between human will and the mind. All of Wundt's ideas are contained in idealistic philosophy, a philosophy of upmost importance to New Thought.

The early twentieth century brought Ivan Petrovich Pavlov and his work with dogs. His theory of conditioned and unconditioned responses and their stimuli parallels in some ways the New Thought theory of objective and subjective consciousness, in that certain responses (subjective reactions) can be elicited by applying certain stimuli (objective will). This New Thought concept is discussed in chapters eight and thirteen.

These later psychologists influenced directly only the writings of the last New Thought founder, Ernest Holmes, though in many instances pieces of their theories rest in antecedent philosophies and psychologies available to the earlier writers.

The changes in scientific and philosophic thought during the nineteenth century produced the three founding forms of psychology. The psychology of consciousness came out of Wundt's work. From Freud's theories came the psychology of the unconscious. And from Darwinism and the evolutionary psychologies came the psychologies of adaptation and behaviorism. Of these psychologies, the first two play roles in the formulation of New Thought philosophy.

We are now ready to begin our study of New Thought and the roads it followed in developing its philosophy.

II.

FINAL PREPARATIONS

*Metaphysics means nothing but an unusually
obstinate effort to think clearly.*
William James (1842–1910)
U.S. psychologist and philosopher
Principles of Psychology

Science without religion is lame, religion without science is blind.
Albert Einstein (1879–1955)
German-born U.S. theoretical physicist
Out of My Later Years

For the reader who is unfamiliar or only nominally familiar with New Thought, two stops must be made before proceeding on our journey. Our first stop provides the questions and answers vital to an understanding of our journey.

What Is New Thought?

New Thought is a system of thinking that virtually everyone is familiar with; they just don't know it. Numerous authors and speakers, even composers and movie producers use New Thought in their works; they just don't call it by that name. To put it simply, New Thought is about right thinking, thinking that leads to positive results—to health, wealth, peace, and happiness. But while right thinking is the hallmark, there is much more to New Thought than that. New Thought is a lifestyle, a metaphysic and a religion.

A 1916 International New Thought Alliance *Bulletin* defines the New Thought system as one that practices what Jesus taught: healing, unity, cooperation, seeing the good in others, and trusting God for all our needs. New Thought is also "a positive, constructive philosophy of optimism, the recognition, realization and manifestation of God in Man" (qtd. in Braden).

Elmer Gifford, an early New Thought minister, writes that New Thought is a term that conveys "the idea of an ever-growing thought." Humans are considered "expanding idea[s] in the Mind of God, . . . held forever in the Mind of God, functioning under and operating through the law of Mind in Action." The God of New Thought "is not an absentee God, but a Universal Mind and Spirit that permeates all nature and finds its highest expression through and as the mind of man, revealing himself to man continually through the reasoning mind and the whispering inward voice of intuition" (Gifford, *New Thought Defined*, qtd. in Braden).

Ernest Holmes, founder of Religious Science, the newest and second largest of the main New Thought groups, defines New Thought as "[A] system of thought which affirms the unity of God with man, the perfection of all life, and the immortality and eternality of the individual soul forever expanding" (*New Thought Terms*).

From these passages it can be seen that New Thought accepts the concept of God in nature and God in humanity. Thus, there is a unity of all things. God relates to us through our minds. God is universal in scope and application; that is, God is everywhere and operates upon the world by use of all-encompassing law. This concept of law is of utmost importance to New Thought and is discussed further in later chapters.

New Thought, in a word, is metaphysics.

What is Metaphysics?

The early New Thought writers used the term *metaphysical* to describe their new philosophy of spiritual healing. Metaphysics is a division of philosophy comprising ontology, cosmology and epistemology and is concerned with the fundamental nature of reality and being. Ontology is the study of the nature of being (existence);

cosmology is the study of the nature of the universe; and epistemology is the study of the nature and the grounds of knowledge.

Writing in 1907, Leander Edmund Whipple, New Thought writer and founder of the American School of Metaphysics and *Metaphysical Magazine*, sees metaphysics as ontology, the science of existence and equates the principles of metaphysics with the permanent laws of the universe. He quotes Aristotle in support:

> Metaphysics is the science of the first principle of Being, the science of the first principle of knowledge and the science of the beginning and the end of all things–the absolute unity of Being and Thought. Metaphysics is mathematical, therefore exact; knowledge of its principles is necessarily scientific understanding. Mathematics, also, is metaphysics and underlies all real law in the universe.

Metaphysical teachings can be found in every culture from the beginning of recorded history. Most of the major philosophers over time have written about metaphysics, and metaphysics has made its way into psychology by way of Carl Jung. All the major religions of the West have mystical branches that are based on metaphysical principles—Christian mysticism, which includes the teachings of Jesus; the Sufism and Baha'i Faith of Islamic derivation; and the Kabbala of Judaism. The religions of the Eastern world do not have mystical branches, for the religions in their entirety are mystical and metaphysical.

Today metaphysics covers a broad spectrum of disciplines all having to do with the ability of the mind to extend beyond the physical realm. Many of these disciplines are discussed in later chapters.

Why is New Thought a Science?

Two of the major New Thought groups have the word science in their names: Divine Science and Religious Science. Though the third group, Unity, does not have science in its name, it does consider its philosophy to be scientific.

Since New Thought is a philosophy about Absolute Reality (God), it naturally falls within the domain of metaphysics and religion. Aristotle considers metaphysics to be science, as those terms were defined in ancient Greece. But since there typically is no God in modern science, how can a philosophy concerning the nature of God and man's relationship to Him be scientific?

To find the answer to that question it is necessary to go back to the beginning of modern New Thought. New Thought began in the mid-1800s as a method of healing the mind and body. This method evolved almost entirely from the work of Phineas Parkhurst Quimby, a clockmaker who became interested in the workings of the mind. Quimby is considered the father of New Thought by many, though New Thought's paternity actually can be found in the distant past, as we shall see.

In 1838, Quimby came in contact with a Dr. Collyer who practiced the art of mesmerism, named for Anton Mesmer, the Viennese physician who developed the practice we know today as hypnotism. Quimby began using mesmerism on volunteer subject Lucius Burkmar, who was able to diagnose illness in other people while in a trance. Quimby soon discovered that he didn't need to actually verbalize his wishes; he could influence Burkmar solely through his thoughts. He had only to concentrate mentally on an act he wished Burkmar to perform, and Burkmar would comply. Quimby performed many experiments and soon deemed that we all have the ability to create ideas that can be seen by a mesmerized person.

These experiments, coupled with his own experience several years prior, led Quimby to question the healing ability of medicines that doctors prescribe. He also felt that doctors often increase the probability of patients becoming sick by suggesting that certain circumstances lead to illness and by suggesting that those already ill are unlikely to get well. He readily perceived that that had been true in his own life.

Quimby entered into his studies after having suffered from tuberculosis and after being told there was no cure. He had recovered somewhat after following a friend's suggestion that outdoor activity would help. But it was not until Burkmar suggested to him that illness was no longer part of his experience that Quimby became entirely well. These events indicated to him that our beliefs play a role in what we experience, and he came to believe that all that is needed for a cure is to change the beliefs we hold in mind.

In time, Quimby found that he could influence a patient whether or not the patient was mesmerized, and so he discontinued the practice. In essence, he had learned that the mind is more powerful than the body, and so he called his methodology *Mental Healing* or *Mental Science.*

Quimby healed hundreds of people and several of those wrote about their experiences and continued their study of mental healing, its origins and its effects. Many of these writings greatly influenced the development of New Thought philosophy. These influences are explored in chapter five.

Though Quimby was skeptical of religious dogma, he said that his method is the same method Jesus used. Writing in 1861, he says:

> This same Christ which you crucify by your theories is the same that Jesus taught eighteen hundred years ago. It was taught by the prophets of old, and has always been in the world, but has never been applied to the curing of disease, although false Christs have arisen and deceived that people, and the true Christ has been crucified by the priest and doctor to this time. Jesus was the oracle, and Christ the wisdom, shown through this man for the happiness of the sick, who had been deceived by the priest and doctor (Quimby, qtd. in Dresser).

Is his method of healing a science? In order to decide, we must define science.

Science did not become a study in its own right until the Renaissance, when the focus turned from theological studies of God and heaven to studies of humanity and its relationship to nature. Prior to that time, science, like mathematics and psychology, had been one of many branches of philosophy. But by the mid-1700s, when Rome and its church had lost its hold on European affairs as a result of the Protestant Reformation, and academic institutions, which stressed scientific rather than theologic viewpoints, proliferated, society was ripe for a scientific revolution.

This revolution changed not only what was considered science but how science was practiced. By the 1830s when Quimby began his experiments, the *positivist* view of scientific investigation prevailed. The positivists assumed a "definable scientific method, . . . a recipe that anyone [could] apply to any problem and thereby become a scientist." Science was seen as "a set of tools, not a set of ideas," which derived "its authority from adherence to its method" (Leahey).

Four decades later another theory arose, one lying at the opposite end of the spectrum from positivism. The theory, *pragmatism*, denies a fixed, permanent truth. For pragmatists, scientific reason is simply using ordinary reason to explain nature, its objects and its effects. We will run across this theory again as we explore the roots of New Thought.

The primary purpose of science is to attempt to explain nature, and two other theories, *logical positivism* and *falsificationism*, arose near the beginning of the twentieth century, claiming their methods best fit this purpose. The logical positivists collected facts and then verified their validity. Falsificationists, on the other hand, focused on finding data that falsified a theory.

The next theory of renown is *realism*, the prominent theory of science today. Within realism there are several views competing for dominance. The more radical forms adhere to specific, unquestionably true, and totally unverifiable concepts. The more accepted viewpoint holds that there is a world, including all objects, their properties and their relations to other objects, that exists entirely independent of any thinking entity.

In general, the theories of realism are intended to literally explain the world, and these theories are accepted as absolutely true. Observed phenomena must be explained, and sometimes it is necessary to postulate the existence of unobserved entities, such as quarks, gravity and intelligence. Because realists assume a theory truly explains how nature works, all the unobserved entities postulated by the theory are thought to actually exist. They are *real* whether or not they can be seen. These concepts of unobserved entities and of reality being mind-independent are important to the study of New Thought and are discussed further in chapter four.

A modern definition of science provided by *Merriam-Webster's* is "the state of knowing: knowledge as distinguished from ignorance or misunderstanding; and knowledge or a system of knowledge covering general truths or the operation of general laws especially as obtained and tested through scientific method." *Scientific method* is defined as "principles and procedures for the systematic pursuit of knowledge involving the recognition and formation of a problem, the collection of data through observation and experiment, and the formulation and testing of hypotheses."

So, over time there have been in the scientific world a number of competing theories all attempting to explain what science is and what science does. How does New Thought fit into this picture? Can this philosophy truly be a science?

During the late 1800s when logical positivism and falsification-ism were the leading theories in scientific circles, Henry Drummond, a minister and natural scientist living in Scotland, noted: "The discovery of Law is simply the discovery of Science. And if the analogies of Natural Law can be extended to the Spiritual World, that whole region at once falls within the domain of science."

Drummond explored the connection between the natural and spiritual worlds during the time the New Thought Movement was being birthed, and though he sympathized with many of its teachings, he was not part of the movement. He quotes Thomas Henry Huxley, the leading advocate of Darwinian evolution during that time, as saying, "By Science I understand all knowledge which rests upon evidence and reasoning of a like character to that which claims our assent to ordinary scientific propositions; and if anyone is able to make good the assertion that his theology rests upon valid evidence and sound reasoning, then it appears to me that such theology must take its place as a part of science." New Thought feels it has done just that, though Huxley would disagree. Huxley says agnosticism, a term he coined, is the only rational stance, as neither atheism nor theism is verifiable.

New Thought writer Whipple states:

> The word *science* literally means knowledge of fundamental law. The foundation of metaphysical healing rests upon science because it is based on theoretical knowledge of principles and the healing theory is constructed on definite understanding of the active laws which proceed from these principles. . . . Metaphysical healing is logical in character because the action is a process of thought in classification, judgment, pure reasoning and systematic arrangement of ideas.

Another early writer, Abel Leighton Allen, says that science is the search for the secrets of nature and the laws that govern the universe. Agreeing with Drummond, he says the laws of the universe and the laws of God are the same laws. Therefore, science, "in its broadest aspect is a search for the knowledge of God."

In science, principle and law have a common meaning. Early Divine Science minister John Murray defines *principle* as "a source of cause from which a thing proceeds, a power that acts continuously or uniformly; a permanent or fundamental cause that naturally or necessarily produces certain results on all occasions." In New Thought this principle is God.

According to Charles Fillmore, cofounder of Unity, "The science that is here set forth is founded upon Spirit. It does not always conform to intellectual standards, but it is, nevertheless, scientific. The facts of Spirit are of a spiritual character and, when understood in their right relation, they are orderly. Orderliness is law, and is the test of true science" (*Christian Healing*).

Obviously, stressing the scientific aspects of mental healing was of great importance during these early years.

Writing in the 1930s, the founder of Religious Science, Ernest Holmes, equates the *Reality* of philosophy, with the *Principle* of science, and the *God* of religion. He says all three refer to the essence and order of the Universe in which we live. In New Thought all of these terms, as well as numerous others, are used interchangeably. Holmes defines science as "the knowledge of facts based upon some proven principle. [When a law] is discovered, experiments are made with it, certain facts are proven to be true, and in this way a science is gradually formulated. *Any* science consists of the number of known facts about its invisible principle" (*Science of Mind*). Remember, scientific realism asserts invisible principles to explain observable phenomena. Henry Wood talks about this, too. He says we are surrounded by invisible energy. "What we can see is but a part of the grand whole." Modern metaphysician Wayne Dyer agrees in saying that all energy sources "are movements orchestrated by an invisible power supply."

Holmes continues: "There is a Universal Mind; but no one ever saw it. We say God is Spirit; but no one ever saw God. The Bible says, 'No man hath seen God at any time, only the Son, he hath revealed

Him'" (John 1:18). According to Holmes, this passage expressed in New Thought language says, "No one has seen Cause; because we see an effect, we know there must be a Cause. Nothing is more evident than the fact that we live; and since we live, we must have life, and since we have life there must be Life. The only proof we have of Mind is that we think. The Eternal Principle is forever hidden."

Writing near the end of the twentieth century, Laurence Doyle, a principal investigator at the SETI Institute, says this about science: "[Y]ou're doing science when you take the evidence of intelligence above the evidence of the senses. . . . [I]f I take a look at the word *science*, to me, it's about looking for something that's repeatable, replicable, reliable. . . . What I get when I boil down the word *science* is a simple three-letter word, *law*. . . . You're doing science when you 'plunge beneath the material surface of things, and find the spiritual cause.'"

In New Thought, God/Reality/Principle is also called Divine Law and is the active truth of all creation. It operates through the principle of cause and effect, known in Eastern philosophy as *karma*. It applies to the physical realm as well as the nonphysical—the mental or spiritual realm—and can be proved by scientific methods. These laws are operating constantly, whether we know about them or not, and they function the same for everyone and everything. They are absolute and unvarying. No one is exempt from Divine Law.

These are powerfully important statements. We can see that the concept of law is an important one, and it is touched on in every road we will follow in exploring the roots of New Thought. Therefore, I reserve discussion of this topic until after we have finished our journey.

We find from the previous discussion that New Thought is indeed scientific. It is positivistic in that it sets forth laws that can be tested and proved valid, and, in a particular sense, it is realistic. There is an invisible entity that exists independent of our thinking or perceiving and that is postulated by theory. That entity is God or Divine Law. New Thought is also pragmatic. "Practicing the presence of God for practical purposes" is taught by Unity. Its founders, Charles and Myrtle Fillmore, call their philosophy *Practical Christianity*. Which leads to another question.

Is New Thought Christian?

Practical Christianity implies Christ. Two of the major New Thought groups consider their churches to be Christian. Many of New Thought's beliefs are derived from the Bible and the words of Jesus, the *Christ*. In his *Metaphysical Bible Dictionary* Fillmore writes:

> Apart from its being a book of great historical and biographical interest, the Bible is, from Genesis to Revelations, in its inner or spiritual meaning, a record of the experiences and the development of the human soul and of the whole being of humankind; also it is a treatise on humanity's relation to God, the Creator and Father. . . . The metaphysical interpretations given in this dictionary are based on the practical teachings of Jesus Christ, as understood and taught by Unity School of Christianity.

So, whether or not New Thought is Christian depends on how the term *Christian* is defined. The Christian status of New Thought is explored further in the next chapter. The relationship between Jesus and New Thought is discussed in depth in chapter nine.

Why is it Called New Thought?

New Thought philosophy is definitely not new, so why is it named such? The movement became known as *New* Thought for the same reason that the experimental, or physiological, psychology of the late nineteenth century was called the *New* Psychology. Both of these systems of thought came into vogue during the same time period, offering new paradigms, new and different ways of relating the mind and the body and inquiring into man's nature, and resulted from new, progressively evolving and advancing minds. They were also considered new because these paradigms were the first to be developed in America by Americans antithetic to the old doctrines that came with the early colonizers from England and Scotland. And the *new* in New Thought also refers to the fact that in order to achieve positive results in our lives, we must keep our thoughts in a constant state of renewal—again and again each day we have *new* thoughts.

The concept of New Thought as science, the Divine Laws and all of the other concepts presented in this chapter are explored further in the following chapters.

But before we begin our travels we must spend some time with the founders of New Thought.

III.

THE PATHFINDERS

Nay, be a Columbus to whole new continents and worlds within you,
opening new channels, not of trade, but of thought.
Henry David Thoreau (1817–1862)
U.S. philosopher, author and naturalist
Walden (1854)

An invasion of armies can be resisted,
but not an idea whose time has come.
Victor Hugo (1802–1885)
French dramatist, novelist and poet
'Histoire d'un crime' (1852)

The New Thought founders separately established churches. Unity is the largest with almost twice as many churches worldwide as the second largest, Religious Science. At a far distant third is Divine Science. It is not known why Divine Science did not keep pace with Unity and Religious Science, since they all teach virtually the same doctrine. Perhaps it is because even though over the years many Divine Science churches were founded, most remained independent of the parent organization and thus suffered from lack of exposure.

Overall, the New Thought churches fall into one of two categories according to where they place their emphasis. Either they emphasize Jesus or they emphasize Law or Divine Mind. In general, Divine Science and Unity fall into the former category while Religious Science falls into the latter. It has been my experience, however, that some Religious Science churches emphasize Jesus and some Unity churches de-emphasize him, according to the background of the ministers and the preferences of their congregations.

While there are other groups that teach New Thought philosophy, I limited my research to these three churches because they are the pioneers of the philosophy on which all other New Thought groups depend.

Divine Science

The first New Thought church to come into being was Divine Science, which actually began as two separate churches, founded independently of each other by different women, one in California and the others in Colorado.

Malinda Elliott Cramer, one of eleven children in a family of Quakers, founded the California church. At age fifteen she became ill from a disease her many doctors considered inherited and incurable. (Divine Science literature does not indicate what disease she suffered). Several years later Malinda's family moved to San Francisco at the urging of her doctors, who felt the change of climate might help. Her doctors were wrong, though, and she suffered for almost 20 more years before she came to an understanding of the Truth that allowed her to heal. She began taking classes with Emma Curtis Hopkins from whom she learned to let go of her old ways of thinking about illness. Of her healing experience she writes, in part:

> It was early one morning in the year 1885, during an hour of earnest meditation and prayerful seeking, that I asked the following questions in faith, believing that they would be answered, with a willingness to abide the decision, whatever it might be. "Is there any way out of these conditions? Is there any power in the vast universe that can heal me?" The immediate and all-convincing response was not an audible voice, but was an intuitive response by the life-giving spirit . . . . From the depths of Divine perception and understanding I was caused to know and realize that if I got well it would be by the power of the Infinite Spirit. . . . I at once saw the unreality of the conditions, and was free from the belief that they had any power, or could control for either good or ill . . . and the old conditions passed away as fast as I disowned them by dropping the old habits of thinking and believing (Cramer, qtd. in "Divine Science Founders").

At the time of her healing she was 40 years old. Because of numerous questions from friends inquiring about her health and whether she truly had been healed, and because Cramer felt it important to enlighten her friends as to the role of thought, both hers and theirs, in the continuing process of healing, she began teaching formal classes in what she called *Divine Science*. She established the Home College of Divine Science in 1888, which offered courses she wrote and taught. In that same year she founded one of the first monthly metaphysical magazines, *Harmony*, for which she acted as editor and writer. Two years later she took her classes to cities around the country, and that is how she came into contact with the other Divine Science group.

Sisters Nona Brooks, Fannie James and Althea Small founded the Colorado church. Born in Louisville, Kentucky, the young sisters moved to Pueblo, Colorado with their family because of their mother's poor health. There Brooks developed a serious throat ailment. While subsisting on a limited diet, by doctor's orders, she deteriorated to just 85 pounds. Her sisters also suffered from various maladies.

One day in the early 1880s, Brooks and her sister Small (whose husband, coincidentally, was a real estate partner of Charles Fillmore just prior to Fillmore's move to Kansas City and subsequent founding of Unity) attended a class taught by Kate Bingham. Bingham's own healing had taken place in Chicago where she had studied with, and received treatment from, the "teacher's teacher"—Emma Curtis Hopkins. She returned to Pueblo three weeks later in glowing health, and because numerous friends inquired about her sudden recovery, she began holding informal classes.

Hearing of the ill-health of Brooks's family, Bingham invited them to attend. During the fourth class Brooks was completely flooded with a light brighter than the sun. She exclaimed, "It filled me! It surrounded me! I discovered that I had been instantly and completely healed."

After her remarkable healing, Brooks and her sisters revised and systematically applied the new teachings to their thoughts, habits and lifestyle. They put their complete attention on the presence of God working in their lives. As they manifested other physical healings and improved their financial situation, they became convinced of the truth of the spiritual principles they termed *Divine Science—Divine,* because "the subject concerns the understanding of God as Omnipotent," and *Science*, "because [the principles] are proved in our experience." Brooks says Divine Science reveals "a Universe that is God and God in action—a Universe in which there is nothing but God—a Universe which is God and God-Idea in expression."

James married and moved to Denver, with Brooks, Small and their families soon following. They began attending Cramer's classes and discovered the similarity between Cramer's Divine Science and their own. Cramer granted them permission to continue using the name Divine Science.

Brooks deepened her understanding of Divine Science by studying at Cramer's Home College. Cramer's school ordained numerous ministers including Brooks and two of the most well-known New Thought philosophers and writers in modern times—Emmet Fox and Ernest Holmes.

While Divine Science considers itself to be a Christian denomination, it recognizes that it is not Christian in the orthodox sense. There are many differences between the beliefs of Divine Science and those of traditional Christian sects.

One major difference involves the Bible. The Bible was written on three different levels: 1) a historical level, which relates facts as to actual people, places and events; 2) a moral level, on which the codes of appropriate behavior are given; and 3) a spiritual or metaphysical level, which relates the story of humanity in its evolution from self-consciousness to cosmic consciousness using symbolism, metaphor, hyperbole, allegory, and parable. Jesus taught on this level, and this is why his teachings are considered to be mystical or esoteric. The creation story in Genesis was also written at the spiritual level. The creation was not an event, but a process. Because many Christian denominations do not understand that most Bible stories are allegorical, they take them as fact. All the founders of New Thought, on the other hand, interpret the Bible almost entirely at the spiritual level.

Someone created an acronym for the word Bible that perfectly expresses its teachings at the spiritual level: **Basic Instruction Before Leaving Earth.**

Another difference has to do with prayer. Divine Science teaches a form of prayer called *affirmative prayer*. Through affirmative prayer the flow of Universal Mind is allowed to manifest in individual lives.

All the goodness of God is available to each of us and awaits our acceptance. We experience this goodness by affirming, believing and then accepting.

Cramer mentions the Hindu *Bhagavad Gita*, the Jewish Kabbala, Hermetic philosophy, and the words of the mystic Jacob Boehme. She later founded the International Divine Science Association, the predecessor of the International New Thought Alliance, an umbrella organization for various New Thought groups.

After Cramer died in 1906, the Divine Science headquarters moved from San Francisco to Denver, and the movement continued to grow. By 1925 churches abounded in numerous large cities around the country. The Divine Science movement weakened after a couple of decades, though, and today there are only a few dozen churches. Though it was the first organized group to promote the New Thought philosophy, the name Divine Science remains unfamiliar to many in the New Thought movement.

Basic Principles of Divine Science

- There is one eternal God and Father, the One Infinite Source and Cause of all that is.
- God is Omnipotent Life, Substance, Intelligence, and Power.
- God is Universal Mind Presence and is not a person.
- The Trinity is Mind, Idea and Consciousness or, in other terms, Spirit, Soul and Body.
- The nature of God is wisdom, love, knowledge, understanding, power, life, and joy.
- We are all embraced within this one Infinite Source.
- All objects of creation are Ideas in the mind of God.
- Humans are immortal, individualized expressions of God and are wholly good like their Creator.
- Jesus of Nazareth embodied the Christ Consciousness; thus, his title of Christ Jesus.
- The healing principles used in Divine Science are the same principles taught and practiced by Jesus Christ.
- Freedom is our birthright.
- There are spiritual or divine laws.

- Evil is the false belief in a presence or power other than God.
- Matter is one aspect of divine energy; the other is Spirit. Matter and Spirit, then, are aspects of the same substance.
- We make our own worlds by what we think, and we are controlled, to some degree, by the thoughts and beliefs of others.

Unity

Unity was the next group to formally organize. Just a year after Cramer founded her school, Charles and Myrtle Fillmore issued their first *Modern Thought* magazine, and Unity was born. The Fillmores incorporated the Unity Society of Practical Christianity in 1903 and the school in 1914.

Myrtle was born in 1845 and Charles nine years later. Both endured physical challenges in their youth. Myrtle suffered from tuberculosis, and Charles developed a disease of the hip that left him with a shriveled leg. They met in Texas in 1876 and married five years later. They came in contact with New Thought in 1886 when they attended a lecture by Dr. E. B. Weeks, who was a student of Emma Curtis Hopkins. Myrtle immediately integrated the ideas presented in the lecture and within two years had completely healed her tuberculosis. About her experience, Myrtle writes:

> I have made what seems to me a discovery. I was fearfully sick; I had all the ills of mind and body that I could bear. Medicine and doctors ceased to give me relief, and I was in despair, when I found practical Christianity. I took it up and I was healed. This is how I made what I call my discovery: I was thinking about life. Life is everywhere. Ah! Intelligence, as well as life, is needed to make a body. Here is the key to my discovery. Life has to be guided by intelligence in making all forms. The same law works in my own body. Life is simply a form of energy, and has to be guided and directed in man's body by his intelligence. How do we communicate intelligence? By thinking and talking, of course. Then it flashed upon me that I might talk to the life in every part of my body and have it do just what I wanted. I began to teach my body and got marvelous results ("History of Unity").

After Myrtle's healing Charles undertook the conscious process of manifesting his own. He also began studying numerous religions and philosophies, including those of Emerson, Thoreau, Shakespeare, Tennyson, Jesus, Christian Science, the Quakers, the Rosicrucians, Spiritualism, Theosophy, Hinduism, and native spiritualities. By1889 he had quit his business and devoted his full energy to learning and then teaching the truths he discovered.

During this period the Fillmores personally studied with Hopkins, who profoundly influenced the development of their form of New Thought. In 1891 Hopkins ordained them ministers of Christian Science, though the Fillmores chose not to use that name for their work, preferring instead *Unity*, which refers to the oneness of all with God and to the fact that they, in the words of Charles, "borrowed the best from all religions," thus uniting truth.

Charles called their philosophy *Practical Christianity*, and considered their church to be Christian, though it would not be considered so using orthodox Christian standards and dogma. The use of phrases such as *Father-Mother God, Christ in you, the Christ consciousness*, and *the divinity of man*, set it outside orthodoxy. Many New Thought writers agree with the Fillmores and assert that New Thought is more Christian than is orthodox Christianity. The reader is invited to make that determination for him or herself after completing this chapter and chapter nine.

Unity's literature states that Unity is the religion *of* Jesus Christ, not the religion *about* Jesus Christ. This is an important distinction, as the teachings of Jesus are key to the Fillmores's philosophy. According to Charles:

> Unity is a link in the great educational movement inaugurated by Jesus Christ; our objective is to discern the Truth in Christianity and prove it. The Truth that we teach is not new, neither do we claim special revelations or discovery of new religious principles. Our purpose is to help and teach humankind to use and prove the eternal Truth taught by the Master (Unity Movement).

Myrtle writes that among the truths taught by Jesus is his method of healing:

Few have dared even to suggest that Jesus applied universal law in His restorative methods; for on the one hand it would annul the miracle theory and on the other it would be sacrilegious to inquire into the miracles of God. So it has been generally accepted that Jesus' great works were miracles and that the power to do miracles was delegated to His immediate followers only. But in recent years a considerable number of Jesus' followers have had the temerity to inquire into His healing methods, and they have found that they were based on universal mental and spiritual laws that anyone can utilize who will comply with the conditions involved in these laws. This inquiry has led to the conclusion that man and the universe are founded on mind and that all changes for good or ill are changes of mind ("Unity History").

This is where the *practical* part comes in—putting into practice the teachings of Jesus, who taught the importance of our thoughts, words and acts. Through the spoken word the creative power of God is made practical. By repeating statements of Truth, what Unity calls denials and affirmations, patterns of right thinking are molded into habits of right acting. This process is similar to the affirmative prayer taught in Divine Science.

The Bible is Unity's primary text, and as with Divine Science it is interpreted metaphysically. Unity also utilizes the textbook *Lessons in Truth* written by Harriet Emilie Cady, though Cady was not associated formally with Unity. As did the Fillmores, Cady studied with Emma Curtis Hopkins, but she chose to remain, in her words, "spiritually independent" and did not join any group. Myrtle came upon Cady's booklet, "Finding the Christ in Ourselves," and was so profoundly impacted that Cady was asked to write for *Unity Magazine* and later to pen their textbook. Like the other minds of the New Thought movement, Cady was inspired by Hopkins, the Bible and the ideas of Emerson.

Basic Principles of Unity

- God is Omnipotent, impartial, infinite, and eternal.
- The Trinity is viewed metaphysically as Mind, Idea and Expression.

- The nature of God is absolute good, love, wisdom, health, and joy.
- Humans are ideas in the Mind of God, created in God's image and likeness. Thus, we are spiritual, divine beings and, as such, partake of God's characteristics. The spirit of God indwells every person, and every person is, in potentiality, the expression of perfection.
- There is only one power in the universe, and that is God (or good). Thus, there are no Satan and no evil. What is considered evil is merely a limited or incomplete expression of God. Evil originates from the ignorance of humanity.
- God desires always to give. The Divine Plan is to manifest good into human experience on a constant and continuing basis.
- Life, substance and intelligence are everywhere. There is nothing but life, substance and intelligence. This is what is real, and it is spiritual.
- Prayer is conscious communion with God.
- There are spiritual laws. With proper use of them we can release the effects of wrong thinking; i.e., sickness, poverty, frustration, loneliness, and pain.
- Jesus was the one person who expressed perfection, thereby becoming the Christ.
- We are given by God freedom of thought and act.
- There are no such places as heaven and hell; rather, they are states of consciousness. Our experience here and now is heavenly or hellish based on our thoughts, words and deeds.
- The only reality is spiritual; therefore, though matter and material conditions appear to be real, they are not.
- Our thoughts and our words affect the condition of our life and affairs. We can, with effort, change our thinking and thus change our experience.

Religious Science

Religious Science, the last major group to organize, is the only main New Thought group whose beginning was not the result of a healing. Moved to search for truth, Ernest Holmes studied every world philosophy and religion he could obtain writings for. He took what he felt was the truth from the many minds he discovered and synthesized them into his Science of Mind philosophy. Because he was influenced by some sources unfamiliar to Divine Science and Unity, his Science of Mind differs somewhat from these two churches.

Holmes entered the New Thought arena much later than did the founders of Divine Science and Unity. Cramer was already teaching classes and Myrtle had already manifested her healing before Holmes was born in 1887.

Early in his search for truth Holmes studied the Bible and Ralph Waldo Emerson's essay, "Self-Reliance," which profoundly influenced Holmes's thought and his life. While a student in Boston, he completed a New Thought course developed by one of its prominent leaders, Christian D. Larson. He also read Mary Baker Eddy's *Science and Health With Key to the Scriptures*. Noticing the similarities between the two philosophies and desiring to learn more about mental healing, he enrolled in, but did not complete, the courses offered by Christian Science. Passionately continuing his reading of Emerson's works, he added those of Walt Whitman and Robert Browning, finding tremendous harmony among in all these works. He then came upon the writings of Thomas Troward, with whom Holmes felt complete accord. From these minds and many more, Holmes developed his form of New Thought philosophy.

In 1918, Ernest and his brother Fenwicke founded the Metaphysical Institute and began teaching what they called Mental Science. As had Cramer and the Fillmores, the Holmes brothers began publishing a magazine. The next year they both published books and began speaking in public. A few years later Ernest decided to move to California and left Fenwicke in the East. From that point on they taught separately.

Ernest continued to read and study, moving into the mystical writings of Meister Eckhart and Hopkins, the latter with whom he also personally studied shortly before her death. It was from these and other great mystics that he learned of cosmic consciousness (intuitive perception of the Whole), which he later frequently experienced, sometimes for extensive periods of time.

He published *The Science of Mind* in 1926, the textbook for the Institute of Religious Science and Philosophy he founded in California. Even though it was not Holmes's original intention, a church later formed around this philosophy.

Because of his voluminous studies, his philosophy was influenced by numerous people and philosophies. Those who impacted him most were Emerson, Hopkins, Troward, Eddy, William Walker Atkinson (aka Yogi Ramacharaka), Plotinus, and the many Idealist and Gnostic writers as well as Hinduism and Taoism. All of these influences are explored in the chapters of this book.

As did Fillmore, Holmes wrote numerous books laying out his philosophy, and with Fillmore, he felt his ideas involved practical living. The method used by Religious Scientists to practice the presence is known as *spiritual mind treatment* and incorporates the use of affirmative prayer. Treatment is "clearing the thought of negation, of doubt and fear, and causing it to perceive the ever-presence of God" (*Science of Mind*). Religious Science also is aligned with the other two New Thought groups in that Holmes sees his Science of Mind as "ethically based and deeply Christian in spirit." In the words of Holmes:

Religious Science is based on a very few simple and fundamental ideas. The basic proposition is that the universe in which we live is a combination of Love and Law, or Divine Presence and Universal Principle. We may call it a spontaneous Self-emergence and a mechanical reaction, or the Law and the Word, or the Personal and the Impersonal, or the Thing and the way It works. Everything we do, say, and teach; our methods of treatment and procedures; all is based not on a duality but on a dual unity or a two-sided unity of one and the same thing.

Our whole system of teaching is based upon Quimby's concept that the things which have to be resolved are mental, not physical. We must be able to reduce everything to mind, or consciousness, because consciousness does not operate upon something external to itself. Consciousness is the one great reality in the universe. . . . [O]ur thought does not spiritualize matter and it does not materialize Spirit. Spirit and matter, or thought and form, are one and the same thing (*Seminar Lectures*).

Interestingly, Holmes says Religious Science is "open at the top" and Fillmore refers to Unity as a philosophy with an "open end." Both of these churches realize the importance of being open to new possibilities, to new ideas and to new beliefs.

Basic Principles of Religious Science

- There is only one God. This God is Love, Law and Spirit.
- God is self-knowing.
- All is Mind or Intelligence.
- God is First Cause. Everything that *is* was created by God's Thought and was created *from* God.
- There are Divine Laws that operate in the world. Love is the nature of God, but "Love rules through Law."
- God is impersonal and impartial. God works the same for everyone according to Divine Law.
- The Trinity is The Thing Itself, The Way It Works and What It Does. The trinity in man is spirit, soul and body.
- Humans were made in the image and likeness of God. God is good, therefore all Its creations are, by nature, good. God is Divine, so all Its creations partake of that divinity.
- We are born free.
- God or Spirit expresses Itself in the world through each individual person according to each person's belief.
- All thought is creative. Each person's thoughts, attitudes and beliefs produce his or her experience.
- Mind is both subjective and objective; the subjective is subconscious; the objective is conscious.
- Spirit is thought, and matter is form. They are made of the same substance, which is God.
- Jesus not only taught these great truths but he embodied them, thus making him the Christ. This Christ consciousness is available to all humans.

- There is no evil because all is God, and God is good. Sin and apparent evil are simply mistakes, the results of wrong thinking.
- Heaven and hell are states of consciousness.

From our visit with the founders we can extract sixteen concepts held in common among these three groups:

- God is Spirit, Mind or Intelligence
- God is Good, Wise, Loving, etc.
- There is only God, and God is always present
- God is the Creator of all that exists and creates from within Itself
- God is a Triune Being
- God is impersonal or impartial
- There are spiritual or divine laws by which God works
- Jesus embodied the Christ consciousness, which consciousness is available to all humanity
- Jesus taught mental healing
- We are created in God's image and likeness; as such, our nature is good, and we are divine
- It is our birthright to partake of God's goodness
- We are given free agency or free will; thus, we are always at choice
- We are the means by which God expresses into the material world
- Our thoughts, attitudes and beliefs produce our experience
- Heaven and hell are states of mind or consciousness
- Evil and sin are simply mistakes resulting from ignorance and wrong thinking

These concepts form the basis of New Thought philosophy and are explored further in chapters nine and fourteen. The four key premises upon which New Thought philosophy relies are examined in the next chapter.

IV.

THE KEYS

Only divine love bestows the keys of knowledge.
Arthur Rimbaud (1854–1891), French poet
"Mauvais Sang"

Men are not prisoners of fate, but only prisoners of their own minds.
Franklin D. Roosevelt (1882–1945)
32nd president of the United States
"Pan American Day address," April 15, 1939

In order for New Thought philosophy to hold together cohesively and logically, four propositions must be true:

- God exists
- Name is nature
- Freedom is our birthright
- Mind is superior to, or more real than, matter

Let's look at the legitimacy of each of these propositions.

God exists

All theistic philosophies rely on the premise that God exists. Inasmuch as God, as we theorize It, is intangible, there have been numerous theories proposed over time attempting to prove Its existence. The four traditional arguments are 1) arguments from (or to) design, also known as teleological arguments; 2) common consent arguments; 3) cosmological arguments; and 4) degrees of perfection arguments.

The arguments *from* or *to* design are the most convincing of the arguments and that is likely why they are the most popular. The arguments start from our experience and our observation of order and regularity in nature and move backwards to conclude that based on that order there must be an Organizer or Designer at work.

The common consent arguments argue from the *almost* universal acceptance of a belief in God to the truth of that belief. That is, in the language of logic, if almost everyone believes *P*, then *P* is probably true. In our case, because the belief in God is held among widely diverse cultures, it is a reasonable belief and is conceivably true. This argument, however, is logically flawed, for just because nearly everyone believes a thing is true doesn't necessarily make it so. For instance, before the Polish astronomer Nicholas Copernicus proved them wrong in the sixteenth century, almost everyone believed that the earth sat in the center of the solar system and that the sun and all the other planets revolved about it. As we know, this is not true. However, in spite of its illogic, this argument is considered to hold some merit because of the universality of the belief involved.

The cosmological arguments hinge on seventeenth century German philosopher Gottfried Leibniz's *principle of sufficient reason*, which states that for any fact there is a reason why it is so and not otherwise. It is a fact that there is a universe; therefore, there must be a sufficient reason (one that needs no further reason) for its existence, the sufficient reason being God, the Creator.

The last of the arguments states, again in the language of logic, that whatever is the most *P* must be the cause of all other *P*. So, in applying this logic to God, because there is goodness in the universe, there must exist the Most Good, which is God, the cause of everything else.

While these arguments all hold some validity, there have been arguments proposed to refute them. These counter arguments, too, have validity. So what are we to do? I believe the acceptance of the proposition that God exists rests entirely on one's experience and one's faith. But is it reasonable to do so?

The rationality of basing one's entire life on faith in God has been, and continues to be, debated in philosophical circles. Of course, there have been arguments for and against the rationality of living by faith. While doing so may not be rational, many of us choose to believe regardless.

Blaise Pascal, the French mathematician, physicist and theologian, put forth an argument in the mid-seventeenth century for those who are inclined to believe in God. Pascal's Wager, as the argument is called, says that given the two possibilities (and he only allows for these two choices) of *theism* (there is a God, and there is a heaven for those who live rightly) or *nihilism* (there is nothing after death), the best choice lies with theism. If there is the slightest chance that there *is* a God, and God has provided a heaven when we die, we are better off to live a life deserving of a heavenly reward. If, in fact, it turns out that God exists, then we have everything to gain by having believed. If, however, there is no God, and nothing to look forward to after death, what would we have lost by betting on the existence of God? Pascal concludes we will have lost nothing. The implication being, of course, that if there is a heaven or hell awaiting us, whatever sacrifices we may have made in order to live rightly, would be far overshadowed by the outcome.

Let's see if we can discover how our New Thought philosophers came to the conclusion that God exists.

Creation myths from every culture across time and around the world assume a Creator of some sort. Stories explaining the existence of the universe passed down orally from generation to generation until written communication developed. Many of these stories are several thousand years old. Of course, being old does not make a thing true nor does the fact that *every* culture has a creation story. But neither is it necessarily untrue.

The most ancient written views about God are found in the Hindu *Vedas*, which, depending on the reference used, were written between 4300 and 1500 B.C.E. (Before the Common Era). (As comparison, the oldest Bible stories are estimated to date to 1000 B.C.E.) The *Vedas* teach that all things issue from one eternal, *self-existing* Principle. The entire universe consists of this one being.

The Bible asserts an Omniscient (all-knowing), Omnipresent (always everywhere present), Omnipotent (all-powerful), eternal, infinite God that created all that exists.

The ancient Greek philosopher Aristotle, who lived between 384 and 322 B.C.E., in seeing God as the *unmoved mover* or *First Mover*, an entity that is the cause, organizer and purpose of the universe, put forth the first teleological argument for God's existence. God is pure spirit, mind or pure thought (*Nous*) and contains only itself. As such, God is perfect and eternal. (Interestingly, according to Baird T. Spaulding, the term for *Father* in the Hindu language of Sanskrit, means *first mover*.)

Plato (427-437 B.C.E.), Aristotle's teacher, states that what is knowable must be eternal, definable and real. For Plato, Reality or God "is not one located in any particular place or time, it does not change, and it *is* in every respect" (Flew).

Leibniz (1646-1716) says the *idea* of God is possible and lays out his theory in the cosmological argument briefly explained above. He also puts forth the First Cause argument, which states that every finite thing has a cause, and that cause has a cause, and that cause has a cause, and so forth. He says a finite thing cannot continue in series in infinitude; therefore, there must be a first term in the series. Since the first term in a series must be uncaused, this first term is first cause. Thus, he determines there is an uncaused cause of everything, and this is God.

It is known that Fillmore and Holmes read the works of these philosophers, the books of Hinduism and the Bible. Brooks writes about Aristotle and often quotes the Bible, as did cofounder Cramer, but it is not known to me if either were familiar with the other writings. Whether the founders of New Thought looked to these philosophers for verification of an already-existing, prevalent belief in God (as in the common consent argument) or whether they determined that God exists because of the above sources or any other source is not known. All we know is that they were familiar with these writings and they did accept the proposition that God exists.

Name is nature

One of the key concepts of New Thought has to do with the *nature* of God and the *name* of Jesus. God is said to be good, wise, loving, all-powerful, etc. It is held that these words describe God's nature. How do we know this?

In the biblical time period it was common practice to name a person or place because of its nature, purpose, or circumstance of being. The Bible is full of such examples. Moses received his name because in Hebrew the word *Moses* means "drawn from the water." Adam named his wife, the mother of all life, Eve because *Eve* means "elementary life or living." The word *Eden* means "pleasure, delight or sensible duration," thus the paradisaical Garden of Eden. Jesus, which is the Greek form of the Hebrew name Jeshua or Joshua, received his name because Jeshua means "deliverance, safety or salvation." He was also called *Immanuel* or *Emmanuel*, which in Hebrew means "God is with us."

Traditionally, many Native Americans and other indigenous cultures receive their names based on nature or deed. In some cultures a given name is changed at puberty, when the youth's nature can be ascertained.

That sort of naming is not done much in the cultures of European decent, though. Commonly, a child's name is decided upon before birth, and long before his or her nature can be determined. Names are chosen to honor someone or just because the parents like the name.

But the names for God *do* indicate nature. Some traditional names for God are Elohim, Jehovah (Yahweh) and Adonai. According to many Bible authorities, the translators of the King James Bible ("KJB") used a simple code for these different Hebrew names.

Elohim is a name that characterizes God as Creator, and the only true God, and in the KJB it is written as "God." *Jehovah* means "self-existent or I am that I am." Jehovah, or Yahweh in Hebrew, is written as "LORD" in the KJB. *Adonai* means "sovereign" or "master" and emphasizes the Lordship of God. It is coded as "Lord."

These three names are used interchangeably throughout the Old Testament for the one true God, and sometimes these names are used in combination. For instance, "The LORD God" is code for *Jehovah-Elohim*, which means "The self-existent one is the true God."

Fillmore writes that Jehovah means *"He-who-is—who-was—who-will-be manifest; the self-existent One; He who is eternal."* He says a word-for-word rendering of this meaning is "I-am–I-was–I-will-be because I-am–I-was–I-will-be the power to be eternally I."

One of the greatest influences on New Thought was Emma Curtis Hopkins, who writes, "Have you ever heard that there is a marvelous power in every word? It contains its own potentiality. . . . God is the name for that Intelligence which out of its own substance bestowed upon you that intelligence you now have." She says that one of the names for God is *Good.* Good can mean support, substance, abundance, health, peace, happiness, joy, or anything else the word *good* represents to an individual.

She also mentions the word *OM*, a Sanskrit name for God in Hinduism. She says OM means "Good beyond Good," indicating that "Far beyond even our ideas of Good, there is Infinite Good, awaiting our words." OM, as God, is discussed further in chapter ten.

Thus we see that the names for God indicate the nature and character of God. This is true for all the names in the Bible. This point is significant, for New Thought speaks much of Jesus and his teachings and interprets his words in light of "name is nature." Jesus, his teachings and the concept of name is nature are discussed further in chapter nine.

Freedom is our birthright

Virtually every philosopher over the past three thousand years has addressed the issue of free will, and every philosopher has decided either that humans freely act or that their actions are predetermined. The concept of freedom implies choice. As humans we are free to choose among a variety of options. Determinism, on the other hand, says that everything is predetermined. All options are decided for us before we are born, and nothing we do can change our destiny.

The religious philosophies are split between these two views. Interestingly, some of the Bible-based philosophies accept determinism, relying largely on New Testament verses, while others support free will, relying mainly on the writings of the prophets of the Old Testament. Compare the first two scriptures below, interpreted as deterministic, with the last two, claimed as supporting free will:

And he will send his angels and gather his elect from the four winds, from the ends of the earth to the ends of the heavens (Mark 13:27; Matt 24:31).

And this is my covenant with them when I take away their sins. As far as the gospel is concerned, they are enemies on your account; but as far as election is concerned, they are loved on account of the patriarchs, for God's gifts and his call are irrevocable (Romans 11:27-28).

. . . choose you this day whom ye will serve (Joshua 2:25).

. . . they have chosen their own ways, and their soul delighted in their abominations . . . but they did evil before mine eyes, and chose that in which I delighted not (Isaiah 66:3,4).

The decision as to whether a verse refers to free will or determinism seems to be whether the words *elected* or *chosen* are used, even though these words have similar meanings. As with many words, interpretations can be given to support numerous different theories.

In 1879, the thirteenth century philosophy of St. Thomas Aquinas became the official philosophy of the Roman Catholic Church. His theory regarding free will follows Aristotle's ethical theory, which holds that moral action is the result of intellectual reflection and *choice*. The argument is this: Humans are capable of rational thought; rational thought leads humans to choose moral acts; therefore, humans must have free will.

Aquinas says we cannot be held responsible for our actions unless we are free to choose those actions. This seems commonsensical, but according to opposing arguments, free will loses all sense when coupled with other doctrines accepted by many Christian churches, including the Catholic doctrines based on Aquinas's philosophy. For instance, the doctrine that holds God as Creator of the world, designer of laws and judge of any violations to those laws, and the doctrine of the Fall, and the subsequent rescue by grace, seem to contradict freedom to choose our actions. Are we held responsible for our actions, or are we saved by grace? Further, if God is Omniscient, which these churches also maintain, and knows every choice that will be made and every act that will be performed, how can our choices and actions be free?

Many unsatisfactory attempts have been made over the years to reconcile this dilemma; that is, to keep free will *and* the orthodox doctrine both as representing absolute truth.

During the Reformation of the sixteenth century, some of the Protestant reformers, John Calvin and his followers being the prime examples, resolved this issue by denying free will. They used specific scriptures, like those shown above, to support this stance, claiming that we are predestined, or elected, before birth to either eternal punishment or reward, and nothing we do while on the earth can change our predetermined destiny. Not all of the reformers, though, took this route. Erasmus and Martin Luther continued to defend free will in spite of the apparent contradictions generated in applying free will to the then-accepted Christian doctrine.

Many subsequent philosophers attempted to harmonize God and free will, but in order to grant full freedom of will to humanity, portions of the orthodox doctrine concerning God had to change. For instance, if our choices and our actions are totally free, then *we* are at cause rather than God, and God is no longer First Cause. Others attribute a partial or conditional freedom to humanity, saying sometimes we act freely and sometimes we don't. Sometimes our actions are based on factors outside our control.

German philosopher Johann Fichte (1762-1814) claimed that freedom is the essence of things and is the highest reality. His compatriot George Hegel (1770-1831) said that freedom is the essence of reason. As rational beings, we are free. Friedrich Schelling (1775-1854), another well known German philosopher of this period, stated that self-consciousness, freedom and will are everywhere in the universe, including within human beings. The French deist philosopher Jean-Jacques Rousseau (1712-1778) introduced the concept of the *noble savage*, "the romantic idea of man as enjoying a natural and noble existence until civilization makes him a slave to unnatural wants and seduces him from his original freedom" (Russell).

In the nineteenth century Transcendentalism arose, spawning a sort of mini-Reformation in which the Western conception of God changed once again. In developing their philosophy the transcendentalists looked to the East and discovered a more pantheistic God, one that is everywhere and everything and that grants to humans perfect freedom. Many of the ideas of Emerson and Thoreau, the two most influential transcendentalists, originated in Taoism, Buddhism and Hinduism. The *Tao Te Ching* speaks of the uncarved block, which is man's natural state, the state of innocence, plainness and simplicity, and represents a state of freedom. The Hindu *Vedas* declare that our real nature is divine and we are pure, perfect and eternally free. God is seen as everywhere, eternally present, and there is nothing but God. God always has been, always will be and dwells within each of us as the divine Self. "The greatest temple of God lies within the human heart" (Vedanta Society). Many of Jesus's teachings were interpreted as conforming to this doctrine; e.g., the kingdom of God is within (Luke 17:21) and Jesus is in the Father, we are in him, and he is in us (John 14:20).

Many of these philosophies are known to have influenced the course of New Thought and will be explored further in later chapters.

Mind is superior to matter

In the world's earliest written records can be found discussions as to the reality of mind or spirit, and matter or body. The Indian *Samkhya* teachings of the eighth century B.C.E. teach of an eternal, infinite and undetermined primal substance from which matter springs and to which matter returns. Two centuries later, Anaximander of Miletus (610-540), one of the earliest Greek philosophers for whom we have records, teaches the exact same concept.

The mind/matter debate generally falls between the realists and materialists on one side and the idealists on the other.

Realism is the thesis that the existence of the universe and everything within it is independent of an observer. It exists whether or not anyone perceives it or knows about it. Materialism is a monistic (one substance) doctrine in that everything that exists is either matter or depends completely on matter for its existence. Thus, the universe contains no spiritually-real dimension. These two doctrines maintain that reality is not dependent upon a thinking entity; that is, material things are real regardless. No conditions are necessary, and no thinking entity, human or divine, is needed for their existence. Realists, as we mentioned in chapter two, think that their theories explain the world as it really is.

On the opposite side of the debate is idealism, which disagrees with the concept that the material world exists independent of a thinking entity. Rather, it views the existence of the world as completely mind-*dependent*. That is, the world we see exists only because a mind exists by which to observe it. All reality depends upon mind. This harkens back to Rene Descartes's famous aphorism—*cogito ergo sum*, "I think, therefore I am." The ultimately real transcends the world of matter—it is above or beyond physical matter. The fundamental nature of reality is mind or consciousness, and the only knowable things are mental states or mental entities. In other words, mind is the only reality and everything outside of mind is a creation of mind. Mind is the cause, matter is the effect or the result.

Within idealism can be found monists, dualists and neutralists. *Idealistic monism* posits a spiritual reality inherent or immanent in all things. *Idealistic dualism* posits both spiritual and material realities with the spiritual being of a higher reality than the material and with both realities known only because of the mind. This is also known as the *double aspect theory*, for mind and matter are two aspects of a single substance. The third type of idealism is neutral. That is, Ultimate Reality or the basic real "stuff" of which all things are made is neither mind nor matter. The term *neutral monism* was coined by American pragmatic philosopher William James in the nineteenth century to identify Ultimate Reality as "the Mysterious Essence and Primordial Source of both Mind and Matter . . . , a Pure, Profound Potentiality" (Laughlin).

Most of the great philosophers across time have been idealists. The ancient realist/materialist philosophies died out and were not resurrected and modified until the eighteenth and nineteenth centuries in reaction to the idealism of George Berkeley (1685-1753), the influential Irish empiricist philosopher and Anglican bishop. These philosophies, however, are peripheral to our study and will not be discussed.

Idealists take the basic conception of matter's existence being dependent upon mind and formulate it in slightly different ways.

Metaphysical idealists see the universe and everything within it as mental realities. Metaphysical Idealism is split into two groups.

1) Platonic idealism postulates an ultimate reality consisting of ideal Forms or Ideas (the real objects of knowledge), which are known only by the mind. The major representatives of this group are Plato, Aristotle and St. Augustine, though their views of ultimate reality are different. Both Plato and Aristotle envision an eternal uncreated substance that is given form by God. God doesn't create, it molds or forms. Contrarily, St. Augustine, whose philosophy forms the basis of Catholic doctrine, views God as creator of the substance of which all things are made.

2) Personalist idealism views ultimate reality as consciousness, mind or personality. The theory is formed from the views of Berkeley and Leibniz. Bronson Alcott, a transcendentalist, is credited with coining the term *Personalism* in 1863. He defines Personalism as "the doctrine that the ultimate reality of the world is a Divine Person who sustains the universe by a continuous act of creative will" (qtd. in Sahakian).

Leibniz posits ultimate entities that he calls *monads*. The term *monad* is Greek for "unity" or "oneness" and is the substance from which all things are made. Each monad is "individual, conscious, active, alive, and ranges in quality from the lower types (matter) through the higher types (souls or mind) up to the highest of all (God, who is responsible for all the rest)" (Sahakian). Monads are spiritual in nature and conform to natural law. The human soul is created from the higher immaterial and eternal monads, the body from the lower monads. The individuality of each monad allows for the diversity of forms and personalities.

Berkeley's form of idealism takes its views from several forms of idealism and is considered separately at a later point in this chapter.

Absolute idealism is the view that not only is reality of the mind, but it is of One Mind. This One Mind is the Absolute and contains all reality, or all reality is made of it. This form of idealism is found in Hinduism and the philosophical writings of Plotinus (204-269), Emanuel Swedenborg (1688-1772), Benedictus Spinoza (1634-1677), George Friedrich Hegel (1770-1831), Josiah Royce (1855-1916), and Frances Herbert Bradley (1864-1924).

For Swedenborg, a Swedish mystic and theologian, matter is spirit made visible to our senses. Spirit, or mind, is the only substance and is the only reality. All material form has a corresponding spiritual form, and together they make up an indivisible whole. For humans the mind is the corresponding spiritual form of the body; and as the mind changes, so does the body. This concept has tremendous importance for mental healing, as clarified in the next chapter.

In Hegel's system "the truth is the whole," and everything comes in threes. A thesis and its opposite, the antithesis, are synthesized into one truth. Applying this system to the mind/body dilemma he unifies all objects of sense and thought into one Absolute Reality or Idea, which is a coherent whole whose nature is ideal, spiritual or mental. This Absolute takes three forms: "the Idea-in-Itself (logic); the Idea-for-Itself or Idea-outside-itself (nature); and the Idea-in-and-for Itself (mind or spirit)" (Sahakian). All the things we see consist of some degree of reality, as aspects of the whole.

The absolute idealism of Hinduism, Spinoza and Plotinus are discussed later in this chapter.

Epistemological idealists identify reality with what can be known mentally, or what can be perceived, and consider what can be known or perceived as spiritual in nature. The leading proponents of this type of idealism are Rene Descartes (1596-1650), the French mathematician and philosopher known as the father of modern philosophy; John Locke (1632-1704), English empiricist philosopher; David Hume (1711-1776), Scottish historian and empiricist philosopher; and Bishop George Berkeley (1685-1753), though each formulates this theory slightly differently.

Rene Descartes was the first to discus in depth the mind/body problem. In fact, it is to his theory, known as Cartesian dualism, that all succeeding mind/body discussions are directed. Sitting at his desk pondering his existence, he realized that he is a thinking entity. "I think, therefore I am." Upon further contemplation he determined that reality consists of two distinctly separate essences— mind and matter, or soul substance and corporeal substance—that together are unified into reality.

While Descartes's real substance is knowable only to the mind, Locke's real substance is wholly unknowable to any of our senses. He calls it the "I-know-not-what," the unknowable thing-in-itself. For Locke, there are real objects existing beyond our perception; however they are unobservable and unknowable.

Hume rejects the existence of any physical objects for he believes that the only "things" that can be known, or that are real, are sensations and ideas. He sees no need to posit an entity or cause to produce them. He is a true sceptic.

Subjective idealism sees the conscious mind, or self-consciousness, as the basis of human knowledge. It also sees material substance as spiritual in nature. Proponents of this form of idealism are Berkeley and Fichte.

Fichte sees mind and matter being of the same spiritual substance. Matter is one form or manifestation of mind or spirit. Conscious mind creates the objects of matter as well as the knowledge by which we know them.

Berkeleyan idealism sees reality as composed entirely of spirit and the ideas of spirit, and in order to be known, must be perceived. Hence the classic questions: If a tree falls in a forest and no one is there to hear, does it make a noise? Does it even exist if no one is there to perceive it? Berkeley would answer "Yes," in a particular sense, because he claims there is an eternal, or divine, spirit that is always perceiving, thus allowing the existence of ideas outside our personal awareness.

Transcendental idealism has to do with the nature of the mind and the connection between our *a priori* mental acts and our *a posteriori* sense impressions. Mental acts come first; they are prior to, or precede, our sense perceptions. The leading proponent of this form of idealism is Immanuel Kant (1724-1804), considered to have been the greatest philosopher since the time of the ancient Greeks. A later form of Kant's idealism emerges with the transcendental movement.

The debate, then, is over the reality of matter. Realists emphatically say "Yes!" Idealists qualifiedly say "No." Some idealists see matter as being completely unreal or illusory. Some forms of pantheism and Hinduism fall into this category, as does Christian Science. All of these systems of thought are discussed in depth in later chapters.

From the previous discussion of the various forms of idealism, we can see that opinion is divided between the idealists who hold mind as the only reality and the materialists and realists who assert that matter is the real substance. The issue is further complicated because within idealism we have monists, for whom there is only one substance that manifests as both mind and matter, dualists who claim that mind and matter are separate substances, and pluralists who posit several substances.

In this great debate between materialism and idealism, New Thought sides with monistic idealism; in particular, with Plato's form of metaphysical idealism; the absolute idealism of Hinduism, Spinoza and Plotinus; the transcendental idealism of Kant; and the blended idealism of Berkeley.

Within Plato's idealism is found his theory of Forms and is an attempt to refute sophistic scepticism, which claims that a search may be made for absolute knowledge about how things are, but such knowledge can never be found. Contrarily, Plato feels absolute knowledge not only can be found but can be known as well. Building on the teachings of Socrates, Plato determines that if a concept represents the reality of things, as Socrates teaches, then reality must be above these things in an ideal realm. Plato substitutes *Idea* or *Form* for Socrates's *concept* and supposes a world of Ideas separate from, and superior to, the world we experience.

Plato combines Parmenides's philosophy of Being with Heraclitus's philosophy of Becoming to create his theory. For Parmenides (c. 550 B.C.E.), the Universe is a single, permanent substance. The ultimately real world is one eternal, uncreated, unchangeable, indestructible substance called Being. There is only One; therefore, the thinker and the thought are one and the same. Heraclitus's (c. 460 B.C.E.) universe is also uncreated, but it is changeable. There is no permanent, immutable substance. Everything is in flux. Ultimate reality is always developing, always Becoming.

Plato's famous allegory of the cave (*Republic*, VII, 514 d) is intended to support his notion of the reality of Ideas (the Being of Parmenides) and the illusory nature of matter (the Becoming of Heraclitus). In the allegory, a group of men are chained facing the wall of a cave in which they have lived since childhood. They are unable to move their heads from side-to-side and so are only able to look straight ahead to the wall. A fire burning above and behind them provides their only light. Between the prisoners and the fire there is a low wall behind which men carry statues and reproductions of animals. As the men pass along the wall their shadows are cast unto the

walls of the cave, and because the prisoners cannot turn their heads to
see the men, they think the shadows are the real forms. If the prisoners
were released from their chains, they would then see that men, not
their shadows, were the reality. And if they left the cave and encountered animals like the reproductions they had seen in the cave,
their first impulse would be to think the animal seen outside the cave
and the shadow they had seen in the cave were the same; that is, they
would ascribe reality to the shadow. Plato says this is what we do. We
take the world of our experience to be real when it is only a shadow
world, a reflection of the real world. The real world is the world of
Ideas, which is not of the senses, but of the mind.

In the absolute idealism of Plotinus, the Egyptian mystic, we
find a spiritual trinity consisting of The One, Spirit and Soul. These
three make up the one Absolute—the one exalted and indescribable
God from which all creation flows. This impersonal It permeates all
creation yet is above and prior to all creation. This Absolute is unity,
the synthesis of mind and matter. The Absolute One, or God, is permanent and unchangeable, but its myriad creations are temporary and
alterable. Enveloped within the Soul of the Absolute is the entire
universe; thus, all creation, including the human body, is immersed
within Soul rather than containing Soul. We each have an individual
soul, and this soul is a facet of the World Soul.

Like Plotinus, the Dutch rationalist Spinoza sees God as the
One, the only eternal and infinite substance from which all things are
made. Although creation seems to consist of separate and individual
forms of matter, there can be no separation when there is only One.
The universe in its myriad forms, then, is an aspect or an attribute of
the One. The myriad creations of the One work together by use of
irreversible laws as an integrated whole. Unlike Plotinus, Spinoza sees
all of Nature as being God; thus his philosophy is pantheistic. By
positing only one substance, of which both mind and body are aspects,
Spinoza attempts to resolve the mind/body problem. Being of the same
substance, the mind and body operate such that an affect on one aspect
triggers an affect on the other. This is an important concept for mental
healing.

I here only briefly touch on the monistic idealism of Hinduism.
Because of its importance to our study, Hinduism is covered in depth
in chapter ten. The Hindu philosopher Sri Aurobindo (1872-1950)

writes, "Divine evolution is the aftermath of a process of involution wherein the Unmanifest Absolute made itself manifest in several levels of reality" (McGreal). Involution means "from within," so God, the Unmanifest Absolute, creates from within all the levels of reality, which, Aurobindo says, includes mind, life and matter. God or *Brahman* evolves as Its creations evolve. Holmes picks up on this line of thought and expounds on it in his philosophy.

Berkeley set out to prove that all reality is mental. In that sense-data are mental, and since "To be is to be perceived," mind, specifically God's Mind, as the perceiver, is the only reality. Thus, he denies any reality to matter. In Berkeley's words, "That any immediate object of the senses—that is, any idea or combination of ideas— should exist in an unthinking substance, or exterior to *all* minds, is in itself an evident contradiction. Whatever is immediately perceived is an idea; and can any idea exist out of the mind?"

Though matter exists only in the mind, Berkeley is not saying the world does not exist. He is saying it only exists because a spiritual being, or a mental being, since mind is spirit, is perceiving it. Thus, the world and all its unthinking constituents are mind-dependent. The world must exist, otherwise we would not be able to experience it.

In the eighteenth century Kant theorized that the world we know and experience is a world interpreted by the mind and is not the ultimately real world, though neither is it simply a creation of the mind. Kant postulated three kinds of reality: 1) the world we live in and perceive—the world of phenomena; 2) the world of understanding; and 3) the ultimately real world—a supersensible world that transcends all senses and is unknowable, though the mind attempts to know it. The real world is thought, "by pure understanding alone, as a thing in itself," and has nothing to do with sense. The real world is based on ideas of reason and they are "transcendent inasmuch as they overleap the limits of all experience" (Kant, qtd. in Sahakian).

These four concepts of the mind and the reality of the world of our senses are important to New Thought, for the concepts of mind as the only reality and mind's ability to affect matter are important to mental healing. I close this chapter with a discussion of the mind/ matter debate as it applies to New Thought.

The founders of New Thought consider matter to be "Mind in form," or "Substance in action," or "Being in manifestation." God is

Mind, Substance, or Being and is the only Reality. God expresses into the world by way of thought—Its thoughts as well as our thoughts. God's thoughts are equivalent to Plato's Forms or Ideas. They are ideal and real. God expressing through our thought is the same concept Berkeley had in mind when he said that reality, or existence, exists by being perceived. This is the way the One works —first in the mind, then in manifest form. And with Spinoza, the founders see mind and body affecting each other.

In *Christian Healing* Fillmore states that the omnipresent Spirit substance is visible only to mind, stands back of and gives support to all our thoughts and words, is always with us, and is ready to be used and manifested.

New Thought disagrees with those who claim that everything external to mind is illusion. True, mind is the only reality. However, as Holmes writes, "our thought does not spiritualize matter and it does not materialize Spirit. Spirit and matter, or thought and form, are one and the same thing" (*New Thought Terms*). The physical universe is Mind in form or Spirit made visible. He quotes Plotinus as saying, "Nature is the great nothing, yet it is not exactly nothing," because "Its business is to receive the forms of thought which the Spirit lets fall into It" (*Science of Mind*).

Brooks writes that by necessity a universal God must be present in Its creation. The entire universe consists of one substance, and that substance is God. Dualism "separate[s] the effect from its cause, the manifestation from its source, creation from the Creator" causing a belief "in two powers, Spirit and matter, good and evil, life and death, sickness and health." Matter is simply Spirit made visible. The truth is that the universe consists of nothing but God and "is God and God-Idea in expression." Hence, since there is no separation, nothing in the universe can suffer any sort of discord or affliction. "If thine eye be single, if it sees only the One Presence and One Power at work in the universe of form, thy body shall be full of health; thy thought shall be filled with light."

Duality is not possible in a universe consisting of only one substance, and a belief in duality is wrong thinking. Holmes tells us that "True philosophy in all ages has perceived that the Power back of all things must be One Power; and the clearer the thought of Unity, the greater has been the philosophy" (*Science of Mind*).

In science almost a century ago, the Cartesian concept of duality perished with the advent of quantum physics. And decades before that, psychologists Gustav Theodore Fechner (1801-1887) and William James (1842-1910) put forth theories of consciousness which held that there is "only one primal stuff or material" from which all things are composed (James, qtd. in Sahakian). In viewing the mind and the brain as aspects of the same underlying reality, Fechner hoped to solve the mind/body problem and remove duality from psychology. New Thought is attempting to do the same for metaphysics and religion.

Now that we see there is a solid history and context, though no definitive proof and continuing debate, for the basis of New Thought philosophy, we return to our three groups, to an exploration of the history of their philosophies, and to their common beliefs.

V.

THE ROAD TO WELL-BEING

Health is my expected heaven.
John Keats (1795–1821), British poet
Letters of John Keats

I find that with me low spirits and feeble health come and go together.
Rutherford Birchard Hayes (1822–1893)
Diary and Letters of Rutherford Birchard Hayes:
Nineteenth President of the United States

As shown in chapter three, the three main New Thought churches essentially teach the same doctrine, though among the groups there is some variation as to content and as to the many minds who influenced each philosophy. These many minds are what I refer to as "the Roads."

The first road we follow is one that all three of our churches traveled, and it leads us to a metaphysical group not considered part of New Thought, at its own insistence. That group is Christian Science. The doctrines of Christian Science and New Thought are virtually identical except in one respect, and that has to do with the reality of matter. This distinction is discussed later in this chapter. The similarity between the two groups is not surprising considering the founders of the three main New Thought groups all studied with and were highly influenced by Emma Curtis Hopkins, a practitioner of the Christian Science philosophy. We begin our journey with Hopkins.

Emma Curtis Hopkins

Not much is known about the life of Emma Curtis Hopkins prior to her studies with Mary Baker Eddy. She was born September 2, 1849, and it has been written that she displayed an affinity for world history and language. She studied the works of the major Greek philosophers in their original language.

Hopkins studied with Eddy and worked for several years for the Christian Science organization, serving at one point as editor of the *Christian Science Journal*. She left, or was dismissed, in 1885, apparently because of conflicts with the autocratic Eddy. Though no longer part of the official organization, Hopkins continued to teach Christian Science doctrine and two years later founded the Christian Science Theological Seminary. Over the next several years she broadened her teachings by adding concepts from mystical and Eastern writings. As an independent teacher not associated with any particular group, Hopkins taught large classes in many cities around the country, in the process influencing numerous New Thought writers and effectuating many healings.

Hopkins taught that the only reality is God and that this reality is known by many names: Substance, Spirit, Intelligence, Mind, Love, and Wisdom, to name a few. God is Infinite and Unbounded and is the Substance of the Universe. Humans are creations of God, and since God is Mind, we are thoughts of God or ideas in the Mind of God, and share in Its nature. (Capitalized nouns indicate characteristics of or synonyms for God.)

Since reality is spirit, matter is the unreal semblance or shadow of the real thing. She says, "All physical things are the semblance only - the out-picturing - of things not yet shown," and "[I]f matter be but the unreal semblance of the real thing or entity, it is easy to say matter is nonentity; and nonentity is nothingness" ("Emma Only"). It is clear that she considers matter (physical objects) to be unreal or imaginary. Though we possess a physical body there is a part of us that is real. Since the only reality is Spirit, the real part of us, the real self, is spirit. She says most ancient teachings tell us that the real self is "indestructible, unchangeable, never yielding to imperfection." Obviously, the real self is not the body.

The purpose of the real self is to manifest itself in ways that prove its excellence. In denying the reality of our fleshly body, the false self, the perfection and divinity of the real self is able to shine through. This is what Jesus means in telling us to let our lights shine. In following this counsel, we prove to everyone that we are of divine origin.

The kingdom of heaven is not a place; it is a state of mind, the state of knowing the Good. The right states of mind consist of perfection—perfect health, perfect wisdom, perfect prosperity, perfect *everything*. When we acknowledge, accept and voice this Truth, it leads us to health, wealth and wisdom, for the perfection that is true of God is true of us. Sickness, pain, death, and poverty are not part of God, therefore, they need not be part of us. So, it may seem like we are living in heaven right here, right now, when our minds are in the right state.

She does not take a literal interpretation of the Bible but rather views its stories from a metaphysical perspective, as did all her teachers. For example, when Jesus speaks of sheep, he is speaking of our thoughts. Thoughts act like sheep in that they are docile and obedient. We are the shepherds of our thoughts, and they go wherever we lead them. Our most obedient thoughts are our thoughts about God, and these ideas of God will lead us to heaven, to the state of right thinking.

Hopkins emphasizes the power of words and teaches that words contain potentiality, the greatest of all potentiality being in the word *God*. This is because within this word is all potentiality—the potential for goodness, health, wealth, and well-being. God is the ideal, for Its "words are life unto those that find them and health to all their flesh." Though for many it is unconscious, the truth is that *"there is Good for me and I ought to have it"* (*Scientific Christian*, emphasis in original). But we won't have it unless we ask for it and then accept it. If we allow our mind to accept this Truth, then we allow the words of God to become part of our being, as God works by means of Truth. We must also expect that God will work in our lives, and actually see in our mind that God is working, for God works in response to our expectation and in response to our requests.

When we understand these Truths, it becomes possible to become one with God. This is what is meant by the atonement—it is at-one-ment, or becoming one mind, understanding that all is Mind, what she calls "the Science of Mind." In recognizing this oneness, she reiterates what mystics have always taught—there is only One, and all things spring from that One; every soul is the direct offspring of Divine Soul or Mind.

Because of her familiarity with the Hebrew scriptures as well as the sacred texts of India, she sees the similarity between these sayings of Jesus, "I and my Father are one" and "ye are the sons of the Most High," and the ancient doctrine of *nirvana*, which is man's union with God. She quotes from the Hindu *Chandogya Upanishad*: "The Man who is conscious of [his] divinity incurs neither disease, nor pain, nor death" (qtd. in Anderson, "Excerpts"). She sees her teachings as consistent with all of these doctrines.

In Hopkins's teachings we find the ideas that thought is creative and can heal; that we are all God's children and as such are divine; that health, happiness and abundance are our birthright; that God is everywhere always; and that the methods of mental healing can be proved by scientific means. As we have seen, these same ideas are basic to New Thought.

Words similar to these of Hopkins can be heard today in any prayer, meditation, or spiritual mind treatment given in any New Thought church. The only difference is the use of modern terminology for *Thee* and *Thou* such as *God, Divine Mind, Infinite Love*, or any of the other names for God utilized by New Thought:

> Facing Thee, there is no evil on my pathway –
> There is no matter with its laws –
> There is no loss, no lack, no deprivation –
> There is nothing to fear for there shall be no power to hurt –
> There is neither sin, nor sickness, nor death.
> Because Thou Art The Unconditioned and the Absolute,
> I also am Unconditioned and Absolute.
> Because Thou Art Omnipotent Free Spirit,
> I also am Omnipotent Free Spirit.
> (Hopkins, qtd. in Anderson, "Contrasting Strains")

As previously mentioned, Hopkins is known as the teacher's teacher. Besides the founders of the three main New Thought churches, many of the early leaders of the New Thought movement were among her students, including several authors, poets and founders of New Thought magazines. It is estimated that she taught

50,000 students before she passed on April 25, 1925. It is safe to say, that Hopkins's bore a tremendous influence on New Thought.

We see in Hopkins's thought traces of other paths. Her philosophy is a union of the teachings of Eddy, the mystics, Jesus, and certain ancient Greek and Eastern philosophies. All of these influences except for Eddy are explored in later chapters.

Mary Baker Eddy

From childhood on, Mary Baker Eddy suffered from poor health, and after the birth of her son in 1843, when her health further declined, she began investigating the many healing techniques available at the time. None of them proved to be of much help, though, until 1862 when she went to Phineas Quimby for treatment. His methods helped her considerably, and Eddy began to study with him. After a time, she became disillusioned with Quimby's philosophy. Though she saw merit in his system of healing, she disagreed with his concept of the mind and was offended by his loathing of religion. For most of her life Eddy had attended regular church services and was a student of the Bible, which she had looked to for strength and hope during her long years of ill health.

While Eddy had been helped by Quimby's method of mental healing, she had not been cured, for she later experienced a relapse in her health and developed doubts as to Quimby's methods providing any lasting cure. She continued her search and began reading the works of the transcendentalists, finding Bronson Alcott's words particularly helpful.

Shortly after Quimby's death in 1866 Eddy fell on the ice, seriously injuring herself. In the depths of despair, and believing that she was dying, she turned once again to the Bible and discovered the spiritual laws that lie behind what she refers to as "the Science of Mind-healing." As to this discovery and her subsequent return to health, she writes:

> St. Paul writes: "For to be carnally minded is death; but to be spiritually minded is life and peace." This knowledge came to me in an hour of great need; and I give it to you as death-bed

testimony to the daystar that dawned on the night of material sense. This knowledge is practical, for it wrought my immediate recovery from an injury caused by an accident, and pronounced fatal by the physicians. On the third day thereafter, I called for my Bible, and opened it at Matthew ix. 2. As I read, the healing Truth dawned upon my sense; and the result was that I rose, dressed myself, and ever after was in better health than I had before enjoyed. That short experience included a glimpse of the great fact that I have since tried to make plain to others, namely, Life in and of Spirit; this Life being the sole reality of existence (*Miscellaneous Writings*).

Eddy had discovered that the true power of the mind, the true healer, is divine Mind working through the human mind. Thus, every effect is a mental phenomenon. In early 1867 she began teaching this newly-discovered truth she called *Christian Science*, which she saw as completely different from Quimby's methods of the same name. She spent the next eight years putting this truth into written form, resulting in the book *Science and Health, With Key to the Scriptures* (hereafter referred to as *Science and Health*). This book, along with the Bible, is the official text of Christian Science. In Chapter 14, Eddy summarizes the Christian Science philosophy as follows:

- As adherents of Truth, we take the inspired Word of the Bible as our sufficient guide to eternal Life.
- We acknowledge and adore one supreme and infinite God. We acknowledge His Son, one Christ; the Holy Ghost or divine Comforter; and man in God's image and likeness.
- We acknowledge God's forgiveness of sin in the destruction of sin and the spiritual understanding that casts out evil as unreal. But the belief in sin is punished so long as the belief lasts.
- We acknowledge Jesus' atonement as the evidence of divine, efficacious Love, unfolding man's unity with God through Christ Jesus the Wayshower; and we acknowledge that man is saved through Christ, through Truth, Life, and Love as demonstrated by the Galilean Prophet in healing the sick and overcoming sin and death.
- We acknowledge that the crucifixion of Jesus and his resurrection served to uplift faith to understand eternal

Life, even the allness of Soul, Spirit, and the nothingness of matter.

- And we solemnly promise to watch, and pray for that Mind to be in us which was also in Christ Jesus; to do unto others as we would have them do unto us; and to be merciful, just, and pure.

In Chapter 6 of *Science and Health* she compacts her system even further into what she feels are the key self-evident propositions:

- God is All-in-all.
- God is good. Good is Mind.
- God, Spirit, being all, nothing is matter.
- Life, God, omnipotent good, deny death, evil, sin, disease. Disease, sin, evil, death, deny good, omnipotent God, Life.

The following list is abstracted from *Science and Health*, Chapters 1, 2, 4, 6, and 14, to lend insight into the basic concepts upon which the Christian Science system is based and, too, so that we may see the clear path from New Thought through Hopkins to Eddy:

- There are many names for, and descriptions of, God—Universal Principle, the only intelligence in the universe, the universal cause, the only power or source, divine Principle, Love, the only creator, infinite, indivisible, the Father-Mother, and Mind.
- God created everything *in* and *of* Himself. As God is Spirit, "possessing all power, filling all space, constituting all Science," (omnipotence, omnipresence, omniscience), matter was never created and is, therefore, unreal. Inasmuch as matter is unreal, so is anything that is associated with matter; i.e., sickness, pain, poverty, and mortality. This "divine Principle is demonstrated by healing the sick and thus proved absolute and divine." Also because God is all and is good, the devil and evil are unreal.
- Humans, being made *of* God in His image and likeness, are spiritual. We are the ideas of God, and we are good.

- There is only one Mind, which consists of God and His thoughts. Mortal man does not have a mind, as Mind is immortal. Christian Science uses the term *mortal mind*, by which is meant all of the emotions and beliefs having to do with the flesh, or matter, which is unreal. There is a sense in which mind in man has meaning, though, and that is as God's idea— the spiritual, or real, part of our being.

- We are healed when we become aware of the errors of our thinking. Jesus said we should have no other gods before us, which Eddy rendered: "Thou shalt have no belief of Life as mortal; thou shalt not know evil, for there is one Life, –even God, good." The only suffering comes from mortal mind, as divine Mind is unable to suffer. "There is no pain in Truth, and no truth in pain; no nerve in Mind, and no mind in nerve; no matter in Mind, and no mind in matter; no matter in Life, and no life in matter; no matter in good, and no good in matter."

- All of God's creations express God yet do not contain the fullness of God. Infinite Mind is not in man, but is reflected by man; that is, the consciousness and individuality of spiritual man are reflections of God. This is what is meant by the *atonement*. Jesus taught the at-one-ment with God, which is the "exemplification of man's unity with God, whereby man reflects divine Truth, Life, and Love."

- The word *Christ* expresses God's spiritual, eternal nature and was not part of Jesus's name. Jesus is called Christ Jesus because Jesus embodied God's nature. As Christ is a spiritual idea it can be, and has been, embodied by others.

- The Trinity is Life, Truth and Love, or "God the Father-Mother; Christ the spiritual idea of sonship; [and] divine Science or the Holy Comforter." By *sonship* is meant God's spiritual idea of man.

- Because of God's goodness, it is not proper to supplicate God for what is already ours. We only need to heed "God's rule," and make ourselves available to the good that already exists by showing gratitude for the good we have and striving daily to "assimilate more of the divine character . . . until we awake in His likeness."

- Jesus did not teach a gospel consisting of creed, ceremony or ritual, but a gospel of Divine Love "casting out error and healing the sick, not merely in the *name* of Christ, or Truth, but in demonstration of Truth." The Christian Science system is based on Jesus's teachings and his methods of healing and "enables the learner to demonstrate the divine Principle, . . . and the sacred rules for its present application to the cure of disease."

Though it can be seen that there are numerous similarities between Christian Science and New Thought, Eddy adamantly insisted that her system of healing was not New Thought, and by the late 1800s when the New Thought Movement was flourishing, she had distanced herself from the other systems of healing based substantially on both her work and that of Quimby.

The major distinction between the systems was alluded to in the last chapter. New Thought sees matter as Spirit made visible while Christian Science sees matter as completely unreal. Because of this, Christian Science encourages its adherents to rely totally on faith in the healing power of God for cure from illness rather than to resort to medical treatment. This, however, is not what is commonly called "faith healing." As with New Thought, Christian Science views any bodily condition as an effect of our conscious and unconscious thoughts. Therefore, all healing needs to take place in the mind rather than in the body.

There are two reasons Christian Scientists rely on faith and prayer rather than the medical profession: 1) Because illness is viewed as illusory, accepting medical assistance tends to affirm the illusion; and 2) Members of the medical profession can have a negative effect on our health because of the suggestibility of the mind. Christian Scientists are not forbidden to seek out medical aid. Rather, they are free to choose one form of treatment or the other, but not both. Experience has shown that combining medical care with the prayers and treatments of Christian Science practitioners tends to lessen the efficacy of both treatments, for we cannot serve two masters. Either we treat the real mind or the illusory body.

We now travel to Quimby's world, delve into his manuscripts and examine the teachings that Eddy and Hopkins in large measure used in developing their healing philosophies.

Phineas Parkhurst Quimby

As mentioned briefly in the second chapter, Phineas Parkhurst Quimby was the first, at least in modern times, to realize the connection between our thoughts and our experiences and to use this knowledge as the basis for healing. In reality, mental healing goes back at least to ancient Greece. In the *Dialogues of Plato*, a Thracian friend of Socrates states, "Let no one persuade you to cure the head, until he has first given you his soul to be cured. . . . For this . . . is the great error of our day in the treatment of the human body, that physicians separate the soul from the body" (qtd. in Braden). In Platonic terms, soul and mind are equivalent.

Quimby also uses Jesus's words in developing a basis for his healing methods and his concept of God. Quimby has been charged by many, including Eddy, with being anti-religion, and it is true that he held very strong feelings against religious dogma, for what he felt were very good reasons. Regardless of these feelings, Quimby was an enormously spiritual man, as we shall see.

Born with a scientific mind on February 16, 1802, he became an inventor. Common to the times, he did not receive much of a formal education. His fascination with how things work, though, resulted in a magnificent self-education. A lover of truth, he preferred to prove truths for himself rather than read someone else's opinions about a subject of interest. His friends, neighbors and acquaintances considered him to be honest and practical. This was important, for as his interests branched into new and untried territory, bordering at that time on quackery, his good character lent credence to his questionable work.

He first became acquainted with mesmerism in 1838 and by 1840 was conducting the experiments with Burkmar discussed in chapter two that led to his theories of the mind and the eventual abandonment of mesmerism. Between 1841 and 1859 he discovered new truths about the mind and the connection between our thoughts and the illnesses we suffer. Based on these insights he gradually formulated the new method of healing he called the *Science of Health*. Most of his manuscripts are dated between 1859 and 1865, and this is also the period when he was most actively engaged in healing the sick. This, too, is largely when his thoughts regarding religious dogma and medical practices were framed. He continued his work, healing hundreds of people, until his death in January of 1866.

From the account given in his manuscripts, Quimby had suffered for many years from tuberculosis and ulcers on his lungs before he began his experiments with mesmerism. He endured constant pains in his back that doctors told him were caused by the disease in his kidneys.

During one of his sessions with a mesmerized Burkmar, Quimby described his pains to Burkmar who then put his hand on the exact spot where Quimby felt pain. Burkmar confirmed the doctor's prognosis. Half of one of Quimby's kidneys had dissolved into a three-inch piece and was connected by just a strand. Quimby believed what Burkmar said because it agreed with what the doctors had told him. He also believed the doctors who said that medicine would not cure him. Something, however, prompted him to ask Burkmar if there was any remedy for his ailments. Burkmar declared that he could reattach the hanging piece of kidney, the entire kidney would grow back, and Quimby would get well. Burkmar placed his hands on Quimby, rejoining the pieces of kidney. The very next day Quimby was free of pain and remained so the rest of his life.

Pondering the events that led to his healing, Quimby came to new insights regarding the mind. He had believed that he possessed the ailments Burkmar described, and he also had believed the doctors who told him nothing could be done to ease his pain. Nevertheless, he had also believed Burkmar when he said he could cure him. Quimby then realized that he had been deceived into a belief that resulted in his sickness and began to doubt that his kidneys in fact had been diseased at all. He then concluded that Burkmar had effected the cure by reading Quimby's mind. After further experiments, though, Quimby decided that his disease and accompanying pain actually had existed but had been of his own making.

In his experiments he also learned about the role imagination plays in a person's experience. Quimby would think of a wild animal, bringing the picture of the animal as vividly as possible into his mind, and without telling Burkmar of the image, Burkmar would become frightened. Telling Burkmar the animal was simply in his imagination did not lessen his fear. This led Quimby to conclude that our minds have the power to create something *seen* from the *unseen*, that ideas can take form. Upon further experimentation, he determined that ideas are not material in nature, but are made from something that can be seen by a person's "spiritual eyes." He began to question the need for mesmerism since one's beliefs create the ideas in the mind.

At this point he discontinued his experiments with Burkmar. Having been shown how a person's mind can be influenced by another's thoughts and beliefs, and having gained insight as to how these thoughts and beliefs can cause disease, he turned to developing a cure. He read many books on mesmerism and examined the different explanations for "mesmeric sleep." He also studied various philosophers mentioning Bishop Berkeley, an idealist, and Lucretius, a materialist, by name. He compared the teachings of the philosophers concerning mind and matter and sided with the idealists, for in reality "there is no matter independent of mind or life."

As he contemplated his previous experiments with Burkmar, he determined that since he was able to influence Burkmar by creating a mental picture that produced a negative effect, it should be just as easy to create pictures that produce positive effects. It also occurred to him that since effects can be produced by suggestion, and illness is an effect, then illness could be cured by suggestion. He determined that it is by suggestion—the suggestion placed in mind by doctors—that medicine effects cures, and so, began to question a need for medicine.

He began experimenting with these new discoveries using people suffering from various illnesses. These experiments confirmed the results of his own healing and convinced him that disease is not real in and of itself, but is a result of erroneous thinking.

These experiments also proved to him that cures can be effected without the use of mesmerism. Using his own intuition Quimby could feel what his patients felt, and he no longer needed mesmerism to induce the body into health. So he abandoned mesmerism for clairvoyance, transforming matter by removing from the mind all beliefs and opinions that tend to create afflictions and replacing them with ideas of health and well-being. He realized that his intuitive power was not unique, that we all have power over the body through the states of our mind, and that our well-being is not dependent upon anyone else, not mesmerist, priest or doctor. All that is needed for well-being is a change in mind as to our beliefs about our illness.

He mentions Emanuel Swedenborg in connection with self-induced mental states, and it appears the formulation of his ideas at this time were influenced, at least in part, by Swedenborg's writings.

Quimby came to believe that there had to be a deeper science than the one proposed by the medical field, and he recognized the connection between the religious creeds we believe and the consequences we create. He already had concluded that disease results from "a deranged state of mind," a mind filled with beliefs and opinions placed there by all the other minds to which a person chooses to listen, and he came now to view the beliefs and opinions of medical and religious authorities as being especially detrimental. He had learned that a patient could be affected simply by suggestion, and depending upon the suggestion, the resulting effect was either enjoyable or regrettable. He felt we could influence all minds wisely, and by developing this wisdom we could free ourselves and others from the negative suggestions that plague society.

Consequently, he determined that all healing "occurs according to one principle: the only principle of healing in every instance whatever, natural and Divine, according to resident energies and unchanging laws" (qtd. in Dresser, H.; emphasis in original). He decided there is no physical science, for the only true science is spiritual. According to Horatio Dresser, Quimby's student, friend and biographer, "Quimby's work from this time on was to expose what he called the deception practiced by physicians, just as he exposed priestcraft, the humbuggery of mediumship, and the fallacies of every sort of imposition turning upon the acceptance of opinion for truth."

Quimby was not against religion per se, but was against the disastrous consequences of believing in various religious doctrines, particularly the doctrines of unpardonable sin and predestination. Many of his patients believed in, and were victimized by, what Dresser calls "the old theology," identified in the manuscripts as Calvinism. Quimby considered the priests and ministers of the time to be "blind guides," and so "he made war on all religious opinions and on all priestcraft." He regarded Jesus as a reformer who had to defeat the old religious beliefs of the people before he could begin teaching them the Truth. Quimby held Jesus in very high regard and considered Jesus to be the founder of spiritual science. In comparing Jesus to the "blind guides," both of whom he refers to as "oracles," he writes:

> Let us now sum up the wisdom which this oracle has delivered. All of his wisdom is founded on an opinion that there is another world and that Jesus came from that world to communicate the fact to the inhabitants of this one. The happiness of man is not increased by this theory, because this oracle cannot cure the sick. Now Jesus cured the sick and said if they understood Him they might do the same. We want a theory like that of Jesus, not of talk but of words, for a theory that cannot be put into practice is worthless.

> My oracle is Jesus: He proves the goodness of wisdom. Jesus was the oracle and Christ the wisdom shown through this man for the happiness of the sick who had been deceived by the other two classes, priest and doctor. God or Wisdom has seen how these blind guides had robbed the widow and the poor of their treasures, deserted them and left them forsaken and despairing, dependent upon the charity of a wicked world. This wisdom developed itself through the man Jesus and He fearlessly stood up and denounced these blind guides as hypocrites and devils (qtd. in Dresser, H.).

Quimby believed he followed in Jesus's footsteps by ridding his patients of their old religious beliefs and then turning them to the truth that heals.

While he didn't look to the Bible for answers as do some of his successors, particularly Eddy, he is well-versed in its doctrines, and he found within its pages corroboration of his mental science. In many lengthy articles concerning biblical interpretation, Quimby attempted to establish the "spiritual Science" that lies beneath the "letter of the Word." He saw Cain and Abel, Law and Gospel, and Saul and Paul as examples of the two forces working within each individual. The Bible is not theological but scientific, containing "a 'scientific' explanation of cause and effect, showing how man must act and think for his happiness." The account of the creation "pertains to man's spiritual development, not to the production of a literal earth." His experience with hundreds of patients showed him that viewing the Bible in a literal sense caused many ailments. In showing his patients the inner meaning of Jesus's sayings, he opened the way for their self-healing, for Jesus taught the true healing principle—the Christ within.

He equated Christ with Truth and Christ with Science, thus his *Science of the Christ*, claiming that Jesus taught the same science of health that Quimby taught. He taught that true scientific wisdom is health, happiness and light. False reasoning, or ignorance, is sickness, death and darkness. Disease, as well as all we call evil, is simply false reasoning, an error, and is unreal.

Quimby equated *God* with *Principle*, the "Principle that never moves, the foundation of all things," and, according to Dresser, he believed deeply "in the indwelling presence of God as love and wisdom. God is a Spirit and not a man. Wisdom is the sower and God the vineyard, and as man is made in the image of God his [inner] mind is spirit and receives the seed of Wisdom." He felt certain that he operated under a guiding Principle, a Principle of Goodness, in his work with the sick, and that everyone has this same ability.

It seems clear that there is a direct line through Hopkins to Eddy, and through Eddy to Quimby. Further, most of the sixteen common themes we find among New Thought churches can be found in Quimby's teachings. Quimby really is, then, the father of modern New Thought.

We visit now the man from whom the teachings of Quimby, in all likelihood, were relayed to the founders of Unity and Religious Science, if not also to Divine Science. In my research I did not find any references to Quimby or Eddy by the women who founded Divine Science, but they did use the term *Christian Science*, and because of their tie to Hopkins, I assume a familiarity with this term's origins.

Warren Felt Evans and Emanuel Swedenborg

Warren Felt Evans, a contemporary of Eddy, and a patient of Quimby, impacted greatly the spread of Quimby's theories of mental healing by means of the numerous books he authored. It is not known how much influence, if any, his writings had on Eddy and Hopkins.

Eddy was acquainted with Evans, though, and some have claimed a connection between the two. Because of this, his tie to Quimby, and his emphasis on *mental* healing, Evans is included in this particular road to New Thought.

Evans, a Methodist minister, came to Quimby in 1863 for healing. He suffered from a serious, chronic condition that had not been helped by the medication administered by his physicians. Quimby's methods healed him. Shortly thereafter, Evans decided that he had sufficient understanding of the healing method to conduct healings of his own. He set up a practice of mental medicine first in Claremont, New Hampshire and then a few years later in Boston, Massachusetts. There he and his wife practiced mental healing for the next twenty years. Though not a medical doctor many, including Eddy, referred to him as "Dr. Evans."

How Evans learned of Emanuel Swendenborg's teachings is not known. Perhaps he learned of them through Quimby as Quimby mentions Swedenborg in his writings, and it was shortly after his visits to Quimby that Evans left the Methodist Church and joined the Church of the New Jerusalem, a church based on Swedenborgian principles. Powerfully influenced by both Swedenborg and Quimby, Evans combined their philosophies into the system of healing he calls *Mental Science*. He intended his numerous books to explain and enlarge this philosophy. His first book, *The Mental Cure*, published in 1869, was the first of many books by many authors on the subject of mental healing.

In creating his mental science Evans uses Quimby's method of healing in combination with Swedenborg's concept of God, His characteristics and His relationship to humanity. Before examining Evans's teachings, it is important that we understand Swedenborg and his concept of God. Therefore, a short detour is required.

Emanuel Swedenborg, called by some the Buddha of the North, was born in 1688 in Stockholm, Sweden. Well-versed in the sciences he developed several theories, some of which have now been confirmed. In the mid-1700s, Swedenborg experienced numerous visions from which he derived his 30 volumes of theology. He believed he had been given new revelations and called to share them with the world. Thus began his twenty-seven years of writing, living in near isolation.

The revelations taught him that God is love, wisdom, goodness, truth, and life. God is infinite, everlasting and unchanging; thus, is everywhere and always the same. God exists in itself, and all things in the universe exist because of God. God is the cause of all nature, is substance and form, and being the only substance It is the underlying reality of all things. All creations in themselves are inanimate and dead. It is the Divine in them that give them life. We all have access to the fullness of God's life, but some of us obstruct it. This Divine Being seeks to share Its goodness and to make Itself known. Inasmuch as we are created *from* God, we contain the nature of the Divine. It manifests Itself to us through personal revelation in dreams, intuitions and insights; through revealed scripture; and through the diversity found in nature.

There is an unseen world and a seen world, and the unseen world is more real. The way we learn about this unseen world, which includes God, is through intuition, or turning within. The seen world is the natural world, and the unseen world is the spiritual world that produces and sustains it. These two worlds correspond to one another by law as cause and effect. All is in Divine Order, and God does nothing arbitrarily. All is directed by law, with natural laws corresponding to higher spiritual laws. This relationship between the two worlds he refers to as the *Doctrine of Correspondence.*

Individuals possess both a natural mind and a spiritual mind, the natural mind being lower, what he calls the "animal mind," or the "mind of a person's world," and the spiritual mind, being higher, is the human mind or the "mind of his heaven." Because our thoughts and feelings are part of the spiritual world they are governed by spiritual laws, and because there is a correspondence between spiritual laws and the natural laws, whatever is thought or felt in the inner, or spiritual, realm, is manifested into the outer realm. A thought thus becomes an act, every changed mental state resulting in a corresponding change in the body. Since we can choose our thoughts and feelings, we determine whether our inner state is pleasant (heaven) or unpleasant (hell). Thus, we literally can experience heaven on earth. The natural mind dies with the body, and the spiritual mind continues on.

Of course there is much more to Swedenborg's philosophy; however, this brief synopsis will suffice for our understanding of his influence on Evans. His mystical teachings are explored further in chapter seven and his many Divine Laws are discussed in chapter thirteen.

It can be seen that many of New Thought's concepts about the nature of God, as well as some of its Divine Laws, derive from Swedenborg's teachings. We can also see similarities between his ideas and those of Quimby, Eddy and Hopkins.

We return now to Evans and his Mental Science.

Evans was obviously well read as he mentions and quotes numerous philosophical and religious minds. Therefore, though his philosophy has been said to be an integration of Swedenborg and Quimby, it really is much more than that. He may have looked to Quimby and Swedenborg in formulating his mental science, but he incorporates many other philosophies in supporting and enlarging it. He designates the idealistic Bishop Berkeley as "the English Plato" and Swedenborg as "the Scandinavian Seer" (Braden).

Evans's God, as is Swedenborg's, is Love and Good, the Alpha and Omega, the First and the Last, the Beginning and the Ending. As with most of the writers who view God as ungendered, he refers to God in the traditional masculine. God is Life, "unoriginated and self-derived," and all other life flows from Him and is in Him. God is Love, Wisdom, Truth, and Divine Mind. God is One, not three. He is both personal and "indefinitely diffused principle." Everything derives from the One in varying degree and form. "[T]he whole universe of created minds are bound up in the same bundle of life" (*Mental Cure*). God, the All-Good, desires to convey his inherent goodness to humanity.

His concept of God broadened in his later writings, and *The Divine Law of Cure*, published in1881, twelve years after his first book, shows the influence of Hermetic, Kabbalistic, and Eastern philosophies as well as that of Emerson. He uses the terms Over-Soul and *atman* and agrees with the mystics that God is not out somewhere in the cosmos but rather is in each human heart.

In *The Mental Cure* he identifies the All from which all things spring as the Christ, the incarnate expression of the Christ being the man Jesus. God manifested through Jesus in the flesh. "This vivid consciousness of the indwelling divine principle, was the marked characteristic of the man Jesus. In him God became man, and humanity divine."

Though he is the greatest example of the embodied Christ, Jesus is not alone in this distinction. "But the Deity was thus manifested in Jesus, in order that through him he might be incarnated in all humanity, so that every man might walk forth consciously to himself as a son of God and say, 'I and my Father are one.'" This oneness of which he speaks is the same concept taught in the Eastern philosophies, by the mystics and by Hopkins. Evans believes the uniting of self with God is the "appointed destiny of every created soul."

Evans compares the objects of nature to those of spirit and depicts them as does Swedenborg—all physical matter is the manifestation of spirit, its underlying reality. As further support for this position, he says idealists Fichte, Schelling, Hegel, and Cousin embrace this same doctrine. Idealism, remember, holds that the only substance is mind and that material objects are real only because of mind and are dependent upon mind for existence.

While mind and matter are both forces, mind is a higher and more divine force. Mind is a spiritual force and is usually thought to be without form; however, mind is substance, so it must have form. Material objects have shapes only because of the action of a spiritual cause.

This truth is important to mental healing, for anything not of spirit is not real of itself, but only as a projection of the mind. Thus, mental states can affect the body. Disease originates in abnormal states of the mind. We release illness or any other kind of suffering by thinking correct thoughts and by remembering that suffering reverses and pain releases when we think properly. The concept of death is also a result of wrong thinking, for the universe is boundless life, and there can be no death.

He claims that mental healing is the same kind of healing that Jesus performed. He also claims the idealists provide a basis for mental healing. He quotes Hegel as saying, "the universe is an expression, a manifestation of the ideas in the Divine Mind," and "Disease . . . is only a wrong way of thinking, or . . . a false belief" (qtd. in Braden).

As Quimby discovered, one mind can affect another, both positively and negatively. So, not only can we heal our own bodies, we can influence the healing of others, *and* we can become well by focusing on healing another. Universal law states that as we give, we receive. When we stop the outflow, the inflow also stops. In becoming absorbed with ourselves, we are not in harmony with Divine Life. But when we bless another, the good sent out returns multiplied. Send out loving, compassionate thoughts and they will return in like kind.

In *The Mental Cure* Evans mentions several ways to assist others in healing. One is through prayer. A prayer is a wish for health and happiness, and the positive mental state enlisted in the giver of this wish affects both the giver and the receiver of the prayer. Through prayer, one spirit, or mind, affects another, for within the being who desires to spread good is "a fraction of the divine omnipotence."

A second way is through love. "Love is the life of all; it is the life of God; it is the divinest and most potential thing in the universe." When we rise above all selfish concerns and desire to do nothing but good, our very presence can effect healing. Evans says this is one of the ways in which Jesus healed. He passed his peaceful, loving state of mind to those around him, and it effected cures.

Another means of healing is through our words. Like Hopkins, Evans says there is power in words. *Logos,* or Word, is the creative power of God, and can create healing. Consider the words of Jesus: "Go in peace; Your sins are forgiven; Be it done unto you according to your faith." With these words Jesus was able to reverse all manner of sickness, even death.

We can see that Evans's thought is the combination of the teachings of Quimby, Swedenborg, the idealists, Eastern philosophies, and his own ministerial studies. Inasmuch as Swedenborg received his information by way of revelation, it would seem that this particular path ends here. However, many of the concepts revealed to Swedenborg apparently also were disclosed to others, as we shall see as we travel the other roads to New Thought. The second path through Evans also ends, for Quimby credits no influence on his ideas other than the words of Jesus. We can assume the influence of Swedenborg and the other philosophers he mentions, but cannot support that assumption. He discontinued his use of mesmerism when he discovered through his experiments that a person can affect another person's actions solely through use of his thoughts. Mesmerism was not practiced by any of his followers, so there is no need to trace the origins of Mesmer's ideas. Except for the trails we will pick up in other roads, the paths through Hopkins to Eddy to Quimby and from Evans to Quimby and Swedenborg end here.

Along this road we discovered that New Thought gained most of its concepts about mental healing from Hopkins, Evans, Eddy, Quimby, and Jesus, and some of its concepts about God and Its divine laws from Swedenborg, Hopkins, the idealists, the mystics, and Eastern philosophies. New Thought's conceptions of mind and matter come largely from Quimby, Hopkins and the idealists.

The next road we travel is highly significant to Unity and Religious Science.

VI.

THE REBELLIOUS ROAD

What is a rebel? A man who says no.
Every act of rebellion expresses a nostalgia for innocence
and an appeal to the essence of being.
Albert Camus (1913–1960), French-Algerian philosopher and author
The Rebel

Man's mind, once stretched by a new idea,
never regains its original dimensions.
Oliver Wendell Holmes, Sr. (1809–1894)
U.S. author and physician

We know from their writings, that both Fillmore and Holmes were greatly influenced by the transcendentalist philosophy exemplified in the writings of its prolific adherents—Frederic Hedge, Ralph Waldo Emerson, George Ripley, Theodore Parker, Orestes Brownson, Henry David Thoreau, Margaret Fuller, Nathaniel Hawthorne, Bronson Alcott and his daughter Louisa May, Walt Whitman, and Oliver Wendell Holmes, Sr. The most influential of these, for our purposes, are Emerson and Thoreau.

The reader may be wondering why the chapter on Transcendentalism is entitled "The Rebellious Road." It is because the transcendentalists were rebels, revolutionaries and reformers reacting against the lifeless intellectualism of Unitarianism, the major religion in the Boston area in the early nineteenth century. Historian Perry Miller writes that the transcendental movement was "a protest of the human spirit against emotional starvation," and an "effort to create a living religion." Charles Braden writes that the movement was a "religious radicalism in revolt against a rational conservatism."

There are other reasons as well for the rise of this movement. According to historian Paul Boller, "chance, coincidence and several independent events, thoughts and tendencies" converged in New England during this time (qtd. in Reuben). The transcendentalists all lived in or near Boston, Massachusetts in the early to mid-1800s, and many were graduates of Harvard University, where the seeds of their revolt were cultivated. Some of the other causes were 1) the splintering of Calvinism into various groups; 2) the secularizing effects of science, technology and industrialization on society and the resulting change in the status quo; and 3) the impact of European ideas on Americans who traveled abroad (Reuben).

Musing in later years, Emerson says of the environment in which Transcendentalism was born:

> It seemed a war between intellect and affection; a crack in Nature, which split every church in Christendom into Papal and Protestant; Calvinism into Old and New schools; Quakerism into Old and New; brought new divisions in politics; as the new conscience touch[ed] temperance and slavery. The key to the period appeared to be that the mind had become aware of itself. Men grew reflective and intellectual. There was a new consciousness . . . (qtd. in Finseth).

Before explaining what Transcendentalism stood for and why it so profoundly affected those who fostered that movement and the ensuing New Thought movement, it is important to understand the religious doctrine to which these revolutionaries reacted. To do that, we must go back several centuries into religious history.

It is interesting to note that the Unitarianism that so repulsed the transcendentalists itself had developed in adverse reaction to Calvinism, specifically to the doctrines of predestination and original sin. And Calvinism, too, was the result of revolution. Along with Martin Luther, Calvin incited the great religious uprising in protest against Catholicism known as the Protestant Reformation. So great was Calvin's influence that he was known in some cities as the Protestant Pope, and Geneva, his base of operations, as the Rome of Protestantism.

Catholic Corruption

We start our brief retreat into history with Christopher Columbus, whose actions in the Americas and the Caribbean were grounded in his country's all-consuming desire for power and riches. This desire translated into conquest and exploitation. According to historian James Loewen, the racial, religious and intellectual superiority that permeate the modern Caucasian world can be traced directly back to Columbus, who introduced "the taking of land, wealth, and labor from indigenous peoples, leading to their near extermination, and the transatlantic slave trade, which created a racial underclass."

Following Spain's lead, from the late 1400s until the American Civil War prohibited slavery, thus eliminating slave trade and all that went with it, nations such as Portugal, Britain, France, Holland, and the United States enslaved millions of indigenous peoples. The actions of the British and the Spanish were particularly heinous, and Haitians and other natives of the Caribbean Islands became the victims of genocide. It is interesting to note that the United States was the last of the offending countries to ban the practice of slavery.

The enslaving of Indians wasn't confined to the Caribbean. Within the American colonies many of the native peoples who had welcomed the colonists to their shores, were enslaved, some even being sent to other lands. Because of the actions of the conquerors in the Caribbean and along the East coast of America, few natives remained to exploit, so the slave traders turned to Africa.

The rationale for this subjugation and carnage was religious. The conquerors based their appalling actions on biblical scripture. The practice of enslaving and plundering seems to be sanctioned throughout the Old and New Testaments in dozens of passages, though in all these instances the term construed as referring to slavery was incorrectly interpreted. The term is actually much closer in meaning to *indentured servant*, though even that term was racially-construed. Throughout history numerous groups of people have kept slaves or servants considered to be inferior because of race or class.

Some scriptures that Christians used to support the practice actually have nothing to do with slavery or indentured servitude. They relied on scriptures that reference a curse. Adam's son Cain was cursed with a mark because he killed his brother Abel. Many interpreted the mark to be black skin. They then deduced that all those who have light-colored skin are superior to those with black or dark skin and that dark-skinned people are evil and cursed and deserving of bondage. Some also used Noah's curse of his son Ham to support the use of slavery, though there is nothing in that scriptural passage to indicate that the curse was anything more than verbal. Certainly, there is no indication that Ham's skin changed color. They conveniently assumed that this curse mimicked Cain's.

Perhaps this whole debacle could have been avoided if the offenders had read the Bible at the spiritual level, understanding that the passages interpreted to sanction slavery are actually allegorical, not literal.

The European world during this time was a Catholic world. There was no separation of church and state; all rulers and leaders were Catholic. Sometimes the civic ruler and the religious leader were one and the same person. By the beginning of the sixteenth century when slavery ran rampant among many European and Middle Eastern countries, some religious people became confused, for the different indigenous groups discovered by the conquerors are not mentioned in the Bible. Orthodox Christianity had no way of explaining their existence or their role in God's plan. They also had no way to explain the animals found in the Americas, for according to the Bible all animals lived first in the Garden of Eden, then in Noah's ark and finally let out on Mt. Ararat when the flood receded. Both Eden and Ararat were thought to be in the Middle East, and there are hundreds of miles of ocean between the Middle East and the Americas. These kinds of issues disturbed many orthodox Catholics, and some historians have determined that this unrest contributed to the Protestant Reformation.

The Renaissance, and all that it encompassed, also contributed to the turmoil. The Renaissance, which comes from the French word for "rebirth," focused on individual achievement in the present life rather than the after life, which had been the focus of previous centuries—the period of time referred to as the Dark Ages. This focus resulted in new optimism in the capacity of humanity to accomplish great things. During this period, 1350 to 1600, Roman culture had become increasingly more secular or materialistic because of its contact with other cultures. Citizens had become wealthy through trade and banking, and in order to glorify their achievements began patronizing various artists; e.g., Botticelli, de Vinci, and Michelangelo. They resurrected ideals of the ancient Greeks and Romans, and literature and philosophy flourished. Scientific theories radically changed in the wake of Copernicus's revolutionary thesis that the earth and the other planets revolve around the sun, rather than the sun revolving around the earth as had been taught by the Catholic church. This thesis, and those yet to come, did not set well with the Catholic hierarchy. In fact, except for the vast wealth they enjoyed, they found objectionable most of the other changes taking place during this time.

The Protestant Reformation

The Catholic hierarchy had been for many centuries in total control of the social, political and religious lives of the Western world. And their abuse of power is well known. The issues that led the German priest Martin Luther in 1517 to post his 95 theses on the door of the Wittenberg Chapel were not unique to Luther. Many in the previous century had been disturbed by the scandalous behavior exhibited by the Pope and his minions but felt unable to act against them. However, with the firm establishment of the new renaissance thinking coupled with the recently established Catholic practice of selling forgiveness, the time was ripe for rebellion.

In the early 1500s the Papacy planned to build the lavish Saint Peter's Basilica and needed to fund the construction. In order to raise the massive funds needed, indulgences for sin were offered for sale and an official appointed for this purpose. Standing at the pulpit, this official "declared that by virtue of his certificates of pardon all the sins which the purchaser should afterward desire to commit would be forgiven him." Repentance was unnecessary. Further, "he assured his hearers that the indulgences had power to save not only the living but the dead; that the very moment the money should clink against the bottom of his chest, the soul in whose behalf it had been paid would escape from purgatory and make its way to heaven" (Hagenbach, *History of the Reformation,* qtd. in "What Started").

Luther was horrified at this blasphemy. Members of his own congregation had purchased these certificates, and when they came to him for absolution, he refused, warning them that without repentance, their sins would follow them into death.

For Luther this was, so to speak, the last straw. He petitioned the Pope in his 95 theses to withdraw himself and other church leaders from the worldly affairs that had corrupted the church and return to the spiritual ways of the early church. He also wanted the church hierarchy to remove themselves as intermediaries between the individual and God. Luther believed that God is available to everyone without mediation. Many historians believe that the papacy desired power and control over the people and this is why all Catholic masses were given in Latin, a language to which few understood, and the Bible was not available for individual study. Luther considered this sacrilege; so he translated the Bible into German, the language of the common people. This act had an enormous impact on the balance of power, for "the new Biblical scholarship that this engendered not only pointed out (minor) flaws in the Latin Vulgate—but gave the new scholars a sense of personal judgment superior to that of the official church" (Hodges).

The hierarchy, of course, opposed Luther's petition and ordered him to cease his challenges. He refused and was aided in his rebellion by Frederick, the imperial elector. With the help of the newly-improved printing press, his movement spread across northern Germany into Scandinavia. Luther's religious rebellion flourished as Rome became known as the anti-Christ.

In 1521 Charles V issued an edict against the expanding Lutheranism, and more than 50,000 Netherlanders were "burned, strangled, beheaded or buried alive . . . for such offenses as reading the Scriptures, refusing to worship graven images, or ridiculing the idea of the actual presence of Christ's body in the wafer" ("What Started"), doctrines Luther had dismissed as false.

Over the next fifteen years free thinkers from other countries joined in the rebellion. Aroused by the teachings of the other leading reformer, John Calvin, the movement spread through Switzerland to England, Scotland, France, Western Germany, Bohemia, Hungary, the Netherlands, and eventually to America. By the seventeenth century it had superseded Lutheranism as the most popular form of Protestantism. It also played a crucial role in the development of New Thought.

John Calvin was born in France in 1509, and before he died in Switzerland in 1564, he and Luther managed to change forever the form and practice of religion. Calvin, of course, was born into the

Catholic faith, and he went to Paris as a young man intending to study for the priesthood. However, his father persuaded him to study law instead, and around 1531 (the exact date is uncertain) he finished his doctorate. Approximately two years later, Calvin experienced a sudden conversion of faith. Unfortunately, next to nothing is known as to the specifics of the conversion that profoundly changed the course of his life and religious history as well.

From Paris he set out to do what he believed to be God's work. Ceaselessly, and unsuccessfully, he petitioned the king of France to abandon Catholicism for Calvin's new theology. The following year, 1536, the local preacher, Guillaume Farel, invited Calvin to Geneva, and, by means of his passionate sermons, he assisted in stirring up that city's already-existing religious factions. Geneva, known in the present time for its pacifist neutrality, was in tumult.

Luther had been interested in reforming religious doctrine and practices, but Calvin wanted complete reform of all aspects of life, and his policies covered political, economic and social activities in addition to theological concerns. According to one historian:

> [H]e gave a theological rationale for the independent-mindedness of the urban commercial class—arming them with Scriptural justification for going their own way within God's creation. Indeed, he encouraged them to establish purified political-economic-social orders as a way of purging Christendom of its corruption and of bringing glory to God in Jesus Christ. He made their soul-searching independent-mindedness a matter of the greatest importance in their standing before God ("Calvinism").

Calvin published his *Institutes of the Christian Religion*, which set forth what he believed to be the true Gospel. Along with eliminating all vestiges of Catholicism in Geneva, his form of Christianity became the law. The new government zealously persecuted Catholics, cast priests into prison, and fined citizens if they did not attend the sanctioned services. In 1552 Calvin declared his *Institutes* to be holy doctrine that no one could speak against. Many "impious" men were imprisoned and executed for opposing this "holy" doctrine. Calvin "founded a little theocracy, modeled after the Old Testament, and succeeded in erecting the most detestable government that ever existed, except the one from which it was copied" ("Calvin"). Indeed, most modern Christians find Calvin's doctrines abhorrent.

The Calvinist Reformed Churches were cold, austere and bereft of any art except music. They celebrated no Christian feasts and radically disliked the "evil" human body. They understood the Bible to be a Code of Law, and the clergy served as judges and juries, deciding upon appropriate punishments for transgressions of its moral laws.

Calvinists believe that God is completely sovereign and in control of absolutely everything; thus they are known as *selective salvationists*. Humans have not been given free will, for if they had, God would not be sovereign. Calvin's *Institutes* require complete obedience to God's will, as interpreted by Calvin. Our actions have nothing to do with our salvation, for we are saved by God's grace through the power of the Holy Spirit. God, in his grace, has selected those whom He will save. This doctrine is known as predestination, and is the main doctrine to which the Unitarians, the Universalists, the Society of Friends (Quakers), and later the transcendentalists and Quimby rebelled.

The Reformation received a boost when the English King Henry VIII, thinking of himself as Defender of the Faith, declared the Church of England to be the official religion of his subjects and appointed himself as the head. In reality, King Henry was not defending faith but his own self-interests. His wife had been unable to provide him an heir and the Catholic church had allowed an annulment of his marriage so that he could marry another. When the second wife also failed to provide an heir, he again sought an annulment, but this time the Church refused. This, of course, infuriated the king, and a new official state religion was born.

As each new king or queen ascended to the throne of England, the official religion shifted back and forth between the Anglicans (English Protestants) and the Catholics. This caused much confusion for the people, as would be expected. Imagine having to shift one's core beliefs and loyalties at the whim of a monarch.

The Catholic church initiated an unsuccessful counter-movement at the Council of Trent in 1545 to arrest the spread of the Reformation. This movement continued into the seventeenth century with the missionary work of the Jesuits and the Inquisitions in Europe and the Americas. In time it became clear that religion, and in particular the

Catholic hierarchy, no longer sustained power over human affairs. The Church reluctantly agreed to a truce, and in 1648 England, Scotland, the Netherlands, Scandinavia, and much of Switzerland and Germany officially became Protestant, while the rest of Europe reverted to Catholicism.

The American Colonies

When the colonists came to America from England in the early 1600s, with them came Protestantism, mainly in the form of Calvinism, though the official established religion of Virginia was the Church of England. With the arrival of the Pilgrims in 1620 and the Puritans in 1628, the religious debates among colonists became rancorous. Banished from Salem, Massachusetts in 1636 for preaching the existence of a personal God, Roger Williams founded Rhode Island. A year later Anne Hutchinson, a popular Puritan lay theologian, joined him after being branded a heretic and excommunicated for her teachings on grace and justification and for claiming that she received direct divine revelation.

Quakers opposed many accepted doctrines, including slavery. Since slavery was widely practiced in the colonies, any Quaker who attempted to settle in certain areas was imprisoned and then deported. Until Quaker William Penn received a charter from King Charles II in 1681 for the land that became Pennsylvania, New Jersey remained the only area open to Quakers.

Puritan New England required every town to establish a church based on Calvinist doctrines (Puritan, Reformed or Congregationalist), but by the end of the seventeenth century numerous groups had broken away and had developed their own religious doctrines. Also by this time German Mennonites, Scottish Presbyterians, French Protestants of various denominations, each with their own form of Protestant doctrine (mostly restatements of Calvinism), and members of the Jewish faith had settled in the colonies.

During the hundred years following the founding of the colonies, much debate took place among the churches concerning the doctrines of the fall of man and everlasting sin. The debate eventually enlarged to include salvation, freedom and the Trinity.

In the 1740s Jonathan Edwards, an adherent of the Calvinist view of predestination, initiated what has been called The Great Awakening in reaction to the apathy and secularization of society. This first wave of revivalism, emphasizing the emotional aspects of personal conversion and commitment, ended just prior to the American Revolution.

In 1776 Thomas Jefferson proposed the first bill that mandated separation of church and state. Nine of the thirteen colonies had established state religions, all various forms of Calvinism or Anglicanism and their off-shoots. It took ten years for the bill to pass.

The 1790s brought the installation of the first Roman Catholic bishop; the breaking away from Calvinism by the Universalists, who received their name because of their belief in universal rather than selective salvation; and the Second Great Awakening, "the most influential revival of Christianity in the history of the United States" characterized by outdoor meetings where participants "barked like dogs, jerked about, and danced in ecstacy" (qtd. in Miller and Faux). It also brought circuit-riding Methodist and Baptist ministers who cultivated churches throughout the South and West where religion was almost nonexistent. In the 1820s, toward the end of this awakening, one of the great revivalist preachers, Charles G. Finney, returned free will to salvation. And the stage was set.

Unitarianism

The term *unitarian* was coined to indicate a belief in God as a unity rather than as a trinity and originated as part of the Protestant Reformation in Transylvania in the late sixteenth century. The first, and only, Unitarian king, John Sigismund, followed the path of many through Catholicism to Lutheranism to Calvinism to Unitarianism.

In the latter part of the seventeenth century in England writer John Milton, scientist Isaac Newton, philosopher John Locke, and numerous lesser-known names championed a more liberal religion. So despite considerable persecution, the Unitarian religion began to organize.

In the late 1700s Dr. Joseph Priestley, a Unitarian minister and discoverer of oxygen, founded the first Unitarian churches in America.

In 1802 the congregation of the oldest pilgrim church at Plymouth voted to become Unitarian.

Unitarian doctrine is virtually identical to that of Universalism, and in 1961 the two groups became one organization known as the Unitarian-Universalists. More evangelical during the nineteenth century than the Unitarians, Universalists actively worked to spread their faith across the United States. Many heeded the words of Universalist publisher Horace Greeley to go west. Universalist Thomas Starr King jestingly defined the difference between Unitarians and Universalists: "Universalists believe that God is too good to damn people, and the Unitarians believe that people are too good to be damned by God" (Harris). Both groups advocate the dignity and worth of all people, and many members actively participate in civil rights and social reform.

Unitarian minister William Ellery Channing delivered a sermon entitled "Unitarian Christianity" in 1819 that lent credence to the Unitarian movement. The American Unitarian Association was organized in Boston six years later with Channing as the head. Those who believed "in free human will and the loving benevolence of God," says Harris, became Unitarian.

Unitarians held rational thought and morality in high regard, but unlike Calvinists, who *demanded* adherence, Unitarians voluntarily chose ethical conduct. They supported "a 'natural theology' in which the individual could, through empirical investigation or the exercise of reason, discover the ordered and benevolent nature of the universe and of God's laws" (Finseth), and then chose the ways they could best observe these laws for the benefit of themselves and society.

As a result of their strong stance on freedom, the various Unitarian groups disagreed on a definitive doctrine concerning God or Jesus. Most see Jesus as an exemplary human whom it would behoove us to follow. He is not a deity, though he lived at a much "higher" level than most humans do. His crucifixion and death did not atone for sin, since no Fall occurred and no original sin resulted. All Unitarians, then and now, hold the belief that the doctrine of the Trinity is found nowhere in the Bible. (Bible scholars agree.) God is Unity; hence, their name. They look to no outside authority for instruction or direction; rather, each follows the dictates of his or her own reason, conscience and experience.

As would be expected, the Calvinists considered the Unitarians and Universalists to be heretics. In Greek, *heresy* means "choice." Because they freely chose the beliefs they practiced, the Unitarians and Universalists unhesitatingly accepted the heretic characterization.

Unitarianism appealed to "upright, respectable, wealthy Boston citizens" (Finseth) as can be seen from the roster of the Unitarians-turned-transcendentalists cited at the beginning of this chapter.

It is no surprise that subgroups arose, and upon Channing's death Theodore Parker, the head of the group considered more radical by some, ascended to leadership. In 1836 Parker began meeting casually with fellow Unitarian ministers Ralph Waldo Emerson, Frederic Henry Hedge and George Ripley, along with other interested parties, to discuss theology and philosophy. They formed a club, known during the four years of its existence by several names—Hedge's Club, the Transcendentalist Club or the Symposium—and unwittingly instigated the Transcendentalist Movement.

One of the main divisions between the transcendentalists and the Unitarians was whether Jesus's miracles proves God's existence. Emerson stood with Ripley against the emphasis placed on these miracles. Ripley argued that "the essential foundation of the Christian faith, or the ultimate test of Christian character" does not rely on such a belief. Andrews Norton, known as the Unitarian Pope, rebuked Ripley saying that such beliefs vitally injure the cause of religion. Norton insisted that the truth of Christianity ultimately rests on the validity of biblical miracles.

Emerson, believing that this position alienates humanity from divinity and diminishes the importance of a personal experience of God, replied that "an intuition cannot be received at second hand" (qtd. in Robinson). Fellow transcendentalist Orestes Brownson identified the implications of the Unitarian position: "There is no revelation made from God to the human soul; we can know nothing of religion but what is taught us from abroad, by an individual raised up and specially endowed with wisdom from on high to be our instructor" (Miller, *The Transcendentalists*; qtd. in Finseth). Thus, Brownson declared the Unitarian position erroneous.

The Transcendentalists

As mentioned at the beginning of this chapter, the transcendentalists who had the most influence on New Thought were Emerson and Thoreau.

Ralph Waldo Emerson was born in 1803 and except for a brief sojourn in Europe he lived his entire life in the Boston area. Along with many of his fellow transcendentalists he attended Harvard Divinity School, where the seeds of their discontent were sown. Upon graduation he served as minister for the Second Church of Boston, a Unitarian church, for three years before resigning in 1832, ostensibly over the serving of communion. His Concord study contained hundreds of volumes in several languages, including the latest in science, history, literature, and the sacred texts of Eastern religions, all of which he voraciously studied.

In 1838, two years after the publication of his first essay, "Nature," Emerson was asked to address the graduating class of the Harvard Divinity School. His famous speech protested "a stale, inherited Christianity," and promoted honor, courage of conviction and personal inspiration. "Wherever a man comes, there comes revolution. The old is for slaves . . . Refuse the good models . . . Cast conformity behind you, and acquaint men at first hand with Deity" ("Divinity School Address"). It was in this address that he expressed his beliefs about miracles. This speech caused a great stir in the community, where he was both praised and ridiculed. Surprised by the adverse reaction, for he felt his words reflected the teachings of Jesus, Emerson made no defense of the speech and refused to debate the issue. His career as a lecturer flourished in spite of the ruckus, though Harvard officials did not ask him to speak again for ten years. He continued to write and lecture until his death in 1882, though health issues forced him to slow down after 1871.

Henry David Thoreau was born in Concord, Massachusetts in 1817. Except for his college years and a short stint in New York while working as a tutor, Thoreau spent his entire life in the Boston area, mainly in Concord. He began visiting Walden Pond when he was just four years old. After graduating from college he obtained a position as a teacher. That career lasted a total of two weeks, for he refused to beat the students in order to maintain silence in the classroom as the authorities required. Failing to find another position, he and his brother started their own school, which was quite successful. They closed the school after three years because Thoreau did not want to continue the school alone after his brother became ill.

Thoreau spent a great deal of time with Emerson, who greatly intrigued him. After closing the school, he lived for two years with Emerson and his family, working as a handyman/gardener for room and board.

Nathaniel Hawthorne, a new resident of Concord, gives this initial impression of Thoreau:

> He is a singular character—a young man with much wild original nature still remaining in him; and so far as he is sophisticated, it is in a way and method of his own. He is as ugly as sin, . . . But his ugliness is of an honest and agreeable fashion, and becomes him much better than beauty. He . . . is a keen and delicate observer of nature . . . and Nature, in return for his love, seems to adopt him as her especial child, and shows him secrets which few others are allowed to witness. He is familiar with beast, fish, fowl, and reptile, and has strange stories to tell of adventures, and friendly passages with these lower brethern [sic] of mortality. Herb and flower, likewise, wherever they grow, whether in garden, or wild wood, are his familiar friends. He is also on intimate terms with the clouds and can tell the portents of storms. It is a characteristic trait, that he has a great regard for the memory of the Indian tribes, whose wild life would have suited him so well (Harding, *Thoreau as Seen*, qtd in "Thoreau: Genius Ignored").

The summer of 1845 began Thoreau's two-year habitation in the primitive cabin he built at Walden Pond. He memorialized this most famous interlude in his book *Walden or Life in the Woods*, the book for which he is most known.

He never married and he spent the rest of his relatively short life with his family, writing and lecturing. He passed from this world in 1862.

Transcendentalism

Transcendentalism, according to a recent edition of *Merriam Webster's*, is a philosophy that stresses the prior conditions of knowledge over current sense experience, or the unknowable transcendent character of ultimate reality. It also views the spiritual and transcendental as superior to the material and empirical.

A 1913 edition of this dictionary defines Transcendentalism in terms of various philosophers. It cites Schelling and Hegel's beliefs as to the absolute identity of the objective and the subjective in human knowledge, and the true knowledge of all things, so far as the mind is capable of knowing them, contrasting Kant's transcendent and transcendental ideas. It also defines Transcendentalism as addressing what is vague or illusive in philosophy.

Transcendentalism, as can be seen from these definitions, is a philosophical term. Though not mentioned in these dictionary definitions, this term is based on the concept of transcendence posited by Plato. For Plato, transcendence is the rising above the ever-changing phenomena of the senses to the changeless real world of the eternal realities—the Good, the Absolute, the Beautiful—Plato's Forms. These transcendent realities can also be called God, because God contains or *is* these eternal realities. The world we observe through our senses is but a reflection of the real world. This real world can only be known through thought or mind, or what some call *intuition*.

Over time several attempts were made to define the difference between *transcendent* and *transcendental*, and Immanuel Kant's distinction attracted the transcendentalists. Kant uses *transcendent* when referring to entities that are beyond our experience and are unknowable, entities such as God and the soul. *Transcendental* pertains to *a priori* thought forms—the innate principles that exist prior to the mind and furnish the mind with the ability to perceive and then understand experience.

Kant laid out his study of the mind in 1781 in his *Critique of Pure Reason*, which study later became known as transcendental philosophy. This philosophy and all others that rely on transcendent and transcendental concepts fall under the branch of philosophy known as metaphysics.

Kant places the origin of the principles of metaphysics solely in the human mind, totally independent of, and prior to, all experience. His arguments are difficult and involved, so I state here only his conclusions. Kant determines that the world we experience through our five senses is not the real world. The ultimately real world transcends our senses and is supersensible or mental; that is, unknowable outside the mind. The real world is "pure understanding alone," a "thing in itself" (Kant, qtd. in Sahakian). There are three necessary, supersensuous things-in-themselves—freedom of the will, immortality of the soul and a Supreme Being.

He calls this view the *transcendental ideality of appearances*, but it has come to be known as *transcendental idealism*, though Kant did not consider his metaphysics idealistic and argued strenuously against that designation. It seems clear, though, that whether he likes it or not, his views are idealistic, for as we saw in chapter four, Idealism is the concept that ultimate reality transcends all sensory phenomena, that the fundamental nature of reality is consciousness (mind or reason) and that the only knowable things are mental states or mental entities.

The transcendentalists were called such, though they preferred to be called idealists, because they accepted the concepts of Kant and other transcendental theorists. According to George Ripley, the leading idea of Transcendentalism is the supremacy of the mind over matter, or the dependence of matter on mind, and the belief in truths that transcend the external senses.

They also accepted as truth an idea borrowed from the Quakers, another Calvinist splinter group, that every person is able to perceive spiritual truth by means of an inner light and has no need of "a jury of scholars, a hierarchy of divines, or the prescriptions of a creed" (Braden) in order to do so. The way to God is through our own divine inner self. Emerson calls this inner light the oversoul, and he calls God the Over-soul. This idea is akin to the view that each of us has a piece (the human soul) of God (Soul) residing within. Because the transcendentalists recognized that everyone contains a piece of the Over-soul, *all* individuals are innately worthy and are to be respected. It follows that all of us are divine and inherently good. Hence, the involvement of many transcendentalists in the social action movements of their day.

Other concepts common to Transcendentalism are the focus on the present life over the afterlife; the innate freedom of all individuals; evil as the absence of good; death as the passing of the individual soul to the Over-soul; the importance of self-knowledge and self-reliance; the oneness or the unity of the universe; and the presence of God in all of nature. Most of these concepts are touched on in Thoreau's *Walden* and in four of Emerson's essays: "Self-Reliance," "Compensation," "The Over-Soul," and "Nature," from which the following exposition of transcendentalist philosophy is drawn.

Eternity is in the present moment, says Thoreau. But, replies Emerson, society lives not in the present, "but with reverted eye laments the past, or, heedless of the riches that surround him, stands on tiptoe to foresee the future." We cannot appreciate the magnificence of the present when we are focused on the past or the future; nor can we know ourselves.

Thoreau entreats us to observe the words of Socrates: "Explore thyself!" He and Emerson stress over and over the importance of finding ourselves. This entails looking inside and deciding who we are and what we want to do with our lives. "Man is his own star," quotes Emerson and then points out the need to be genuine, to never imitate. "Accept your genius and say what you think."

Especially are we not to worry about the opinions of society nor let them hinder our dreams. We are to pay no attention to those who measure by "what each has, and not by what each is." Thoreau tells us to heed our own drummer and honor the music we hear. Each life is meant to be unique. "It is easy in the world to live after the world's opinion; it is easy in solitude to live after our own; but the great man is he who in the midst of the crowd keeps with perfect sweetness the independence of solitude."

Not only are we to know ourselves, but we are to trust ourselves and the connections between events—the seeming coincidences we experience in life. Especially we are to trust our hearts, for the heart speaks for the soul, and the soul is always right. Our true power comes from within—from our experience—never from without. For those who rely on outside sources are mere spectators of life. Too often we dismiss our thoughts simply because they are *ours*. Emerson admonishes us to listen to and follow that still, small voice within, the voice of God that speaks through our hearts and through our souls. "Abide in the simple and noble regions of thy life, obey thy heart." We can know ourselves and know God by going within, for God *is* within. Eternity and omnipresence dwell in our souls. The "absolutely trustworthy" resides in our hearts and works through our hands. "A man is the facade of a temple wherein all wisdom and all good abide. . . . When [the soul] breathes through his intellect, it is genius; when it breathes through his will, it is virtue; when it flows through his affection, it is love." We are never to give up on ourselves for we do not know of what we are capable until we make the attempt.

This is what Emerson means by *self-reliance*. He is declaring that we are to rely on the self, the eternal, divine, real self that lies within.

Emerson tells us that everything has a common origin and follows innate universal laws. "We first share the life by which things exist, and afterwards see them as appearances in nature, and forget that we have shared their cause." And "Innate universal laws . . . , while they exist in the mind as ideas, stand around us in nature forever embodied." The phrase "appearances in nature" in the first quote leads to another transcendentalist concept—reality is of the mind. We tend to see only the surface of things and take that for reality. As Thoreau notes, "[w]e think that that *is* which *appears* to be," and Emerson says, "The world is mind precipitated and the volatile essence is forever escaping again into the state of free thought." With other idealists, the transcendentalists accepted the proposition of mind above, beyond or superior to matter.

We learn from Emerson that there can be no evil because it is impossible for the universe to be wronged. The universe is perfect and good. The apparent evils we see are of our own making. We make our lives much harder and more miserable than they need to be because we "miscreate our own evils" by interfering with the natural optimism of nature. At its heart, nature is God, and God is all that is good. Nature, then, is divine. This explains why the transcendentalists viewed nature as spiritual and the experience of being in nature as transcendent. This is eminently illustrated in this passage from *Walden*:

> I went to the woods because I wished to live deliberately, to front only the essential facts of life, and see if I could not learn what

it had to teach, and not, when I came to die, discover that I had not lived. I did not wish to live what was not life, living is so dear; nor did I wish to practice resignation, unless it was quite necessary. I wanted to live deep and suck out all the marrow of life, to live so sturdily and Spartan-like as to put to rout all that was not life, to cut a broad swath and shave close, to drive life into a corner, and reduce it to its lowest terms, and, if it proved to be mean, why then to get the whole and genuine meanness of it, and publish its meanness to the world; or if it were sublime, to know it by experience, and be able to give a true account of it in my next excursion.

Emerson, too, eloquently writes of the transcendence experienced in nature:

The solitary places do not seem quite lonely. At the gates of the forest, the surprised man of the world is forced to leave his city estimates of great and small, wise and foolish. The knapsack of custom falls off his back with the first step he makes into these precincts. Here is sanctity which shames our religions, and reality which discredits our heroes. Here we find nature to be the circumstance which dwarfs every other circumstance, and judges like a god all men that come to her. We have crept out of our close and crowded houses into the night and morning, and we see what majestic beauties daily wrap us in their bosom. . . . The tempered light of the woods is like a perpetual morning, and is stimulating and heroic. The anciently reported spells of these places creep on us. The stems of pines, hemlocks, and oaks, almost gleam like iron on the excited eye. The incommunicable trees begin to persuade us to live with them, and quit our life of solemn trifles.

Since God, the Over-Soul, is inherent in nature and within man as soul, God is everywhere in everything. This implies a connectedness of man and nature. In Emerson's poetic words, God is "that great nature in which we rest, as the earth lies in the soft arms of the atmosphere; that Unity, that Over-soul, within which every man's particular being is contained and made one with all other." He also says,

> [W]ithin man is the soul of the whole; the wise silence; the universal beauty, to which every part and particle is equally related; the eternal ONE. And this deep power in which we exist, and whose beatitude is all accessible to us, is not only self-sufficing and perfect in every hour, but the act of seeing and the thing seen, the seer and the spectacle, the subject and the object, are one (emphasis in original).

A consequence of the belief in the connectedness of all things is the concept of doing no harm—being aware of the possible consequences of our actions. For this, Thoreau set the standard. He willingly and peacefully went to jail rather than submit to a law that was harmful to another—the Fugitive Slave Law, which allowed a fine for anyone who helped an escaped slave and accepted the word of a slave owner as proof that a black person was an escaped slave. The non-violent protests by Mahatma Gandhi and Dr. Martin Luther King, Jr. can be traced directly back to Thoreau's example.

Doing no harm applies to everything, not just people. Thus, the admonishment to live simply, to appreciate and cooperate with nature, to respect and honor all aspects of life. This belief led the transcendentalists to attempt several practical reforms.

One of the ways the group honored lesser forms of life was by not eating them. Their attempt at vegetarianism appealed to some more than others. Thoreau writes much about the repulsive practice of eating animals and the virtues of abstinence. He writes in *Walden*, "I have no doubt that it is a part of the destiny of the human race, in its gradual improvement, to leave off eating animals, as surely as the savage tribes have left off eating each other when they came in contact with the more civilized." Emerson writes that he tried vegetarianism for awhile, but it did not work for him.

George Ripley announced at a meeting of the Transcendental Club in October 1840 his plan for reforming social life. He envisioned a commune called Brook Farm, which would be "a cooperative enterprise founded on Associationist principles," and would include a small farm and a school or college of the highest quality. He intended to match the work necessary to support the community with the inhabitants' desires and talents, creating a "classless, noncompetitive society" in which "every individual would both find personal fulfillment and contribute to the well-being of the group." This rearrangement would "insure a more natural union between intellectual and manual labor" and "guarantee the highest mental freedom" (Robinson). The commune operated for six years with limited success before being destroyed by fire.

Nathaniel Hawthorne lived at the farm for a while and we learn from letters to his sister that he at first liked it, but after a few months he writes:

> Of all the hateful places that is the worst, and I shall never comfort myself for having spent so many days of blessed sunshine there. It is my opinion, dearest, that a man's soul may be buried and perish under a dung-heap, or in a farrow of the field, just as well as under a pile of money. The real ME was never an associate of the community (qtd. in "Transcendentalism"; emphasis in original).

Communal life is not for everyone. Hawthorne fared much better at the quasi-literary colony formed by Emerson, Thoreau and others of their group.

Many of the members involved themselves in the temperance and suffrage movements. They pressed for educational and economic rights for women and urged the reform of corrupted politics and unfair trade policies.

Some transcendentalists were involved in the Underground Railroad. Thoreau involved himself in declaring that the Fugitive Slave Law makes as much sense as does petitioning Congress to make men into sausages. Though not actively involved in the anti-slavery movement, Emerson, too, recognized this law as a "filthy enactment," and rose with Thoreau to the defense of John Brown, a white man soon to be hung for leading a slave uprising. Says Thoreau, "I plead not for his life, but for his character. . . . Some eighteen hundred years ago Christ was crucified; this morning, perchance, Captain Brown was hung. These are the two ends of a chain which is not without its links. He is not Old Brown any longer; he is an angel of light." Once the Civil War had begun, Emerson joined in the efforts to emancipate the slaves.

Influences on Transcendentalism

As mentioned, the transcendentalists, though highly educated, well read and intellectual, found unappealing the intellectualism offered by Unitarianism and Universalism, which Emerson viewed as "corpse-cold." Though the Unitarians did not offer much by way of spiritual and emotional experience, they did provide solid grounding in rationality and morality.

We know that Emerson studied the works of the ancient Greek philosophers and the writings of the modern idealists, romanticists and Platonists. He also read the *Bhagavad Gita*, the *Sayings of Confucius*, and the sayings of Buddha, comparing these teachings with those of the West. He questioned the truth of a God who reveals his truths to only one culture and allows the rest of the world to wander in darkness, and came to believe that there is truth in the scriptures of both East and West. Because of this and other unorthodox beliefs about God, he and the other transcendentalists preferred the designation of *theist* rather than *Christian*.

Soon after resigning his ministry in 1832, Emerson traveled to England and met with philosophers Thomas Carlyle and Samuel Taylor Coleridge and poet William Wordsworth, all of whom were involved in the Romantic movement. Searching for a level of passion missing from their Victorian England, these men had discovered the writings of the romanticists, especially those of Goethe and Schelling, the leading exponents of romanticist ideas: the celebration of the self, the mystery of nature, the unknowability of Kant's world of thought and the transcendent, and the power of the imagination. The latter is best expressed through art because it is the primary means of knowing our inner self. In fact, according to Schelling, art is the highest medium of philosophical reflection.

Oliver Wendell Holmes, Sr. describes the path taken by the romanticists and transcendentalists in accepting Kant's transcendent beliefs. These beliefs embrace "the doctrine of pre-existence; a doctrine older than Spenser [sic], older than Plato or Pythagoras, having its cradle in India, fighting its way down through Greek Philosophers and Christian fathers and German Professors, to our own time" (qtd. in "Selections"). The romantics and transcendentalists also followed in the footsteps of the Neo-Platonists, Plotinus being its main proponent, and Swedenborg.

Braden cites Octavius Brooks Frothingham, a transcendentalist and author of *Transcendentalism in New England,* as saying that their philosophy sprang from a combination of Kant's *Critique of Pure Reason,* Jacobi's mysticism and Fichte's tendency towards heroism, which I believe is a reference to Fichte's belief that man has a moral duty to perfect himself and to reach his potential.

Quaker and Hindu writings inspired the transcendentalist belief that God can be found through an inner search of self. The existence of an indwelling, immortal soul is taught by Christianity and most other religions. It is also a concept familiar to the ancient Greeks. Emerson equates *atman* with the individual psyche and *Brahman* with God, which he calls the "over-soul, life-force, or prime mover." The Hindu *Upanishads* say, "[S]elf-knowledge, especially intuitive self-knowledge, moves a person ever deeper into the Absolute, for *Atman* is *Brahman.*" We see in this passage also the idea of the oneness of our inner self and God.

The oneness or connectedness of all nature has been posited by many philosophers. Among the oldest is Hinduism, though this concept has been taught by philosophers in the West for over two thousand years. Leibniz writes that all matter is connected and that everything that happens in the universe has an effect on everything else. Hegel, who studied mysticism, believes the only reality is the whole, which is actually a complex intelligible system, much like an organism—one whole consisting of dynamically interrelated parts. He calls this whole the Absolute, and sees it as spiritual in nature. Parmenides and Spinoza have the same concept of reality as Hegel except that they conceive the whole as a simple substance. What we take for individual souls and separate pieces of matter are actually aspects of one substance—the divine Being. Schopenhauer, who studied the Hindu *Upanishads,* says that the appearance of separateness is simply *maya* or illusion, for in reality all things are one.

Closely connected to the idea of allness being wholeness or one-ness is the idea of reality. Hegel's Absolute is the only reality. In this view, time and space, being concepts of sense and separation, are not real. Kant also accepts this view, as does Plotinus and Hinduism.

The concept of doing no harm can be found in the "yogic" Ten Commandments, which consist of the *yamas,* or ethical disciplines. The highest of these ethical disciplines is the practice of nonviolence, expressed in the Hindu Sutras as *ahimsa*, "without harming." There is more to this discipline, though, than just avoiding violence in our interactions with others. The practice involves the conscious avoidance of *anything* that might possibly cause harm, including our words and our thoughts (Moyer).

Many of the ideas of Transcendentalism can be traced back to the Cambridge Platonists who were associated with the University of Cambridge in seventeenth century England. Obviously, the philosophy of Plato and neo-Platonism shaped their thought, but numerous other philosophers contributed to their philosophy. They relied largely on the works that make up the perennial philosophy spoken of in the introduction to this book.

The Cambridge Platonists primarily emphasized religious and moral issues, defended the existence of God, the immortality of the soul and the freedom of the will. They accepted as true Kant's concept of a human mind capable of moral reasoning. They were dualists in accepting the views of Kant, Plato and others who believe that the visible world is the reflection of the invisible world and that there are two kinds of knowledge—intuitive knowledge and knowledge gained by the senses, with intuitive knowledge being superior. They also agreed with the view of Aristotle, Kant, Newton and numerous others that spirit is the cause of nature and its operations.

Transcendentalist "Heresy"

The transcendentalists, like the Unitarians before them, were considered to be heretics because they rejected many traditional concepts of Christianity and accepted many teachings of Eastern religions, including mysticism and pantheism. Many also accepted the concept of reincarnation, the belief that we are born again and again, each time into a new body, having new experiences, usually with the same core group of people, until we gain the awareness needed to return to the One. They did not take the charge of heresy too seriously, though, as can be seen from Emerson's comments in a letter to his brother Charles: "They say the world is vexed with us on account of our wicked writings. I trust it will recover its composure."

It is interesting that the transcendentalists were branded such, for pantheism and mysticism can be found in most religions, even in Christianity. In fact, any religion that holds transcendental or idealistic beliefs is pantheistic.

The mystics, whom we will discuss further in the next chapter, teach that each of us can commune directly with God mind-to-mind or spirit-to-spirit. They also teach, as do the pantheists, that there is only One, and all things spring from that One. In pantheism, though, because of the differing strains, the One can be viewed slightly differently. The division lies between the monists and dualists and/or between the world-denyers, world-affirmers and world-negaters.

Basically, pantheism is the belief that the universe and everything lying within are a part of God and therefore divine. The term derives from Pan, one of the gods of the ancient fertility religions. Pan's original name was *Paon*, which means "the feeder or shepherd," but was interpreted to mean "the All-God" by the Athenians in the fifth century B.C.E.

As we discussed in chapter four, monists believe that there is only one substance in the universe and everything is made of that substance. Dualists claim two types of substances of which things are made. These two substances are mind and matter.

World-negating pantheism holds that the visible world of separateness and multiplicity is unreal and that the real world is an invisible unified whole. This type of pantheism is found in ancient Hindu and Buddhist writings and the ancient Greek works of Xenophanes and Parmenides.

World-denying pantheists are dualists, holding the belief that the universe consists of matter and soul, both of which are real, with soul being superior to matter. For some, union with the One can only occur after death when the soul leaves the body. For others it is possible for the human soul to unite with God during life. Examples of this kind of pantheism can be found throughout Christian history. The first kind can be found in the Gospel of John, the writings of St. Paul, St. Thomas Aquinas, and the Gnostics, and the second in the writings of Meister Eckhart and other mystics. The second form can also be found in Plotinus, who technically was not Christian.

World-affirming pantheists may be monists or dualists, some believing God is the universe and the universe is God, while others believe that while the universe is God, God is more than the universe. Examples of the first type of pantheism can be found in the works of Heraclitus, Taoism, and some forms of Buddhism, and the writings of Emerson. The romantics, following in the footsteps of Spinoza, are examples of the latter.

Believers in the second form of world-affirming pantheism and most world-denying pantheists technically are *panentheists.* Most of the Islamic, Christian and Platonic philosophers have been panentheists. The difference between pantheism and panentheism, which are both forms of idealism, is the value placed on humans, the earth and the universe. Something that is only part of God seems to be of less importance than a thing that is totally God. Therefore, humanity has a higher standing in pantheism.

Warren Felt Evans wrote of a form of pantheism called *Christian Pantheism,* though as philosopher Alan Anderson points out, this pantheism really belongs in the panentheism category. Evans writes in *The Divine Law of Cure*: "The highest development of religious thought and feeling is that of a Christian Pantheism, not the cold, intellectual system of Spinoza, but one nearer to that of the warm and loving Fichte, who exhibited the blessedness of a life in God." He considers this type of pantheism to have been accepted and taught by Jesus and iterates further what is meant by this term:

> [A[union with God so complete in every department of our being that we can say: "The Father is in me and I am in the Father," and "I and my Father are one." A Christian Pantheism which does not destroy the individuality of man, nor separate God from the universe which he continually creates out of Himself, nor sunder Him from the activities of the human soul by the intervention of second causes, is the highest development of religious thought. An intuitive perception of the unity of the human with the Divine existence is the highest attainable spiritual intelligence, and one which raises man above disease and the possibility of death (qtd. in Anderson, *The New Thought Movement*).

The secondary causes mentioned in this passage are discussed in chapter eight.

In describing panentheism, Anderson perfectly describes the feeling and experience the transcendentalists sought in their religion:

Panentheism recognizes that everything shares God's being (or becoming) but that God's being operates from innumerable relatively freely-choosing centers or perspectives of existence. God and the world, which is God's body, are interdependent. To be is to be free, to be choosing, and to be enjoying (slightly or greatly, positively or negatively) the process of selecting from among competing influences. To be doing this is to be alive (Anderson and Whitehouse).

Summary

Transcendentalist philosophy accepts a monistic universe, one in which God is immanent in, yet distinct from, nature. Spirit and matter are of the same essence or substance, but spirit is superior to matter. Their world is a pantheistic one, and so all of nature, including people, is divine. This divine world allows for communion with God and such communion can occur from a mere walk through the forests, and calls for absolute honor and respect. We are all one, yet we are unique, and it is important for us to discover and celebrate this uniqueness, and trust that the God within is guiding our experience.

We can see that the transcendentalists traveled the Platonic road that stretched from Plato to the neo-Platonists, to the Cambridge Platonists, to Kant and all his disciples, to Carlyle and Coleridge, and finally to Emerson and his companions. Their road also passed back through Unitarianism and Protestantism, through the Eastern and Western mystics and pantheists to their most ancient beginnings in Hinduism.

Some have said that Transcendentalism is an ideal theory because "it presents the world in precisely that view which is most desirable to the mind" ("Transcendentalism"). But despite its desirability and the solid basis for its beliefs, the movement did not catch on, and lasted just twenty-five years or so. Some say the movement died with Thoreau and Emerson. Mark Twain called it "the Gilded Age," and said it died because of the American culture's emphasis on materialism.

A form of transcendental philosophy called *personalism* did carry forth, though. As mentioned in chapter four, the term was coined by one of the original transcendentalists, though personalistic ideas can be found in ancient Greece in the writings of Anaxagorus and Plato, and in the more modern thought of St. Augustine, Schleier-macher, Berkeley and Leibniz. Personalism is "the doctrine that the ultimate reality of the world is a Divine Person who sustains the universe by a continuous act of creative will" (Sahakian).

Walt Whitman also carried forward this philosophy in his poetry and essays. Whitman stated in so many words that Emerson's tran-scendental writings were his muse: "I was simmering, simmering, simmering; Emerson brought me to a boil" (Trowbrigde). The influ-ence of Transcendentalism can also be seen in the works of Nathaniel Hawthorne, Emily Dickinson, and Louisa May Alcott, daughter of one of Transcendentalism's founders. It was also carried forth by the German philosopher Hermann Lotze in his attempts to integrate Pluralism with Monism, and Realism with Idealism. In the nineteenth and twentieth centuries, the New Thought founders furthered this theme in their philosophies.

We turn now to the most misunderstood road that New Thought followed.

VII.

THE ESOTERIC ROAD

They that approve a private opinion, call it an opinion;
but they that mislike it, heresy:
and yet heresy signifies no more than private opinion.
Thomas Hobbes (1588–1679), British philosopher
Leviathan

All great truths begin as blasphemies.
George Bernard Shaw (1856–1950)
Irish playwright and critic

Esoteric is a word used to describe knowledge that only a few possess or understand. The major Western religions all have branches that are esoteric; e.g., Christian Mysticism and Esoteric Christianity, Jewish Kabbalism and the Sufi and Baha'i derivations of Islam. These same branches are also considered to be mystical and occultic. These three words are largely synonymous.

As mentioned in chapter three, Ernest Holmes studied all the major religions and worldwide philosophies in formulating his Science of Mind. Of those that fall on this road he specifically mentions Hermetic philosophy and the Kabbala, as does Malinda Cramer, founder of Divine Science. He also mentions a number of mystics, three of whom we have encountered on other roads. It is also apparent from his writings that he was familiar with Theosophy. Fillmore, too, studied many philosophies and religions, mentioning Theosophy, the Rosicrucians and Spiritualism. He also included articles by theosophists and spiritualists in his magazine. Emma Curtis Hopkins, teacher to all our founders, mentions all these various sources in the first chapter of *High Mysticism*.

All of these esoteric philosophies are part of the large group of metaphysical systems known as the Occult. This much-maligned term simply means "unrevealed, secret, hidden from view, concealed, or not easily understood." When used with "the" as in *the Occult*, it refers to "matters regarded as involving the action or influence of the supernatural or supernormal powers or some secret knowledge of them" *(Merriam Webster's)*. Sounds rather benign doesn't it? Especially when *supernatural* and *supernormal* are considered as an integral part of the spiritual world, which is the concern of religion. It is because the broad system of the Occult includes many dark practices that the term has been so misunderstood. New Thought does not sanction these black practices. *The Esoteric Road* refers to those influences that fall into the supernatural or supernormal category—the mystical and esoteric philosophies mentioned in the previous paragraph, all of which orthodoxy considers heretical.

We begin our journey through the Occult with the most recent of these philosophies, for as with the other roads, the newer philosophies build on the older.

Spiritualism

Spiritualism developed during the waning years of the transcendentalist movement and while Quimby conducted mental healings. The word *spiritualism* has two meanings. In the first, spirit is viewed as the prime element of reality. It can readily be seen that any philosophy or religion that views the spirit as more real than the body holds this meaning of spiritualism. All the idealistic philosophies and psychologies fall in this category. In the second meaning, spiritualism refers to a movement comprised of religious organizations that emphasize the belief in communication between the living and the spirits of the dead, often through the use of a medium. In the strictest sense of the word, the second meaning applies to John Edwards and any of the others who claim to channel messages from the spirit world. In the broadest sense, all who believe that a spiritual entity, including God, speaks to them fall into this category. I believe New Thought encompasses both meanings.

In the mid-1800s Herbert Spencer and Charles Darwin separately proposed theories of evolution which further eroded already fading religious beliefs. Spiritualism arose in response, just as in the previous century Romanticism had emerged in reaction to the mechanical view of man and the universe put forth by science. A number of scientific minds of the nineteenth century accepted Spiritualism as a serious discipline. During this period dominated by naturalism and materialism, the scientific and nonscientific-minded alike turned to the occult for spiritual comfort.

We briefly discussed in the introduction to this book that the consequences of science's mechanistic and evolutionary views horrified Frederic Myers. He designed his work to prove wrong the mechanistic view and to prove a spiritual world and the immortality of the soul. His work also bears a connection to Spiritualism.

Myers wrote that "[t]he discovery [of] a life in man independent of blood and brain would be a cardinal, a dominating fact in all science and in all philosophy" (qtd. in Leahey). In pursuit of that life (the soul) Myers gathered massive amounts of data and founded with philosopher Henry Sidgwick the Society for Psychical Research. He studied all forms of abnormal behavior and unusual psychological phenomena, including the receipt of messages from the dead.

Disturbed by science's erosion of spirituality, the general public lent tremendous support to Myers's work. As a result of society's need for assurance of life after death, numerous fake mediums and various forms of quackery abounded. Because this lessened the legitimacy of Myers's work, to this day the serious science of the paranormal remains controversial.

The Spiritualist community believed in Myers's work. Not only did they accept the notion of the immortality of the soul but they claimed it eternally evolved as well. During this evolution each soul progresses through planes of ever-increasing perfection until it eventually reaches Paradise—the Summerland. During the time our souls are progressing through these planes, the earth is progressing, too, becoming more and more perfect.

Andrew Jackson Davis, the most well known and charismatic of the spiritualists, taught a doctrine opposed to that of orthodox Christianity. As had Swedenborg, the transcendentalists and the romanticists before him, Davis taught that the spiritual realm is not far off in the cosmos but is within us, in nature, and is governed by natural laws.

Born in Orange County, New York in 1826, Davis grew up in poverty and received very little schooling. As a teenager it was discovered that he possessed extraordinary clairvoyant powers. Although uneducated he could discuss fluently medical and psychological subjects.

In the spring of 1844 he fell into a sixteen-hour trance during which he claims to have conversed with Galen, a second century philosopher and physician who gave him a magical healing staff, and Emanuel Swedenborg, the eighteenth century visionary we met in chapter five, both of whom promised to instruct and guide him.

Beginning in 1845, and for the next fifteen months, Davis dictated his first book while in a trance. He avoided a charge of witchcraft under the 1735 Witchcraft Act (which was not repealed until 1951) because he did not use a medium in his work. This book, *The Principles of Nature, Her Divine Revelations, and a Voice to Mankind*, contains definite Swedenborg influences. It begins with a description of the beginning of the Universe:

> In the beginning . . . [t]here was one vast expanse of liquid substance. It was without bounds - inconceivable - and with qualities and essences incomprehensible. This was the original condition of Matter. It was without forms, for it was but one Form. It had no motions, but it was an eternity of Motion. It was without parts, for it was a Whole. Particles did not exist, but the Whole was as one Particle. There were not suns, but it was one eternal Sun. It had no beginning and it was without end. It had not length, for it was a Vortex of one Eternity. It had not circles, for it was one infinite Circle. It had not disconnected power, but it was the very essence of all Power. . . . Matter and Power were existing as a Whole, inseparable. The Matter contained the substance to produce all suns, all worlds, and systems of worlds, throughout the immensity of Space. It contained the qualities to produce all things that are existing upon each of those worlds. The Power contained Wisdom, and Goodness, Justice, Mercy and Truth. It contained the original and essential Principle that is displayed throughout immensity of Space, controlling worlds and systems of worlds, and producing Motion, Life, Sensation and Intelligence (Stefanidakis).

By1850 Davis no longer relied on the mesmeric state for inspiration. During the next five years he wrote the five-volume *The Great Harmonia*, which provides the intellectual framework for Spiritualism. The book influenced many religious, social, educational, and medical systems of this period. Many of Davis's ideas parallel those of the romanticist, transcendentalist, and utopian communities that flourished during that period. They all felt that the spiritual evolution of the individual is intimately entwined with the evolution of society.

Thus, the Spiritualists considered education of utmost importance. In 1863 Davis founded schools called Lyceums based on the Summerland schools he had been shown during trance. Every child, being the image of an "imperishable and perfect being," contains infinite possibilities. Thus, the schools encouraged individual learning based on each child's innate potential. Though Davis's Lyceums no longer exist, a number of private schools today follow a similar ideology; e.g., Montessori, Waldorf and Sudbury.

During the forty years of his ministry, Davis wrote more than 30 books on cosmology, health and the after life, many of which were immensely popular, one actually attaining 34 editions. He spent the last few years of his life as a proprietor of a small book shop.

As to Spiritualism's connection with New Thought, Fillmore defines clairvoyance as intuitive perception or clear vision. He explains that everything that happens in the manifest world happens first in the realm of thought. It is entirely possible to know what is to occur if one is tuned in to the acts created by thought (*The Revealing Word*).

Thomas Troward, whose teachings we encounter in chapter eight, writes: "From mental healing it is but a step to telepathy, clairvoyance and other kindred manifestations of transcendental power . . . which follow laws as accurate as those which govern what we are accustomed to consider our more normal faculties" (*The Edinburgh Lectures*). In *The Law and the Word* he writes that many things labeled as supernatural are actually known laws working under unknown conditions (Brodeur). Indeed, as science fiction writer Arthur C. Clarke noted, "Any sufficiently advanced technology is indistinguishable from magic." What science has now proved as conforming to natural law ancient societies attributed to the supernatural.

Davis equates God with Divine Mind, Infinite Principle, Infinite Mind, and Positive Mind. As we have seen, the New Thought founders use these terms, too, though Holmes is more consistent in emphasizing Mind and Principle. With Spiritualism's emphasis on Swedenborg and its parallels with Romanticism and Transcendentalism, its connections with New Thought are obvious.

Theosophy

The word theosophy comes from the Greek *theos*, meaning god or divinity, and *sophia*, meaning wisdom; thus, theosophy means divine wisdom. The word itself has been in use in the Western world for two thousand years, though the movement known as Theosophy did not begin until the 1870s. The theosophist's goal is to acquire the knowledge and wisdom of the divine consciousness and then apply it to his or her life. Such knowledge and wisdom are attained through insight, experience and intellectual study.

Modern Theosophy, which in many respects is a form of Spiritualism, is claimed to be part of the perennial philosophy—the wisdom that underlies many of the world's religions, sciences and philosophies. Modern Theosophy has quite a colorful history due to the flamboyance of its founder, Helena Petrovna Blavatsky.

Born into a wealthy family in Russia in 1831, Blavatsky spent her childhood protesting against the injustice and cruelty she witnessed among people in her culture. She also spent a great deal of time in nature, for which she felt immense love and affinity. In the language of awe and appreciation the rocks, trees and birds spoke to her. Thrust into an arranged marriage at the age of seventeen, she found herself in Armenia, where her husband was stationed. But the free-spirited Blavatsky could not be contained and fled her marriage after only a few months. She wandered Europe and the Middle East for several years before moving to New York and becoming involved with Spiritualism. She joined with Henry Steele Olcott in 1875, and together they founded the Theosophical Society, whose members came largely from the spiritualist community. The Society claimed three purposes: 1) to form a universal human brotherhood that ignores race, creed, caste, or color; 2) to encourage study of comparative religion, philosophy and science; and 3) to investigate the unexplained laws of nature and the latent powers within humanity ("Theosophy").

Blavatsky claimed to receive messages on the spiritual plane from Eastern masters living in Egypt. Unlike the typical medium, Blavatsky communicated with live messengers. She called them Masters and contended they belonged to the Brotherhood of Luxor, a fraternity based on Masonic principles. Interestingly, there existed at the same time in Cairo a Brotherhood of Luxor based on Hermetic principles.

In 1877 Blavatsky wrote her first major work, *Isis Unveiled*, which is a criticism of many beliefs of that time, especially of Darwin's evolutionary theory and the ensuing scientific and theologic responses to it. Since 1859 when Darwin published his theory, there had been a major upheaval in the world of religion. Blavatsky's book agrees with the spiritualists and romanticists and views evolution as including more than just the physical world. She also says there are natural laws that apply to the spiritual world just as there are in the physical world.

Blavatsky and Olcott sailed to India in 1879 under the guidance of the Masters. There the two spread the teachings of Theosophy and gained many British and Indian adherents. The Society spoke out against the misuse of religious teachings, naming the caste system as a prime example. Blavatsky didn't present her teachings as of strictly Hindu or Buddhist origin; rather, she taught that they contained the essence of the truth that lies behind all religions and sciences.

During Blavatsky's time in India, the name of the Masters's order changed to the Himalayan Brotherhood of the Great White Lodge, the Masters relocated to Tibet and were now incorporeal beings. Some say that she spent a period of time in Tibet where she received spiritual training from the Masters. Perhaps it is fair to say that Theosophy, as with all things, was evolving.

The Masters communicated with the theosophists in various ways, sometimes in person, other times through mental telepathy, and through letters which mysteriously materialized in diverse and curious places. A huge furor arose over the letter writing claim and after much investigation Blavatsky was branded a fraud. It wasn't so much the content of the messages that was objectionable, but the claimed means in which the messages were given. Regardless, Blavatsky took offence and left India in 1885. She then went to London where she wrote *The*

Secret Doctrine, which contains a description of the universe and humanity's evolution through various planes that is similar to Davis's. She died in London in 1891.

Blavatsky wrote much that does not apply to New Thought. However, in her writings lay commonalities with New Thought, primarily because both systems of thought comprise the perennial philosophy. I include here only ideas common to both groups.

One of the primary ideas of Theosophy is the essential oneness of everything. All life throughout the cosmos originates from the same unknowable divine source and is essentially divine. All matter is alive and contains consciousness. The spiritual, or astral, body is birthed first and is the model for the physical body. All of humanity is intimately joined through, and impacted by, its thoughts and feelings. We all receive promptings from inner, and higher, sources. By following these promptings we are able to benefit both ourselves and all of humanity. Because we are rooted in divinity, we are capable of judging truth and falsity, reality and illusion, right and wrong, and need not look to any other authority. The following quote is reminiscent of Quimby's certainty that physical illnesses are caused by adherence to the "authority" of doctors and religious dogma.

> Have we not been told again and again that we must consult our consciences before we accept anything? In order to do that, we have to think; we also know that even if in doing so we should, *through our own blindness or incapacity*, reject a truth offered to us, we shall nevertheless have done aright, because we have been faithful to ourselves and to our consciences, . . . the inner man understands, and the truth in time will dawn in faithful hearts (de Purucker, *Fundamentals of the Esoteric Philosophy*, qtd. in "H.P. Blavatsky"; emphasis in original).

Blavatsky sets out three fundamental propositions involving the birth of the universe. The first depicts an "ultimate, unknowable cause from which everything is born and to which all things eventually return." The second says that the universe is an eternal and unlimited plane which is governed by fundamental laws. The third proposition depicts the relationship of the individual soul with the "Universal Over-Soul," and states that every soul by necessity progresses through the "Cycle of Incarnation" according to "Cyclic and Karmic law"

("Some Basic Concepts"). One human is no more privileged than another. Some just seem more privileged because they have persevered and gained in consciousness through numerous reincarnations. In New Thought terms, some of us seem more privileged because we understand the relationship between thought and action, reality and illusion, and God and humans, and because of this we have an understanding of how life works that others do not.

She uses the Sanskrit word *akasha*, which means "space," the kind of space one would find inside an empty suitcase or cupboard. Blavatsky views akasha as a medium for vibrations of various magnitudes. The Masters refer to the akashic records as comprising a nonphysical realm within which all thoughts and actions move, leaving behind impressions that can be read by sensitive people.

Swedenborg writes in *The Anatomy of Our First Nature* that the soul enlivens the physical body by use of vibrations which exist in a stretched membrane. Similarly, Quimby says the mind, being spiritual matter, is "a subtle, ethereal substance, wonderfully impressionable or responsive," upon which opinions, fears and beliefs are impressed (Dresser). Holmes includes akasha in his *Dictionary of New Thought Terms*. And Fillmore compares a trumpet's "sharp vibrations in the ether, which cause disintegration when they impinge upon an object in the mental or material realms" with mental or audible words which "send into the ether a spiritual force that shatters the fixed states of consciousness holding millions in evil ways." Though the concept of ether is no longer considered a valid scientific theory, Fillmore's interpretation of vibrational waves is not affected. Troward writes of "grooves of thought" on our brains that allow the "vibrations of the cosmic currents" to flow through them and react upon the mind. While these descriptions do not seem to mirror *exactly* what Blavatsky and the Masters teach, they show in parallel ways the impact the nonphysical realm has on the physical and vice versa.

In setting forth in the two volumes of *The Secret Doctrine* the ideas that make up Theosophy, Blavatsky provides over 1,200 quotes from all the major scriptures as well as ancient and modern authors from the Far East, Middle East, and West, proving her thesis that Theosophy comprises the perennial philosophy.

It can be seen that many ideas in New Thought are comparable to ideas espoused by Theosophy, though Theosophy covers a much wider range and includes ideas foreign to New Thought.

Rosicrucianism

Blavatsky's idea of a society devoted to the betterment of humanity using esoteric means follows in the footsteps of the Rosicrucian order, a seventeenth century secret society founded by Christian Rosencreuz. The Order derived its name from the Latin words *rosae*, meaning rose, and *crux* or *crucis*, meaning cross and was shrouded in mystery out of necessity. As we have discussed, science, logic and reason ruled the seventeenth century. All things esoteric and spiritual had been relegated to the past, and adherents risked persecution.

The Order published three Manifestos explaining the purpose of the organization: to guide humanity to "spiritual truth and personal enlightenment" by reforming the "educational, moral and scientific" aspects of society. Traditional Rosicrucians feel nothing but love, compassion and tolerance for their fellow beings and hold to a higher standard than do many people. "They seek the Truth within, and they live according to that truth. For the Rosicrucians purity is essential, clear direction a must, and selflessness is the act. . . . Traditionally and historically, the Rosicrucian movement has always fought for the establishment and perpetuation of freedom—the freedom of mind, spirit, and soul" ("Rosicrucianism [1]").

According to Gary L. Stewart, Rosicrucian Imperator, the process of enlightenment is alchemical and spiritual, not material. Spiritual alchemy is transforming, refining, and transcending the self to reach a more evolved state. The goal is Truth, the Truth that leads to freedom.

Rosicrucianism is not a religion, and a student does not have to give up his or her current religion in order to study Rosicrucian principles. One can follow the Rosicrucian path while adhering to any religion, for the path is simply the means one uses to awaken. Along the path the student learns the natural laws, the application of which produces an experience of Divine unity.

Rosicrucian teachings center on mastering life, a concept in which we succeed through using our "mental imaging powers to bring forth concrete reality." Through a series of lessons students learn to image things like health, wealth and happiness. They also learn that humans are both physical and spiritual, or psychic, beings. The lessons help the students become aware of their psychic capabilities and cover topics such as "The Creative Power of Visualization," and the "Influence of Thoughts on Health" ("Rosicrucianism [2]").

It is believed that the philosophers Spinoza and Descartes were members of the Rosicrucian order. As we have seen, there are many commonalities between their philosophies and that of New Thought and between New Thought and Rosicrucianism.

Ella Wheeler Wilcox, known as the New Thought Poetess, was a student of Emma Curtis Hopkins. Wilcox's numerous poems encompass the New Thought viewpoint and its optimism. Probably her most famous line is "Laugh, and the world laughs with you; weep, and you weep alone." She also credits Hinduism for inducing many of her ideas.

Wilcox pursued several esoteric practices around the turn of the century. An avid spiritualist, she claimed to receive messages from her departed husband. She also actively participated in Rosicrucian mysticism. Wilcox, H. Spencer Lewis, and book publishers Frater Elbert Hubbard and J.K. Funk, of Funk and Wagnalls fame, founded the New York Institute for Psychical Research in 1904 as a guise for the Rosicrucian Research Society, as they were not chartered to use the Rosicrucian name until 1915. At that time Lewis became Imperator and appointed Wilcox a member of the first Supreme Council of the American Rosicrucian movement, an office she kept until her death.

Troward incorporates several Rosicrucian principles in his philosophy that Holmes later uses in composing his Science of Mind. Troward posits a Universal Subconscious Mind from which the human subconscious was made. Our subconscious is also universal and infinite and is a conduit of Its expression. The human experience is one of evolution, and "the ultimate aim of the evolutionary process is to evolve individual wills actuated by such beneficence and enlightenment as shall make them fitting vehicles for the outflowing of the Supreme Spirit." We evolve by consciously cooperating with universal laws. He ends *The Edinburgh Lectures* with a lengthy reference to the founder of the Rosicrucians from whom we can learn the process of realizing "unity in the full development of all its powers."

Mysticism

Like *occult* and *esoteric*, the term *mystic* is often misunderstood, and it is easy to see why. According to *Merriam-Webster's*, a mystic is someone who follows a mystical way of life. That doesn't tell us much. Mystic, used as an adjective, means "of or relating to mysteries or esoteric rites; mysterious, obscure or enigmatic; inducing a feeling of awe or wonder." That helps. But Holmes provides a much more meaningful definition in *The Science of Mind*: "A mystic is one who intuitively perceives Truth and, without mental process, arrives at Spiritual Realization. Spirit alone is their Teacher." So, the great mystics understand Truth through Spirit alone. We might say truth comes to them by way of revelation—spirit communing with spirit.

The mystical experience has a long history, having been an integral part of religious experience in the East for several thousand years and part of Western traditions since the first Church Father Origen (c.185-254 C.E.) taught that humans have the capacity to reach the highest state—the absolute absorption into God. The Christian tradition produced a number of mystics—Meister Eckhart, St. Teresa, and St. John of the Cross being the most well known. In Judaism we find the Kabbala, and in Islam the Sufis and Baha'i Faith. From the ancient Greco-Roman pagan world comes Plotinus, one of the greatest of all mystics. In the East we find the mystical Tao of Taoism. The Hindu *Vedas* speak of the mystical experience known as *nirvana* or enlightenment. And Buddhism began with the mystical experience of Siddhartha Gautama, the Buddha or Enlightened One. These Eastern concepts are discussed in chapters ten and eleven.

Regardless of its many forms, there are four elements common among the many types of mystical experiences: 1) a unitary consciousness; 2) inexpressible feelings; 3) a sense of timelessness and unboundedness; and 4) feelings of blessedness (Stace).

Within religious mysticism there are two theories of Divine Reality—emanation and immanence. The emanation view, called theistic mysticism, holds that everything comes forth from God; that is,

God is creator. Examples of theistic mysticism can be found in Christianity, Judaism, Sufism, the Baha'i Faith, and some forms of Hinduism. Swedenborg is an emanationist. He writes that even though the Divine is in everything, "there is in their being nothing of the Divine in itself; for the created universe is not God, but is from God" (*Divine Love and Wisdom*; qtd. in "Writings").

The immanentists are monists and see the universe as contained within God. Monistic mysticism is found in Taoism, with its unknowable and unnameable Tao; in Plotinus, who referred to God as an impersonal It and an ultimate and unknowable God called *the One*; and in the *Upanishads* of Hinduism which speak of God as *Brahman* "which is mind and life, light and truth and . . . enfolds the whole universe" (*Chandogya Upanishad*; qtd. in *Bhagavad Gita*). The immanence view is pantheistic and is the view accepted by most New Thought adherents.

A form of monistic mysticism is naturism, in which the mystic discovers God by unifying him or herself with nature. The boundary between object and subject disappears and the mystic feels part of nature. Emerson and Thoreau are mystics of this type. Also included in this group are various Goddess and Native American religions. In the words of Starhawk, "Immanence means that the Goddess, the Gods, are embodied, that we are each a manifestation of the living being of the earth, that nature, culture, and life in all their diversity are sacred. Immanence calls us to live our spirituality here in the world, to take action to preserve the life of the earth, to live with integrity and responsibility" ("Immanence").

The great mystics across time have taught the same truth—there is but one Life in which, said St. Paul, "we live and move and have our being" (Acts 17:28). The One Life, the only Reality, is here, now. It is up to each of us to turn within and realize that we are surrounded by It, embraced by It, guided by It, provided for by It, and filled with It. There can be nothing less than perfection in our experience because Perfection is all there is. And because there is only Perfection, evil is not real. There is nothing to fear. We experience what we call evil because we misuse our God-given freedom. When we realize the truth of our being and correct our errors in thought and deed, evil disappears. Suffering no longer exists. Poverty and disease vanish. Peace and happiness reign. We are immortal beings and we all receive salvation. In the eloquent words of Holmes:

> [The mystics] have all agreed that the soul is on the pathway of experience, that is, of self-discovery; that it is on its way back to its Father's House; and that every soul will ultimately reach its heavenly home. They have taught the Divinity of Man. . . . They have told us that man's destiny is Divine and sure; and that creation is complete and perfect *now*. They have all agreed that man's life is his to do with as he chooses, but that when he turns to the One, he will always receive inspiration from on High. They have told us of the marvelous relationship which exists between God and man, and of a close Union that cannot be broken; the greatest of the mystics have consciously walked with God and talked with Him, just as we talk with each other. . . . They have taught the "Mystical Marriage," the union of the soul of man with the Soul of God, and the Unity of all Life. The great mystics while sensing this Unity have also sensed the individualization of Being and the individuality of Man as a Divine Reality (emphasis in original).

The mystical experience itself has been described as a flash of illumination, a feeling of being immersed in a flame or rose-colored cloud, and/or a feeling of ecstasy. Moses is portrayed with a glow about him as he comes down from the mountain after speaking with God. Pictures of Jesus nearly always show a halo, or golden glow around his head. Emerson became conscious of the cosmic light while walking in Concord. Whitman describes it as "ineffable light, light rare, untellable, light beyond all signs, descriptions and languages" that felt like a forked tongue piercing his being ("Mysticism"). Tennyson describes it as clearness of mind and "a state of transcendent wonder" (James, *Varieties*). Plato depicts it as a shudder that flows through the body followed by a creeping awe. Jacob Boehme says he was "surrounded by the divine light, and replenished with the heavenly knowledge" ("The Image"), and in just fifteen minutes he learned more than he had in many years of study. George Fox, founder of the Society of Friends (the Quakers), tells of a similar experience.

In this state the substance of which humans are made can be seen. The person understands that life goes on forever, all life is connected to the One, the One is always present, love conquers everything, all evil will be overcome by good, and there is no need to fear death. In speaking of the mystical state Plotinus writes: "Everything there is eternal and immutable . . . [and] in a state of bliss" (*Enneads*, qtd. in Leahey).

For many, the experience of mystical consciousness comes on unannounced and lasts for just a short period; however, for others it lasts for several days. Plotinus, Swedenborg and Holmes all experienced lengthy periods of illumination and bliss. But whatever the length, the mystical experience is felt as "an eternal moment" (Stace).

Though mystical union can come on unannounced, it isn't an experience that appears out of nowhere; it must be sought actively. Our souls are divinely created by God but during the human experience (because of free will) they become mired in the body and other objective matter and in earthly affairs. It takes conscious effort on our part to raise our consciousness to the point where we can once again experience the eternal oneness and blissful ecstacy of our true condition. Knowing or rationally thinking about this true reality is just an intermediate stage in the soul's quest for home. Plotinus says that the soul "yearns to be godlike, . . . to experience [an] immediate ecstatic contact with and vision of God," that this is our "noblest goal" (Sahakian).

The word ecstacy is from the Greek *existanai*, meaning "displace, or drive out of one's mind." The mystical experience of union with the One is quite literally an experience of being out of one's mind. Such an experience is felt rather than thought.

In New Thought the mystical state is sometimes called *cosmic consciousness, superconsciousness,* or *Christ consciousness.* This state is achieved by very few, but over time with the evolution of humanity into higher states of consciousness, this cosmic state will become the norm.

Fillmore writes, "If the superconsciousness, or the Christ Mind, is not developed, the people will destroy one another in insane warring for the fleeting things of the world. Preaching the glories of heaven will not reach a mind that has no capacity for the enjoyment of heaven." The way we experience the superconscious state is by going into the silence or meditating. Holmes calls it Cosmic Light, cosmic consciousness, and with Hopkins and St. Paul, as "the mind that was in Christ Jesus" (Phil. 2:5). Brooks writes of it as going into the light.

Historical figures who are considered to have had such experiences and are possessed by cosmic consciousness are Buddha, Jesus, St. Paul, Plotinus, Mohammed, Dante, Las Casas, St. John of the Cross, Francis Bacon, Jacob Boehme, William Blake, and Walt Whitman. Most of these mystics are mentioned by the New Thought founders in their writings, along with Hopkins, Eckhart, Swedenborg, Homer, Socrates, Plato, Moses, David, Solomon, Browning, Tennyson, and Wordsworth. In fact, Holmes says that all the great poets and spiritual philosophers are mystics. Many of these mystics have been, or will be, discussed within the chapters of this book.

Within Christianity, mostly from the Catholic tradition, there have been a number of mystics, all of whom were considered heretics, for the knowledge they gained in the mystical experience often contradicted official Church doctrine. In reality, these mystics were not heretics, for we find these truths in the teachings of Jesus, as we shall see in chapter nine.

Considered the greatest of the Christian mystics, Johannes Eckhart, better known as Meister Eckhart, was born in Germany in 1260. At the age of 15 he entered the Dominican order. Charged formally with heresy by the archbishop of Cologne, he and his writings escaped the burning suffered by other mystics. Pope John XXII published a bull in 1329 which condemned 28 of Eckhart's propositions.

Eckhart taught that God is intellect or thought and is a unity (as opposed to the Trinity). Because there is only One, God is everywhere and all things are contained within this One. For God, there is only the present moment. In the hierarchy of spiritual beings, the human soul is higher than angels, and the nature of humans is the same as God's nature. It is possible to experience oneness with God for there is a light within the human soul that is uncreated and that "wants to penetrate to the simple ground, to the still desert" within which there are no distinctions (Eckhart).

Probably the most well-known Protestant mystics are Jacob Boehme and Emanuel Swedenborg.

Jacob Boehme, known as the "chosen servant of God," was born into a pious Lutheran family in 1575 in Alt Seidenburg, Germany. Throughout his formative years Boehme spent enormous amounts of time considering how to ensure the salvation of his soul. He studied the Bible but found its teachings about God incomprehensible and perplexing. After much prayer and supplication the mystical experience mentioned earlier in this section came upon him. He writes, "for seven days I was in a continual state of ecstasy, surrounded by the light of the Spirit, which immersed me in contemplation and happiness." In 1600 he received another vision in which he understood "the heart of things, the true nature of God and man, and the relationship existing between them." Ten years later he began compiling all that had been revealed to him. Over the next 12 years he wrote thirty books, for which he suffered severe persecution and a trial for heresy. Shortly before his death in 1624 the nobility of Germany began to accept his writings as having been inspired, and Boehme died "happy in the midst of the heavenly music of the paradise of God" ("The Image").

Boehme's teachings parallel those of the other mystics and address the paradox mentioned by Stace earlier in this section. In answer to the question as to how one is to comprehend the "void of all Self," Boehme writes, "If thou goest about to comprehend it, then it will fly away from thee; but if thou dost surrender thyself wholly up to it, then it will abide with thee, and become the Life of thy Life, and be natural to thee" ("The Image"). Mystical experience cannot be understood by rational thinking. It is sensory in nature. That is why it is called an *experience*. This kind of paradox runs throughout mysticism and the philosophies of the East and is discussed further in chapter ten.

Swedenborg was born in 1688 in Stockholm, Sweden. His father, a professor of theology and dean of the cathedral, later became the Bishop of Skara. In this post he served as chaplain to the royal family and as such considered a nobleman. Thus, Swedenborg spent his youth among the social elite. Because of his father's profession, the Swedenborg home was filled with both reverence and zeal. At the age of 56 Swedenborg began having dreams and visions, some frightening, others inspiring. After a year of these experiences he received a visit from a spirit announcing Swedenborg would "serve as the means by which God would further reveal himself to men in somewhat the manner of the biblical visions of the Old Testament" (Tafel, *Documents Concerning Swedenborg*; qtd. in Synnestvedt). He spent much of the rest of his life writing the 30 volumes of doctrine given him by God and His messengers. (His core teachings were iterated in chapter five.)

In 1769 when he was 81 years old, prelates of the Lutheran state church charged him with heresy. Dean Ekebom, the ranking prelate, considered Swedenborg dangerous and proclaimed his doctrines "corrupting, heretical, injurious, and in the highest degree objectionable" (Synnestvedt). It took a year for a decision to be made. Swedenborg's works were impounded and clerics ordered to discontinue teaching his doctrines. Swedenborg protested this decision, even petitioning the King. In response, the King's court asked several universities to study Swedenborg's works. They found nothing to censure, and after three years the situation quietly dissolved.

Interestingly, just prior to this commotion Immanuel Kant, whose philosophy we discussed in chapters four and six, wrote to Swedenborg. Kant's somewhat contradictory rational and transcendental views caused him distress in respect to Swedenborg's much-acclaimed clairvoyant and visionary powers. His rational side wanted to discount Swedenborg's abilities, while his transcendental side inclined to support them. It is not known how Kant resolved this dilemma. I mention it only because Kant and Swedenborg are both so important to New Thought.

Kabbala

Kabbala, variously spelled Kabalah, Caballa and Qaballah, is a Hebrew mystery religion based on the Jewish Torah and passed orally from teacher to student. *Kabbala* in Hebrew means "that which is received," and is understood to refer to the means by which a deeper understanding of the teachings of the Torah are achieved. Many of the books of Kabbala were written in a certain way so that only those familiar with the teachings of the Torah could understand. The term Kabbala, introduced by the Spanish philosopher Iba Gabriol in the eleventh century, originally referred to specific secret mystical teachings. Today Kabbala refers to all Jewish mystical practices.

Legend holds that originally God taught the Kabbala to some angels, who taught it to Adam after the Fall. From Adam it passed orally to Noah, then to Abraham, and finally to Moses, who included it in the first four books of the Pentateuch (the first five books of the Old Testament). Moses then initiated seventy Elders and those Elders initiated others. Some think that this knowledge passed to David and Solomon. At some point the Kabbalistic knowledge was written down.

It is believed God gave the Kabbala to Adam to assist humanity's return; in essence, to save them from the Fall. The purpose of studying the Kabbala, then, is to enlighten the self in order to enlighten humanity so that everyone may be saved.

There is much to the Kabbala but, as with the other systems in this chapter, I describe only the commonalities with New Thought. Keep in mind that while the concepts are the same, their presentation and mythology are not.

The Kabbala teaches that in the beginning there existed only God. From within himself he sent an emanation outward. Some see this emanation as light. Nine more emanations evolved from this one light. These ten emanations together are called the *sephiroth*—wisdom, insight, inexorableness, cognition, strength, power, justice, right, love, and mercy—and compose the sacred name of God. The sephiroth are parts of God, and also parts of the universe, since the universe is made from God. This is a pantheistic concept.

Others see the emanation as sound. According to Carlos Suares, a mystic and Kabbala master, the universe arose from "the vibrational sound patterns of three Hebrew letters: *aleph*, or the void—spirit wanting to become aware of itself; *mem*, or matter projected from that void; and *shin*, the wave movement of consciousness" (Lemley). Ultimately, everything is vibration, and within these vibrations is unlimited potential. This concept of vibration is similar to that of the theosophists.

Gerald Schroeder writes that the first word in the book of Genesis, *Be'reasbeet*, is mistakenly translated "in the beginning." *Be'reasbeet* is a compound word—*Be'*, meaning "with," and *reasbeet*, meaning "first wisdom." The two thousand year old Jerusalem translation into Aramaic says "With wisdom God created the heavens and the earth."

The Hebrew words translated as "unformed and void" in Genesis 1:2 are *tohu* and *bohu*. The Kabbala teaches that tohu is "the solitary primordial substance, created at the beginning from absolute nothing, the substanceless substrate from which all that is material was to be formed"; and that *bohu* is a composite word— *bo*, meaning "in it," and *hu*, meaning "there is." Thus, instead of the English "The earth was unformed and void" we have the Hebrew "In it [in the *tobu*] there is [potential]." Created at the beginning is the one and only substance filled with potential and from this substance came all that exists.

In the book of Isaiah is found the idea of creation as the Divine act of *tzimtzum*, God's "spiritual contraction" (45:7). The "undifferentiated simplicity of God is fractured, yielding in its stead the variety of our universe. With this Divine contraction comes the release that allows for our choices of free will and leeway for the seeming imperfections and meandering courses found in nature" (Schroeder).

For Kabbalists sin is not wrongdoing to be punished by God, but is ignorance resulting in separation from God. Knowledge of God unites us with God, and those who have this knowledge are to share it.

Over time the original Kabbalist principles were modified and reinterpreted. A practical Kabbala that provides methods of prayer, contemplation and meditation appeared in Italy and Germany in the tenth century. Ecstatic practices and magical rituals began at this time, too. It spread to France and Spain in the thirteenth century, being further modified in transit. The Spanish Hebrews introduced the *Sefer ba-Zohar*, the Book of Splendor, in which God is without end and is knowable only by its representations. God created the universe from himself. There is no independence, as everything is connected. The goal of humanity is complete union with God. Since nothing is independent of anything else, this is accomplished by elevating or enlightening the self. In doing so, everyone else is elevated. The sixteenth century brought the Christian Kabbala, which added alchemical elements. Some also affiliate numerology, astrology, and the Tarot with the Kabbala.

Many early New Thought adherents practiced astrology, and Troward mentions in his Lectures the "Pack of Cards," which I believe is a reference to the Tarot. As mentioned at the beginning of this chapter, Cramer and Holmes read the Kabbala and we can see its influence in their writings.

Hermeticism

The Hermeticists were the original alchemists (transcendental chemists), astrologers (transcendental astronomers), and transcendental or mystical psychologists.

As with other philosophies of great age, the exact date of the beginning of Hermeticism and the author(s) of its teachings are not known with certainty. The traditional author of the treatises known collectively as the *Corpus Hermeticum* is thought to be Hermes Trismegistus ("Thrice-Greatest"), the Master of Masters. Some believe he was an actual person who lived in ancient Egypt and taught Abraham, the Old Testament prophet. Others believe he is the mythological Egyptian god Thoth. Still others feel that several early Christians or gnostics wrote the treatises using the pseudonym Hermes Trismegistus. Regardless of their source, legend holds that the manuscripts resided in the magnificent library at Alexandria. When the library burned, most of the manuscripts were lost.

Hermeticism is also called the Western Esoteric Tradition and is believed to consist of the perennial philosophy. Its teachings contain elements of Kabbalism, Eastern and Neo-Platonic philosophy, Christian and Gnostic mysticism, and alchemy and magic. The Christian church banned Hermeticism during the early centuries because it threatened church authority. Not wishing the truth to be lost, Hermetic affiliates buried in a secret location the fragments that survived the Alexandrian fire. Others furthered Hermetic principles in the Middle East through the mystic and Kabbalistic traditions, and through the philosophies of the Far East, which some believe to be their original source.

Hermeticism returned to the Western world in the fifteenth century when Cosimo de Medici obtained a copy of the treatises and had the Platonic philosopher Marsilio Ficino translate them into Latin. Its blending in the seventeenth century with Rosicrucianism, in the eighteenth century with Freemasonry, and in the nineteenth century with Theosophy and New Thought further advanced its influence.

Hermeticism holds both the emanation and transcendent viewpoints. From the transcendent Divine One emanates a multitude of manifestations that exist on many different planes and in varying degrees of life. The lowest degree of life is crude matter and the highest is Spirit. Though the human body consists of matter, within each body is Spirit. When we realize this indwelling Spirit, we begin advancing through higher and higher degrees of life until we reach the highest degree of all, that of the Divine Spirit or the All. At this point the Creator and the created become one.

According to *The Kybalion*, a text written in the 1930s to explain the Hermetic teachings, there are seven principles that form the basis of the Hermetic philosophy:

1. *The Principle of Mentalism.* The All is the Substantial Reality underlying all things apparent to our material senses. This Reality is Spirit and is unknowable and undefinable. Creation is a mental process. Through meditation or contemplation the All projects its aspect of Will toward its aspect of Becoming. Since the All is Mind and creates through thought, the created world is mental.

2. *The Principle of Vibration.* All things vibrate at various frequencies (the number of times a wave completes a full cycle in a period of time). Between the densest forms of matter, which vibrate at very low frequencies, and the highest forms of spirit, which vibrate at extremely high frequencies, (both of which appear not to be vibrating at all), are millions of forms vibrating at medium range frequencies. These myriad forms exist on various planes, including the physical, energetic, mental, and spiritual.

3. *The Principle of Correspondence.* This principle applies to the entire universe; thus, it is a Universal Law. This principle states that there is a correspondence between the many planes of existence, and because of this correspondence we are able to know the planes that exist beyond sense awareness. This principle contains the most familiar of the Hermetic axioms: "As above, so below; as below, so above." This phrase is found at the beginning of *The Emerald Tablet,* and is believed to be the key to all mysteries. What is true of the macrocosm is true of the microcosm. What is true of the All is true of humans.

4. *The Principle of Polarity.* All manifest things contain two poles consisting of apparent opposites. This principle explains the paradoxes that result from the belief that

apparent opposites are actual opposites (duality). In reality, these opposites are just two extremes of the same thing, differing not in kind but only in degree. Just as with stories, everything has two sides. The same thing can be both hot and cold, dark and light, large and small, high and low, hard and soft, or good and bad. There is no definitive cutoff point between these extremes. For instance, between hot and cold are varying degrees of hot, warm, lukewarm, cool, and cold. Where does hot leave off and warm begin? Where does warm end and cool begin? Further, in this principle we find the paradoxical concept that things are and aren't at the very same time.

5. *The Principle of Rhythm.* All things exhibit an in-and-out, back-and-forth, rise-and-fall, or outflow-and-inflow motion. For every advance there is a retreat. For every action there is a reaction. In regard to mental phenomena there are two planes—the lower plane is the unconscious and the higher plane is the conscious. The swing of the rhythmic pendulum-like motion applies only to the lower consciousness; therefore, by rising to a higher state of consciousness, the effects of swinging from pole to pole are avoided. By polarizing at whichever pole is desired, by "refusing" to allow the swing in the opposite direction, or by "denying" its influence on our position, we can remain resolute in our polarized position. The Law of Compensation, discussed in chapter thirteen, is a counterbalance; that is, the amount of swing in one direction is the same amount in the other direction. Rhythm compensates. However, the compensating swing does not necessarily have to take place during the same lifetime. One who masters this principle escapes the swing in the undesirable direction by rising to a higher plane.

6. *The Principle of Cause and Effect.* For every effect there is a cause. There is no such thing as chance, luck, or accidental happenings. What seems like chance and accident are actually the effects of causes beyond human awareness or understanding. Hermeticists understand that it is possible to rise above the plane of cause and effect through

mental effort and to become the cause rather than the effect. By understanding that Universal Law governs everything, that the higher law always prevails over the lower law, they use the higher Universal Law to overcome all other laws and their ensuing effects.

7.   *The Principle of Gender*. All things consist of gender. In fact, all things consist of both genders. Within every male or masculine thing, there is a female or feminine aspect, and vice versa. The word *gender* derives from a Latin root meaning "to beget, to procreate, to generate, to create, or to produce." Thus, creation at every level, be it physical, mental or spiritual, adheres to this principle. The mind of every person contains a dual aspect—the "I" and the "Me." The "I" represents the masculine principle or the aspect of *Being* and the "Me" represents the female principle or the aspect of *Becoming*. The feminine principle receives while the masculine principle gives. The feminine principle also relates to generating new ideas and imaginations, while the masculine principle is associated with the Will. We can see this principle at work in the common sayings that God is Father and Nature is Mother. These are two aspects of the One.

The Hermetic concepts of God and Its Creations are summarized in the following paraphrased statements from five of the treatises of the *Corpus Hermeticum*:

"Poemandres, The Shepherd of Man" –

- The All-Father Mind is Life and Light. He created humans as coequal to Himself. God loves us and considers us to be His children. We are created in his image and contain the same characteristics as God.

- We are two-fold: the body makes us mortal, but the "essential man" (spirit) makes us immortal.

"The Cup or Monad" –
- The Oneness is the Source and Root of all. Nothing exists outside of the Source. The Source is of Itself.

"The Sacred Sermon" –
- God is both Mind and Nature.

"In God Alone is Good" –
- Good is God Himself eternally.
- He needs nothing.

"About the Common Mind" –
- The Mind consists of God's very essence. The Mind is not separated from God, but is united with it.
- The Mind of humans is God; thus, "their humanity is nigh unto divinity."
- God said: "Gods are immortal men, and men are mortal gods."
- Soul and Mind, and Life and Soul are the same thing.

The Kybalion sums up the Hermetic philosophy in saying that even though Reality is mental, the manifest universe must be treated as real. This is the Divine Paradox, that the Universe both Is and Is Not. There are two poles of Truth—the Absolute and the relative. In viewing the universe from the Absolute pole, the universe is an illusion, a dream, or a thought of the All, for nothing is real except the All. But there are always two sides, and the other side is the relative. From the relative viewpoint, which is the view from humanity's finite minds, the universe is thoroughly real and must be treated as such. In a manner of speaking all aspects of life are relative. We see matter is being solid and at rest, but to a scientist matter consists of atoms vibrating in a constant circular motion in vast amounts of empty space. Musical sounds seem to be real, but actually exist only of vibrations of waves. Though it is necessary for us to view the world as real, we must remember that the only true Reality consists of "things as the mind of God knows them." We must use the principles and laws to rise from the lower relative point of view to the higher view of the Absolute. This is the process of divine alchemy or transmutation. Transmutation is one of the main purposes for studying the words of Hermes Trismegistus. According to *The Kybalion*:

> Mental Transmutation is the art of changing and transforming mental states, forms and conditions into others. Every thought, emotion or mental state has its corresponding rate and mode of vibration. And by an effort of the will of the person, or of other persons, these mental states may be reproduced, just as a musical tone may be reproduced by causing an instrument to vibrate at a certain rate. By a knowledge of the Principle of Vibration, one may polarize the mind at any degree he wishes, thus gaining a perfect control over his mental states, moods, etc. In the same way he may affect the minds of others, producing the desired mental states in them.

In the words of Fillmore, transmutation is "changing in action and in character from the mortal into the spiritual. . . . [T]he mind is the crucible in which the ideal is transmuted into the real."

There are two other esoteric systems that influenced New Thought: Gnosticism and Esoteric Christianity, both of which comprise the mystical and metaphysical words of Jesus. These highly important systems of thought are discussed in chapters nine and twelve.

We turn now to the most recent road that New Thought followed.

VIII.

THE ROAD
OF THE INTELLECTUALS

*The whole of natural theology . . . resolves itself into one simple, though
somewhat ambiguous proposition, that the cause or causes
of order in the universe probably bear some remote analogy
to human intelligence.*
David Hume (1711–1776), Scottish philosopher
Dialogues Concerning Natural Religion

More than any of the other founders, Ernest Holmes took an
intellectual approach to New Thought. Also the most widely read, he
incorporated ideas unique to his Science of Mind. His synonyms for
God have more to do with mind and law than those of the other two
New Thought groups. This in large part is due to the road that he
alone followed.

Referring to Holmes and the members of this road as intellectuals in no way minimizes the intelligence of the other founders or
of the many minds encountered along the other roads. *Intellectual*
refers to mental, psychological and analytical activities, which is the
emphasis of this road.

As we saw in chapter three, Holmes was a synthesizer. He integrated the truths contained in all the varying philosophies from around
the world into one definitive philosophy of mind. Because he studied
and wrote thirty years later than the other founders, works from minds
not yet on the scene when Divine Science and Unity originated were
available to Holmes. In addition to the many minds we found along
the healing, rebellious and esoteric roads, which Holmes also followed, he includes in his Science of Mind the thinking of Aristotle,

Thomas Troward, Robert Browning, and several late nineteenth and early twentieth century idealists, psychologists and other New Thought writers.

Holmes began writing and teaching in the decade following the first World War. As mentioned in the introduction to this book, in the years subsequent to the founding of the other two churches, the world had radically changed. The Cartesian-Newtonian view of the world as mechanistic no longer reigned as the leading scientific theory. Albert Einstein's new theories showed that Newton's laws did not explain the expanding universe nor the new field of quantum mechanics. New theories in psychology brought new ways to view the human mind, how it works and how it influences behavior.

The Science of Mind

Before we start down this road, it is important to understand Holmes's Science of Mind so that we can see the influence of these other minds on his form of New Thought.

Holmes writes that the study of the Science of Mind is a study of God, the Ultimate Stuff from which everything is created. This Stuff he calls the Thing-Itself. The core teaching of Science of Mind is that we are made from, and surrounded by, the Thing-Itself; that the Thing-Itself is Good, works by Law and is governed by thought; that all this goodness is available for our use, and that we will have as much of this good in our experience as we can accept.

The Thing-Itself is universal and contains a threefold nature— Spirit, Soul and Body. Spirit is Self-Knowing or Self-Conscious and is the Cause of all that exists. Soul is the Medium by which It works and is an automatic, impersonal force having no will of its own. It simply obeys the Will of Spirit. Body is the result of Spirit's action on Soul. These three are One Power.

Creation takes place within Spirit, and is the result of Its thinking, contemplating, or imagining. Spirit and Soul exist together always and never change. The only changing thing is form.

Holmes uses many words and expressions for the same concepts. The chart on the following page may be helpful in understanding these concepts.

THE THREEFOLD NATURE OF GOD

SPIRIT	SOUL	BODY
Unconditioned, Self-knowing, Self-conscious, Self-existing Synonyms: Conscious Mind, Life, Intelligence, the Word, Absolute, the Infinite, Father-Mother-God, Parent Mind, First Cause	The neutral, creative medium through which Spirit works Synonyms: Subconscious Mind, Subjective Mind, Mental Medium, Law, Impersonal Law, Universal Subjectivity	The effects of Spirit acting through Soul by use of Law Synonyms: Creation, Form, Multiplicity, the Manifest Universe

Humans duplicate the divine threefold nature of the Universal Being. We are self-knowing in our conscious mind, creative through our unconscious reactions, and we have a body. Our real Essence is eternal and in complete unity with the Whole. The human spirit is the part that is aware of this unity and is the only part of the self that has will and free choice.

Working through Law, Spirit creates us as individuals, and then lets us freely discover the secrets of life in whatever way we choose. Perfection is attainable; in fact, it is our natural state. However, because of the free will given us we make choices that sometimes seem to be imperfect. As we evolve, we begin to awaken to our self-consciousness, realizing that mental law acts upon our thoughts, which causes a reaction in our body. As we gain in awareness, we discover that our thoughts can also cause reactions in other people's bodies, for we are mental mediums through which thought operates. We are thinking centers in Universal Mind, and everything in the visible world is an effect of the ideas we think.

We have at our disposal in our subjective minds a Limitless power, an Intelligence, a Mind that governs everything, and which acts through us. This is how God expresses into the world—by acting through each of us as we allow. Our intelligence is Universal Mind functioning at whatever level we can conceive.

This is the key to happiness and to all mental healing. It is not God's will that we suffer illness, evil and poverty. Limitation of any sort occurs as a result of the way the One Power is used. Law works automatically in the direction it is sent until we consciously change its course. Sickness is not a spiritual reality; it is simply an experience, or an effect. The body cannot think or experience sensation. It is the mind which thinks and feels, and we have the ability to control these thoughts and feelings.

God is a Universal Presence, an impersonal Observer, a Divine and impartial Giver, and It is forever giving of Its goodness. We are the receivers of all this goodness, and it is our responsibility to first acknowledge that this good exists and then to accept it into our experience. Jesus said if we would ask, it would be given. This is the Law, and as Jesus also said, it is the truth that will make us free.

What we now are and what we are to become depends upon what we think. Any condition can be changed by Law if we can conceive it as changed. We are surrounded by an Infinite Mind, which reacts to our thoughts according to Law. Thought attracts. Like attracts like and repels unlike. We draw to us what we think and mentally imagine. Thoughts *are* things.

Most of us sleepwalk through our lives, allowing Law to operate on an unconscious level, but when we awaken, and we understand how Law works, we can begin to consciously attract what we desire. This happens through a process Holmes calls *demonstration*. We must see in our mind the thing we desire, what he calls a *mental equivalent*, before we can demonstrate it into our experience. Holding a strong picture or concept in mind and *believing* in the outcome results in a manifestation of thought into thing.

Holmes uses three catch phrases that sum up his philosophy of mind: "Change your thinking, change your life"; "The Law can do *for* us what it can only do *through* us"; and "Principle is not bound by precedent," meaning what *was* or what *is* does not need to continue to be. The last two phrases come directly from the words of Thomas Troward, whose philosophy is discussed later in this chapter.

Now let's explore the path Holmes trod in formulating this philosophy.

Henry Drummond

Holmes's brother Fenwicke writes in his biography of Ernest that the Holmes family consistently utilized three books: *The Bible*, *The Story of the Bible*, and Henry Drummond's *Natural Law in the Spiritual World*. Drummond's book, with its focus on law, is probably the earliest influence on the development of Holmes's concept of God as Law.

Henry Drummond was born in Scotland in 1851. He received an evangelical Presbyterian upbringing and committed himself to Christ at a young age, a commitment he never broke. He studied science at the University of Edinburgh before beginning his training for the Free Church ministry. He was powerfully influenced by the writings of John Ruskin and Ralph Waldo Emerson, from whom he gained an appreciation for nature.

In 1873 Drummond read a paper to the Theological Society of his college wherein he declared that practical religion could be treated as an exact science. His book based on the same premise, *Natural Law in the Spiritual World*, was published in 1883. He deeply believed that science and religion complement each other and that both reveal God to man. "Science has to deal with facts and with all the facts, and the facts and processes which have received the name of Christian are the continuations of the scientific order as the facts and processes of biology are the continuation of the mineral world."

He wrote several other religious books and booklets that encourage humanity to focus on the good in life rather than the bad, to "seek out all those perfections through which we can make good our claims to a likeness to God" (Nicoll). He also emphasized the absolute capacity of Jesus Christ to meet all the needs of the soul. Drummond unquestioningly believed that we can change our lives by relying on Christ.

His most well-read booklet is *The Greatest Thing in the World* written in 1874 and is a meditation concerning the two great commandments of God—to love God and to love each other. This booklet has sold more than 12 million copies and is still read today.

Drummond wrote *Natural Law in the Spiritual World*, from which the following summation is derived, in the second decade after the evolutionary theories of Spencer and Darwin had burst upon the scene and when positivism had become the scientific method of choice. As discussed in chapter two, positivism is the theory that only observable phenomena and the laws which explain them can be known. In the years prior to the publication of Drummond's book the positivistic scientific method had been extended to sociology and politics, but religion and metaphysics still were considered well outside the scope of science. Drummond's thesis, therefore, was revolutionary.

Being a minister as well as a scientist, Drummond agreed with Francis Bacon, the first of the great British empiricist philosophers, who in the early seventeenth century wrote, "This I dare affirm in knowledge of Nature, that a little natural philosophy, and the first entrance into it, doth dispose the opinion to atheism; but, on the other side, much natural philosophy, and wading deep into it, will bring about men's minds to religion."

What is necessary, then, is a deep foray into natural philosophy wherein will be found natural theology. Drummond believed that such a study would disclose the naturalness of the supernatural. "Thus, as the Supernatural becomes slowly Natural, will also the Natural becomes slowly Supernatural, until in the impersonal authority of Law men everywhere recognize the Authority of God." Note the phrase "the impersonal authority of Law." This is the New Thought concept of an impartial, impersonal God. In support of this concept, Drummond quotes the poet Robert Browning, as does Holmes much later: "I spoke as I saw. I report, as a man may of God's work—*all's Love, yet all's Law.*"

As further support of his basic thesis that theology rests on nature rather than solely on authority, he points out that the laws of nature are nothing more than statements of the constant order observed in nature. These laws say nothing of the causes of observed phenomena, they "originate nothing, sustain nothing; they are merely responsible for uniformity in sustaining what has been originated and what is being sustained. They are modes of operation, therefore, not operators; processes, not powers." For instance, the Law of Gravity says nothing of the origin of gravity or how it works. It simply states that a gravitational force has been observed.

As far as scientists have been able to ascertain, these laws extend throughout the entire universe. Drummond feels this uniformity we observe in the laws of nature is intentional, so that we may understand the whole by observation of the part. He also feels that the invisible creations of God can be understood in the visible realm and cites Plato, Jesus, Plotinus, Swedenborg, Bacon, Pascal, and Carlyle in support, names we have run across before in our journey.

After showing that the spiritual laws are analogous to the natural laws, he makes the further claim that they are not just analogous but that they are the same exact laws. The natural laws do not leave off with the visible and another set of laws take over in the invisible realm. The same laws cover the entire spectrum of reality, from matter at one end to spirit at the other. "Law in the visible is the Invisible in the visible. And to speak of Laws as Natural is to define them in their application to a part of the universe, the sense-part, whereas a wider survey would lead us to regard all Law as essentially Spiritual."

He feels the continuity of nature proves this, as does the work of John Herschel and James Clerk-Maxwell, pioneers in the fields of astronomy and electromagnetism during the mid-eighteenth century. According to their theories, the unseen exist prior to the seen.

> [T]the atoms of which the visible universe is built up bear dis-
> tinct marks of being manufactured articles; and, secondly, the
> origin in time of the visible universe is implied from known facts
> with regard to the dissipation of energy. With the gradual
> aggregation of mass the energy of the universe has been slowly
> disappearing, and this loss of energy must go on until none re-
> mains. There is, therefore, a point in time when the energy of the
> universe must come to an end; and that which has its end in time
> cannot be infinite, it must also have had a beginning in time.
> Hence the unseen existed before the seen.

He describes how science has progressed over time, adding more branches as each new field is discovered. He feels this follows an evolutionary pattern, and since theology is the highest of the sciences, it will be the last to become known. "Science will be complete when all known phenomena can be arranged in one vast circle in which a few well known Laws shall form the radii—these radii at once separating and uniting, separating into particular groups, yet uniting all to a common centre."

Herbert Spencer set forth a theory of evolution a decade before Charles Darwin, neither of whom had religion in mind when developing their theories. However, Drummond sees in Spencer's definition of evolution a place for religion. In analyzing the various relations between the environment and what is called life, Spencer determines there are gradations or degrees of life. He shows why organisms live and die and sets forth the conditions in which an organism might never die but would "enjoy a perpetual and perfect Life," what Drummond terms "Eternal Life."

Drummond explains what Spencer means by the various degrees of life in terms of correspondences. An organism corresponds to its environment according to the level of complexity of the organism. Thus, an amoeba, being a "mere sac of transparent structureless jelly" relates to its environment in very few ways, while an insect, having the capability of the senses of sight, hearing and touch, relates in added ways, and a human, having the most complex structure of all, relates or corresponds, in numerous ways. Because the insect corresponds to its environment in more ways than does the amoeba, it has more life. Similarly, humans have the most life because they have the most correspondences. "[T]his law, that the degree of Life varies with the degree of correspondence, holds to the minutest detail throughout the entire range of living things. Life becomes fuller and fuller, richer and richer, more and more sensitive and responsive to an ever-widening Environment as we rise in the chain of being."

In order to reach Eternal Life an organism must be so complex that its correspondences pass beyond the finite realm of matter to that of spirit, or the eternal, where the environment is perfect. According to Spencer's definition, Drummond says, "Perfect correspondence would be perfect life. Were there no changes in the environment but such as the organism had adapted changes to meet, and were it never to fail in the efficiency with which it met them, there would be eternal existence and eternal knowledge." He then compares that definition of eternal life to the one laid out by Jesus: "This is Life Eternal that they may know Thee, the only true God, and Jesus Christ whom Thou hast sent" (John 17:3). In this statement, Eternal Life does not mean "to live forever" as is commonly thought, but it is "to know God." According to Spencer's definition, knowing God is the same thing as corresponding with God, and a correspondence with God is a correspondence with a perfect environment. Drummond ties knowing

God to evolution and states that evolution culminates in knowledge. He feels he has thus proved eternal life.

Next he sets out to prove the spiritual world. He says there must be something back of the correspondences of the spiritual organism just as there is something back of natural correspondences. An organism exhibits a variety of correspondences. But what, he asks, determines them and organizes them? It is a Principle of Life. In the biological world it is a biological or organic principle, and in the spiritual world it is a spiritual principle. Because of spiritual correspondences, humans can know God. And since it takes an entity of equal or greater affinity to know another entity, it takes the Divine to know the Divine. Therefore, there must be an element of divinity in humanity. He says this analogy is no different from saying that on the scale of life we must be at the level of human or higher in order to understand humanity.

He feels he has found a correspondence that bridges the grave and satisfies the demands of both science and religion:

> In mere quantity it is different from every other correspondence known. Setting aside everything else in Religion, everything adventitious, local, and provisional; dissecting in to the bone and marrow we find this—a correspondence which can never break with an Environment which can never change.

It satisfies science because science, specifically the theory of evolution, states that the environment has the power to form or transform organisms, to develop or suppress their function, and to determine their growth. The influence of the environment increases as the complexity of organisms increases. And with the most complex organisms, environment is able to influence not only the body but the mind and the soul. He reasons that just as evolution moved from the aquatic to the terrestrial, it also moves from the organic to the spiritual. Spiritual man is but the continuation of evolution.

Drummond's influence on Holmes can be seen in Holmes's concepts of God as Law and Principle, as the visible being formed from the invisible, as the invisible being prior to the visible, as the spiritual part of man being divine and eternal, and as to the relationships between the various forms of nature being one of correspondences.

Christian D. Larson

As mentioned in chapter three, Holmes participated in Eddy's Christian Science classes and studied the works of his contemporary, Christian D. Larson, noting similarities between these two systems of thought. Though Eddy's contributions belong to the Road to Well-Being, Larson's, because they are unique to Holmes, pertain to the Intellectual Road.

Larson was an influential New Thought teacher and author of New Thought books. He believed that we all have latent powers that coupled with a positive attitude can be used to achieve success in all areas of life. He organized the New Thought Temple in Cincinnati, Ohio in January 1901 and later that year began publishing *Eternal Progress*, a well known New Thought periodical. In 1929, Larson became associate editor of Holmes's magazine *Science of Mind* and also a frequent contributor.

He is known to this day for his Optimist's Creed, which originally appeared in his book *Your Forces and How to Use Them* published in 1912. Optimist International adopted it for its creed in 1922.

Promise yourself . . .

To be so strong that nothing can disturb your peace of mind.
To talk health, happiness, and prosperity to every person you meet.
To make all your friends feel that there is something in them.
To look at the sunny side of everything
and make your optimism come true.
To think only of the best, and expect only the best.
To be just as enthusiastic about the success of others
as you are about your own.
To forget the mistakes of the past
and press on to the greater achievements of the future.
To wear a cheerful countenance at all times
and give every living creature you meet a smile.
To give so much time to the improvement of yourself
that you have no time to criticize others.
To be too large for worry, too noble for anger, too strong for fear,
and too happy to permit the presence of trouble.
To think well of yourself and to proclaim this fact to the world,
not in loud words but in great deeds.

To live in the faith that the whole world is on your side
so long as you are true to the best that is in you.

Without delving into any of his other writings, we can see
Larson's deep belief in the power of right thinking. This under-
standing of the power of the mind is Larson's main contribution to
Holmes's Science of Mind.

In *Your Forces and How to Use Them* Larson speaks of the ego
but gives it a definition different from that of modern psychology. For
Larson, and Holmes, too, the ego is the I AM of the Bible, the perfect
idea of God. It is "the ruling principle in man, the center and source
of an individuality, the originator of everything that takes place in
man, and that primary something to which all other things in human
nature are secondary."

It is a human tendency to think of the body when we hear the
terms *me* or *myself*. This erroneous perception places the body equal
to our thoughts or physical states. In order to have any control in our
life, we must be above it. Therefore, the *I* or *me* cannot consist of our
physical states. The real *I* or *me* is the I AM, the center of action
which resides in our consciousness. The I AM directs the mind, and
the mind directs everything else.

The mind has tremendous power—the power of the will, of
desire, of feeling and of thought, in fact, of *all* conscious and subconscious action. In properly using the mind, we direct all this power
toward whatever goal we desire. This is not an occasional activity, but
a constant and clear focus so that our desire can be seen by the mind's
eye. This kind of focus allows us to control our life affairs rather than
letting them control us, and is the type of thinking that is used in New
Thought for healing, creating abundance and joyful living.

Ralph Waldo Trine

Ralph Waldo Trine, another major influence on Holmes's philosophy, was born in 1866. Trine studied history and political science
in college, specifically emphasizing social and economic problems. He
worked as a newspaper correspondent while, reminiscent of Thoreau,
he built a cabin alongside a forest in which to live the simple life.

A contemporary of Holmes, he began writing near the end of the nineteenth century. As with the others on this road, he was influenced by Emerson and Drummond, as well as the German philosopher Fichte. In turn, he influenced millions. His writings were accepted by those in New Thought as well as the general public, who had no idea they were New Thought. Henry Ford credits his success in the automobile manufacturing business to Trine's book *In Tune with the Infinite*. Of all Trine's works, this, too, is the book that most influenced Holmes. Trine died peacefully at the age of 91, a well-loved philosopher, mystic, teacher, and author.

Trine's influential message is that within each person resides the power that determines the course of his or her life. The world we experience is the world we have created. Our exterior life is formed by our interior thoughts and beliefs. He sees the exterior as material and the interior as spiritual. Thus, he accepts the Hermetic teaching of "As above, so below" or "As within, so without."

There are laws that govern our interior or spiritual thought forces, and we can make use of them. There is also a divine will at work within and above the human will. To live in harmony with this will and all the higher laws and forces so that they all work cooperatively is the secret of all success. We attract all the goodness life has to offer when our thoughts harmonize with the Divine will, for it is the will of the Divine that we experience the good. When we realize that we contain a power that can make of our lives whatever we wish, we can begin to attract only those things that we truly desire. Says Trine, "it is a changeless law, from which no soul can sway or swerve, we have that in us which will draw whate'er we need or most deserve."

We work out everything in the invisible spiritual realm before we manifest it in material form, "for the effective causes are in the realm of the unseen, the effects in the realm of the seen."

All truth exists in the present and waits for us to recognize this fact. Everything we need is available for the asking or the accepting. Nothing is forced on us, but will be given upon our acceptance. In *What All the World's A-Seeking,* Trine writes:

> Each individual life is a part of, and hence is one with, the Infinite Life; and the highest intelligence and power belongs to each

in just the degree that he recognizes his oneness and lays claim to and uses it. The power of the word is not merely an idle phrase or form of expression. It is a real mental, spiritual, scientific fact, and can become vital and powerful in your hands and in mine in just the degree that we understand the omnipotence of the thought forces and raise all to the higher planes.

The blind, the lame, the diseased, stood before Christ, who said, "receive thy sight, rise up and walk, or, be thou healed"; and lo! it *was so*. The spoken word, however, was but the outward expression and manifestation of His interior thought forces, the power and potency of which He so thoroughly knew. But the laws governing them are the same today as they were then, and it lies in our power to use them the same as it lay in His (emphasis in original).

Trine's influence on Holmes can be seen in his emphasis on law; his assertion of a power that lies within each of us, just as it existed in Jesus; to create whatever we focus our minds on; and the concept that all good is waiting for us to enjoy, but first we must ask for it and then accept it.

William Walker Atkinson

A contemporary of Holmes, William Walker Atkinson, who wrote under the name Yogi Ramacharaka, took much of his thought from the yogic traditions.

Not much is known of Atkinson prior to his involvement with the New Thought Movement. Born in Baltimore, Maryland in 1862, he began a law career in 1884. The stress of his profession induced a complete physical and mental breakdown, resulting in financial ruin. He began searching for healing, which he found in the late 1880s. Using the principles of New Thought, he rebuilt his health and his finances. His articles about the truths of Mental Science were published in several New Thought periodicals, including the Fillmores's *Modern Thought* magazine.

He moved with his wife and children to Chicago in the early 1890s where he worked as an associate editor of a New Thought journal while writing his first book, *Thought-Force in Business and Everyday Life*. In 1901 he became the editor of the well known *New Thought* magazine, and wrote numerous well-received articles concerning New Thought. He also founded the Psychic Club and the Atkinson School of Mental Science.

During the early 1900s, Atkinson began reading works of Hindu thought, and met and collaborated with Baba Bharata, a pupil of the late Yogi Ramacharaka. Together they wrote several books that they attributed to Ramacharaka before Atkinson took the name as a pseudonym. As Ramacharaka, Atkinson wrote numerous books on the subject of yoga that are still in print today.

He also wrote numerous well-received books on New Thought. During the period 1916-1919 he was editor of the journal *Advanced Thought*, and before passing in 1932, he served as honorary president of the International New Thought Alliance.

Atkinson's influence is addressed further in chapter thirteen.

Thomas Troward

Noticing the similarities between Eddy, Larson and Trine's ideas concerning the mind, Holmes delved deeper into the study of the powers of the mind and came upon the writings of Thomas Troward.

Troward was born in India in 1847 while his father, a colonel in the Indian Army, was stationed in the Punjab. Troward received his schooling in England and after graduating from college with honors in literature, he studied law before returning to India at age 22 to take the Indian Civil Service Examination. He passed the test and moved quickly through the ranks to become Divisional Judge in the Punjab, a post he served for 25 years. After his retirement from the Bengal Civil Service in 1896, he returned to England and began a serious study of the Bible and a second career writing and lecturing.

While in India he learned the language and studied all of the sacred books of India's religions—Hinduism, Buddhism and Taoism —as well as the scriptures of all the major world religions. It is likely that this is also where he became familiar with the concepts of Theosophy, for Blavatsky and Olcott taught throughout India during Troward's tenure there. It has been written that he received a vision during this time concerning the development of a system of philosophy that provided to each person peace of mind, physical health and happiness.

Upon his return to England, Troward began writing for the New Thought publication *Expressions* and presented a series of lectures at Queens Gate in Edinburgh, Scotland. He compiled these lectures into the book *The Edinburgh Lectures on Mental Science*, in which he spells out his philosophy. He died on May 16, 1916 at the age of 69.

Troward based his theories on his readings and his own intuition, intellectual processes and deductive reasoning. By the time he began writing, the term *mental science* had been in use for more than thirty years. However, his Mental Science, like Quimby's, does not rest on religious doctrine. He considers it purely scientific.

As with Drummond, the influence of Troward's work on Holmes is substantial and so an explanation of his theories is by necessity quite detailed. The following synopsis is culled from his Edinburgh lectures. Missing are Troward's many lengthy arguments and examples. Therefore, I highly recommend that the serious student of New Thought read the entire book, which can accessed on the Internet.

Troward writes that the purpose of Mental Science is to discover the relationship between the individual power of volition and the cosmic law that maintains and advances humanity. He believes that Mental Science provides a sensible basis for believing that we each have power over our life.

He first sets out the conception of a primary substance underlying all things. This primary substance is inherent intelligence or spirit, self-forming, and lies under and gives rise to all manifestation. In other words, Spirit (the unseen) differentiates into individual forms (the seen). Universal spirit and individualized form are totally opposite in nature yet are not opposed to each other, as each is the complement of the other. Both are necessary, and together they constitute reality. Troward feels the idealists err "in trying to realize an inside without an outside"; that is, all spirit and no matter. And the materialists err "in trying to realize an outside without an inside"; that is, all matter and no spirit.

The chart on the following page compares the qualities of universal substance (spirit) with its individualized forms (matter). From this chart we see that life consists entirely of spirit or thought. It is infinite and eternal, and there is only one of it—it is unity.

SPIRIT	MATTER
Distinctive quality is thought - Living - Control of motion - Invisible (but its effects are visible) - Omnipresent (independent of time and space) - Abstract - Unconditioned (it controls conditions) - Absolute - Cause - Contains the primary life substance in itself - Infinite - a Unity	Distinctive quality is form - Dead - Inner motion (atoms) - Visible - Extension in space - Limited by boundaries - Bulk, distance, direction - Concrete - Conditioned - Relative - Effect - Made from the primary life substance - Finite - Multiplicity

Within the category of life we find what Troward calls the *livingness* of life, which he measures by the degree of intelligence possessed by any individual life form. The greater the intelligence of an organism, the higher up on the scale of livingness it is placed. Thus, animals are higher than plants, with humans being the highest of the animals. This concept is similar to Drummond's correspondences and his various levels of life, though Troward's level of livingness is determined by the level of intelligence it contains. For Troward, then, life is intelligent. As seen in the previous chart, life is also spirit and thought.

Troward next turns to the concept of primary substance as Universal Mind. Just as the intelligence within humans is universal in nature, the human mind is also universal. Universal Mind, being spirit, is subjective in nature, which means it is creative and suggestible. Subjective Mind "is amenable to any suggestion, and will carry out any suggestion that is impressed upon it to its most rigorously logical consequences." The law of subjective mind is that "as a man thinketh in his heart so is he" (Prov. 23:7).

There is only one mind, but within humans it functions in a dual manner. These two functions Troward refers to as the subjective mind and the objective mind, and for ease of description he treats them as two minds. The chart on the following page sets out the characteristics of these two minds.

SUBJECTIVE MIND	OBJECTIVE MIND
The inner mind (the subconscious) - reasons deductively (from general to particular) - the builder of the body (the creative power) - impersonal - suggestible	The outer mind (the conscious) - reasons deductively (from general to particular) and inductively (from particular to general) - controls the subjective mind

Our subjective mind is our own innermost self and is *the same* subjective mind that produces the myriad natural forms in the universe. Each individual subjective mind is a personal portion of the universal mind and is connected to both the universal subjective mind and the individual objective mind. It is the bridge that connects the internal with the external, the absolute with the relative.

The subjective mind, being suggestible, builds our body in response to the ideas we place into it. Thus, our body represents our beliefs. If we believe that the body can be influenced by external forces outside our control, then subjective mind will produce bodily effects that correspond to that belief.

The importance our thoughts play in this scenario is obvious. The kind of health we enjoy, in fact the kind of *life* we enjoy, is strictly based upon the thoughts we place into subjective mind. Thus, the quality of our life is completely within our control.

Troward speaks of creating a spiritual prototype, which is the same concept as Holmes's mental equivalent. Whatever experience we desire in the material or external plane must first be conceived in the spiritual or internal plane. He cites Plato, Swedenborg and Jesus as having taught this same concept. Mark 11:24 records Jesus as saying, "All things whatsoever ye pray and ask for, believe that ye *have* received them, and ye *shall* receive them" (emphasis added). We don't just ask, but we believe that it *already has been accomplished.* In seeing in our mind's eye that what we desire already exists, we "magnetize our minds to attract into manifestation" the experiences we desire. Using all of our senses—seeing, hearing, tasting, feeling, and smelling—increases the effectiveness of our thoughts.

Subjective Mind works by means of law and is universal in scope. Universal Law is impersonal; that is, it relates the same way to all people. No one is judged as more deserving than anyone else. But while it is impersonal it also contains an element of personalness. By this Troward means that we each personalize or individualize the Law in the various ways we make use of it. It is our personal beliefs to which Law responds and acts. We need not concern ourselves with how our desires will be manifested; that is Law's job. Our only concern, as Jesus said, is the asking and the believing.

Troward holds the same concept of natural law as does Drummond. The law does not change but works always the same everywhere. This means that there is no difference between natural law and spiritual law.

Troward calls the action of Subjective Mind in the individual mind *relative first cause*. Subjective Mind in the Universal Mind is *Universal First Cause*. *Secondary causes* result from the information received by our outward senses. These secondary causes produce further conditions, and those conditions produce even more conditions, and so on, creating a series of secondary causes. By making our decisions from the plane of secondary causation we set up for ourselves "an endless train of antecedent conditions coming out of the past and stretching away into the future." This is due to the fact that the outward senses deal only with the limited, the relative and the conditioned. However, by using our internal power rather than our external senses we can work from first cause and create the exact experience we desire.

Working from first cause is a *conscious* practice in that we make *conscious* use of the law. Remember, law is always working. By becoming conscious of the law we can direct it to create a certain desired effect. Our lives then become one of cause rather than of effect, mastery rather than servitude, freedom rather than enslavement.

The concepts of first and secondary causes are extremely important for mental healing. In order to experience health we must remember that the ideal is what is real, not what is outwardly manifested. We work with the real when we work from first cause. Allowing circumstances to dictate effect is not working from first cause. In viewing circumstances as causal, we are working from the level of secondary causation, which is the region of doubts, fears and limitations. If our focus is at this level, so will be our effects. In recognizing this we can place our focus in the realm of first cause and allow law to create conditions of health. These words of Troward sum up this process:

In actual practice we must first form the ideal conception of our object with the definite intention of impressing it upon the universal mind . . . and then affirm that our knowledge of the Law is sufficient reason for a calm expectation of a corresponding result . . . . The intelligence [of universal mind] not only enables it to receive the impress of our thought, but also causes it to devise exactly the right *means* for bringing it into accomplishment. This is only the logical result of the hypothesis that we are dealing with infinite Intelligence which is also infinite Life. Life means Power, and limitless power moved by limitless intelligence cannot be conceived of as ever stopping short of the accomplishment of its object; therefore, given the *intention* on the part of the Universal Mind, there can be no doubt as to its ultimate accomplishment (emphasis in original).

According to Alan Anderson, a modern-day philosopher who has written extensively about New Thought, Troward's concepts of objective and subjective mind are the same as Thomson Jay Hudson's. Anderson believes that Hudson's *The Law of Psychic Phenomena* influenced Troward's concept of the "impersonal, deductive, mechanical, automatic 'Law' side of God."

Other than Troward's few references to the words of Jesus, and his one reference to the Great Pyramid, the Pack of Cards, and the Rosicrucians, Troward does not refer to any particular doctrine in support of his theories. Even so, we can see clear evidence of his familiarity with ancient Greek and Eastern philosophies.

Intellectual Influences

Holmes quotes a number of minds in support of the concept that thoughts are things. The Bible says, "As a man thinketh in his heart, so is he," and William Shakespeare writes, "There is nothing either good or bad but thinking makes it so." According to Aristotle and Demosthenes, 'What we expect, that we find," and, "What we wish, that we believe" (*Science of Mind*).

Holmes gained many of his ideas from the idealists. In "A Treatise Concerning the Principles of Human Knowledge" Berkeley says that the soul is always thinking. Hegel's God is Absolute Idea—

thought thinking about itself. In *The History of Philosophy* he writes that God is Reason and Reason is Substance and Infinite Power. Reason is the substance of the universe from which all natural and spiritual life originates. Idea or Reason is the True and the Eternal.

Frances Herbert Bradley, the most influential British Absolute Idealist of the nineteenth century, defines reality as the Absolute. It is unity or wholeness. There is a difference between reality and appearance. Appearance is fragmentary, relational and ever-changing. Error, evil and sin exist in appearance, not in reality. The goal of life is fulfillment of the self—realizing that the self is part of an infinite whole, and the whole is in the self. A contemporary of Bradley's, Josiah Royce, views God as perfect universal thought or Absolute Mind. The universe is intelligent, rational and orderly. Error or sin is simply an incomplete thought. There is only Absolute Mind; therefore, all the minds in the universe are essentially the same mind and so is the world of one self. Thus, That art Thou. This concept of "That art Thou" comes from Hinduism and is discussed in chapter ten.

Aristotle, a student of Plato and tutor to the young Alexander the Great, was and still is the most influential philosopher of Western thought. Aristotle taught that God is pure thought and absolute spirit and consists of nothing but itself. It is perfect and wants for nothing. God acts by self-contemplation; that is, God acts by thinking. Aristotle set forth the first teleological argument for the existence of God in positing an unmoved mover that is both first and final cause and that gives the universe its design and purpose. God's existence is one of complete eternal bliss, and it is the purpose of humanity, through use of the mind, to attain this same state. Aristotle's God is not a personal God but is simply Thought thinking about Itself. Interestingly, these teachings of Aristotle condemned during the Dark Ages by the powerful Catholic church were later declared by this same church to contain the true doctrine.

Isaac Newton refers to God as Universal Law, Principle and Divine Mind. He says there is a spiritual world corresponding to the natural world as cause and effect. This spiritual world produces and sustains the natural world.

According to the great American philosopher and psychologist William James, who wrote and lectured during the formative years of New Thought, "no mental modification ever occurs which is not accompanied or followed by a bodily change" (qtd. in Leahey). He feels that the greatest discovery of his time was that we can alter our lives by altering our attitudes and our mind. He devotes an entire chapter in *The Varieties of Religious Experience* to New Thought and, in his view, the badly-needed optimism and hope it brought to the "harshness and irrationality" of orthodox Christianity. He calls the new "mind-cure movement" the religion of the healthy-minded.

Being a pragmatist and always looking for the practical application of psychological and philosophical ideas, James admired the practical aspects of New Thought. He also greatly respected the writings of Horatio Dresser and Henry Wood, two of the earliest New Thought writers.

James regards Troward's writings "uncommonly clear" and a "classic statement" of his philosophy. A concept of Troward and Holmes's parallels one of James's. James writes that one of the laws of psychology states that by holding in mind a picture of what you desire to have or be, and keeping that picture in constant awareness, the picture will become reality. This is Troward's spiritual prototype and Holmes's mental equivalent. James's admiration of the new movement is not surprising for he was raised with Swedenborg's philosophy. His father, Henry James, Sr., a respected philosophical theologian, based his own philosophy on the teachings of Swedenborg, and James's pragmatist mentor, Charles Sanders Peirce, also was a Swedenborgian.

Sigmund Freud's pioneering work with the unconscious came too late to have impacted the founders of Divine Science and Unity, but his work greatly affected Holmes. While the idea of an unconscious was not a new one, the concept of repression—ideas and memories that are purposely unknown to us—and that these repressed ideas and memories affect our health and our behavior was new, at least to the field of psychology. The concept of repressed ideas existing in an unconscious state had been posited in the philosophies of Arthur Schopenhauer (1788-1860) and Friedrich Nietzsche (1844-1900). During the time these philosophers wrote, what constituted the unconscious was open for debate. Some, including Freud (1856-1939), saw it as an actual place. Others saw it as a state of mind.

Freud's main goal was attaining the knowledge of reality. Such knowledge is gained when the forces that lie in the unconscious have been dominated and controlled. Since reality is only found in the unconscious, in that which is repressed, and since most people deal almost exclusively with the fictional and delusional conscious, what most people consider "reality" is actually a distortion of the real.

This goal of becoming conscious of what is unconscious, then, is an expansion of the consciousness. It is an understanding of truth, both intellectual and affective, and an awareness of what is real. As the post-Freudian psychoanalyst Eric Fromm noted, this expanding or "raising" of consciousness is synonymous with awakening or becoming enlightened (as used in the East), leaving the cave (as in Plato's allegory), and bringing light into the darkness (as often used in a religious sense).

Psychoanalysts after Freud differed in their views of the unconscious and the conscious. Freud viewed the unconscious as the "seat of irrationality" while his student Carl Jung considered it as the "seat of the deepest sources of wisdom." Eric Fromm, on the other hand, speaks of the conscious and unconscious as states of "consciousness-awareness and unconsciousness-unawareness" (Suzuki, et al.).

Though Freud's concept of the unconscious is different from that of Holmes's, his theory that all human behavior is determined by forces within, forces that often are unknown or unacknowledged, and therefore that no behavior is purely accidental, helped Holmes to formulate his own concept of the unconscious, which he calls the subconscious. Holmes's subconscious is not a place but a state of mind. Interestingly, Jung and Fromm, writing during the same time period as Holmes, were influenced in their psychologies by some of the same philosophies which influenced Holmes—Taoism and Buddhism. Jung, Fromm and Holmes took Freud's basic ideas and using differing terminology developed them into similar psychologies of the mind.

As can be seen, this road unique to Holmes focuses on the intellectual and psychological aspects of spirit and is why Religious Science is considered by many as more cerebral and less emotional, and as placing less focus on the role of Jesus (and therefore as less Christian) than the other New Thought churches. I believe, however, that the following chapter will show that even though Religious Science addresses left-brained aspects of mind more than right-brained ones, it does rely heavily on the enormously important teachings of Jesus. In effect we could say that all roads lead to Jesus.

IX.

ALL ROADS LEAD TO JESUS

JESUS, there is no dearer name than thine
Which Time has blazoned on his mighty scroll;
No wreaths nor garlands ever did entwine
So fair a temple of so vast a soul.
There every virtue set his triumph-seal;
Wisdom, conjoined with strength and radiant grace,
In a sweet copy Heaven to reveal,
And stamp perfection on a mortal face.
Once on the earth wert thou, before men's eyes,
That did not half thy beauteous brightness see;
E'en as the emmet does not read the skies,
Nor our weak orbs look through immensity.
Theodore Parker (1810–1860)
An American Anthology, 1787–1900

As we have seen, Jesus's effect on New Thought is immense. The founders of the New Thought groups spoke very specifically about Jesus and his teachings, as did other early New Thought writers and many other influential minds.

We first encountered Jesus in chapter three in enumerating the core beliefs of the three major New Thought groups. From that discussion we can extract sixteen common concepts held among these groups. These are:

- God is Spirit, Mind or Intelligence
- God is Good, Wise, Loving, etc.
- There is only God, and God is always present

- God is the Creator of all that exists and creates from within Itself
- God is a Triune Being
- God is impersonal or impartial
- There are spiritual or divine laws by which God works
- Jesus embodied the Christ consciousness, which consciousness is available to all humanity
- Jesus taught mental healing
- We are created in God's image and likeness; as such, our nature is good, and we are divine
- It is our birthright to partake of God's goodness
- We are given free agency or free will; thus, we are always at choice
- We are the means by which God expresses into the material world
- Our thoughts, attitudes and beliefs produce our experience
- Heaven and hell are states of mind or consciousness
- Evil and sin are simply mistakes resulting from ignorance and wrong thinking

The first six concepts are related. Since there is only God, and God is infinite and eternal, then everything that exists is God or made of God, and God is everywhere always. Also, since there is only God, in order for God to create, it must be self-aware and must create from within. God works by Divine Law, and because Law is constant and unchanging, God is impartial or neutral in the way It works.

Let's briefly recap these concepts about God, and then we will see what Jesus had to say.

God is Spirit, Mind or Intelligence

In *The Science of Mind* Holmes defines each of these three synonyms for God. *Spirit* is the Self-Knowing One, the Conscious Universe, or the Absolute. The *One Mind* is all of Truth. There is only Mind, and it is both conscious and subconscious. *Intelligence* is the same as Mind, God-Mind or Universal Mind. Holmes and Fillmore also refer to God as *Father-Mother God*—the Universal Parent Mind. All of these terms are interchangeable.

Holmes refers to a Feminine Principle, which is the Universal Soul. "It gives birth to the Ideas of the Spirit, and is therefore the Feminine Principle of Nature." The Masculine Principle is the Assertive Principle of Being, the "Projective Principle of Life, impregnating the Universal Soul with Its ideas and concepts."

Fannie James writes that God is Love, Life, Spirit, and Intelligence. Spirit is everywhere, filling everything with knowledge. Therefore, the "one Spirit is all and its intelligence is everywhere."

God is Good, Wise, Loving, . . .

The one idea about God that all theistic religions agree upon is that God is good. The many other synonyms for God—Love, Wisdom, Benevolent, Grace, Peace, Joy—are merely derivatives of *Good*.

Hopkins, who we encountered along the Road to Well-Being, equates God with Good in saying "My good is my God." All of the founders of New Thought accept this concept.

There is only God and God is always present; God is the Creator of all that exists and creates from within Itself

There is only God. God is everywhere, always present, and because God creates from within, we are a part of It. God is everywhere and everywhen. "God is All and in All." This idea of God was called Christian Pantheism by Evans, the early New Thought writer we discussed in chapter five, even though the Christian churches considered pantheism a heresy. As we discussed in chapter six, pantheism is the idealistic concept that God is all-inclusive; that is, all of God's creations, including all of nature and its underlying laws and forces, are a part of God and are elements of its Being.

There are numerous examples of these concepts in the writings of the founding New Thought philosophers. I include here but a sampling.

Fillmore writes that God cannot be located in geographical space, for Mind is everywhere and everywhere-present (*Christian*

Healing) and "creates and moves creation through the power of mind" (*Teach Us to Pray*).

James writes that God is said to be Omnipresent. Therefore, God is everywhere, always present, for that is what *omnipresent* means. Divine Science cofounder Brooks continues along these same lines in writing that even though we often are unaware, we are always in the presence of God, for God fills "heaven and earth with His presence, His life, and His abundance."

Holmes says that we live in a spiritual Universe that is "pure Intelligence and perfect Life, dominated by Love, by Reason and by the power to create" (*Science of Mind*).

God is a Triune Being

There is only One, but that One has three aspects, which are identified by the founders variously as Mind, Idea and Consciousness; Spirit, Soul and Body; Mind, Idea and Expression; or The Thing Itself, The Way It Works and What It Does. There is but One Mind or Spirit—The Thing Itself. This Mind creates through Thought or Idea by use of Divine Law—The Way It Works, and Its creation is Consciousness or Expression—What It Does.

God is impersonal or impartial

There is a common perception that in saying that God is impersonal, we are saying that God is uncaring. This is not at all what is meant. *Impersonal* has two separate connotations: 1) God is not a person, and 2) God is impartial or neutral. In the first sense, God is an impassive, timeless eternal in which there is neither past nor future. This is the Hellenistic concept of God discussed above. In the second, God is neutral. Its gifts are available equally to everyone. God does not play favorites. It treats everyone the same.

For many, God being neutral does not seem to be a reality. We can point to numerous people and circumstances as proof that everyone is not treated the same, that we aren't given the same blessings or opportunities, and that some prayers are answered and some are not. The response to these statements involves several of New Thought's concepts about God's creations. Therefore, God's impartiality is discussed at a later point in this chapter.

There are spiritual or divine laws by which God works

Because the discussion of this topic is lengthy, it has been given a chapter all its own: chapter thirteen.

Jesus and His Teachings

Before we begin our discussion, it is important to remember that the Bible was written on three levels: historical, moral and spiritual or metaphysical. As we discussed in chapter three, New Thought interprets the Bible's teachings primarily at the spiritual level.

Now let's see what Jesus had to say about these concepts of God*.

Jesus taught that God is Spirit (John 4:24), that there is only One who is good (Matt.19:17), that this One is our Father (Matt. 23:9); that God, the Spirit of truth, and His kingdom are in us and around us (Luke 17:21, John 14:16-17, 23); and that God is impartial—It causes the sun to shine equally on the evil and the good, and sends rain to fall on both the righteous and the unrighteous (Matt. 5:45). In numerous instances Jesus teaches the oneness of all things. He says that if we know him, we know his Father (John 8:19, 14:7); that he and the Father are One (John 10:30); that he is in the Father and the Father is in him (John 10:38, 14:10-11); that whomever sees him also sees the One who sent him (John 12:45, 14:9); and that he is in the Father, we are in him, and he is in us (John 14:20). In all these instances, *One* means a unity or one essence.

Trine explains the importance of Matthew 23:9: "And do not call anyone on earth your father; for One is your Father, He who is in heaven." If God is the Father of everyone, then we are all his children, and together we form the great brotherhood of humanity. This statement implies not only the oneness of all humanity, but also the oneness of humanity and God.

Jesus uses the term *Father* in two senses. First, as the cause of all life, the one source of all things. God is Father of all that exists because It is the cause. The second sense is the awareness of God as

---

* All quotations attributed to Jesus are from the New American Standard or King James versions of the Bible.

a living presence within. It is because Father holds a masculine con-
notation that Jesus uses the pronouns *He*, *Him* and *His* in referring to
the genderless God, as does virtually all religious literature. It is important to remember, however, that God is not a He or a She. God
does contain both masculine and feminine aspects, but It is not male
or female in the sense that humans are one or the other gender. God
transcends such human classifications.

Jesus also teaches of a God who is a loving parent, one who
watches over us, and provides for our needs. In return, all God asks is
that we love—love God, love our neighbors and love ourselves.
Jesus's teachings about God and Its relationship to humanity are
explored further in the next section.

The German philosopher Leibniz summarizes nicely Jesus's
teachings about God:

> Jesus Christ has revealed to men the mystery and the admirable
> laws of the kingdom of heaven, and the greatness of the supreme
> happiness which God has prepared for those who love him. . . .
> He alone has made us see how much God loves us and with what
> care everything that concerns us has been provided for; how God,
> inasmuch as he cares for the sparrows, will not neglect reasoning
> beings, who are infinitely more dear to him; how all the hairs of
> our heads are numbered; how heaven and earth may pass away
> but the word of God and that which belongs to the means of our
> salvation will not pass away; . . . in fact how everything must
> result in the greatest welfare of the good, for then shall the
> righteous become like suns and neither our sense nor our minds
> have ever tasted of anything approaching the joy which God has
> laid up for those that love him.

We turn now to the other nine concepts common to New
Thought—those concerning God's creations—and explore the nature
and role of humanity in the Divine Plan.

The first two concepts deal with Jesus and come directly from
the spiritual level New Testament teachings. Agnes Lawson writes:

> Someone has said that the greatest discovery of the nineteenth
> century was Jesus Christ. He was rediscovered and rescued from
> the superstitious misconceptions regarding him, in which he was

thought of as a superman of extraordinary powers which were, and ever would be, beyond the rank and file of the race. A new interest was given Christianity with the rescue of the thought of its founder from a supernatural being to that of a man who was but a member of the human family with powers not extraordinary, but the ordinary powers all men possess will they but believe in them and use them.

Jesus embodied the Christ consciousness, which consciousness is available to all humanity

Jesus is the name of a person, the child born of Mary in Bethlehem. *Christ* is a title, or more accurately a perfect idea of Mind. In Greek, *Christ* means "anointed, the anointed, or the Messiah." It is true there is only one Christ, but that does not mean there is only one person who can embody the Christ. The Christ is available to all.

In his *Metaphysical Bible Dictionary*, Fillmore writes:

> Jesus is the name that represents an individual expression of the Christ idea. . . . Christ is the only begotten Son of God, or the one complete idea of perfect man in Divine Mind. This Christ, or perfect-man idea existing eternally in Divine Mind, is the true, spiritual, higher self of every individual. Each of us has within him the Christ, just as Jesus had, and we must look within to recognize and realize our sonship, our divine origin and birth, even as He did.

The Christ of the New Testament is the I AM of the Old Testament. The I AM and the Christ are interchangeable names for the same concept. The I AM and the Christ are also called the Son of God, which is another term for the essential spirit, that part of all humanity which was made in the image of God. The I AM, Christ or Son of God lies within each of us, but for most it lies beyond awareness. Those who do become aware of this divine self, this image of God, are said to embody the Christ consciousness.

As discussed in chapter four, Jehovah, literally JHVH in Hebrew, is the name given for God in the Old Testament. Fillmore tells us that JHVH, as translated by students of Hebrew, is "the ever living male-and-female principle." Thus, Jehovah, Christ, Son of God, and

I AM all relate to the portion of the Absolute that resides within each of us.

Jesus also refers to this indwelling spirit as Father. He recognized that he embodied this divine self and called upon it in doing his work. Numerous scriptures tell of his magnificent works, and always he credits the Father within him or the faith carried within the other for accomplishing the deed. Of himself he takes no credit. That is because Jesus the man did nothing. It was the Christ or the I AM within doing the works.

Jesus says in John 14:6, "I am the way, the truth, and the life. No man comes to the Father except through me." This has been incorrectly interpreted to mean that the gospel based on Jesus's words is the only way to salvation. According to the book *The Mystic Christ*, the Greek word for "comes" is *erchetai* and indicates present tense. In the Aramaic language of Jesus, the word for "I" in this scripture is *ena-ena* or I-I. This is the I AM THAT I AM of the Old Testament. Thus, Jesus is saying that he is the representative of the I AM for the people to whom he is speaking. This scripture can be construed to mean either that Jesus is the means of salvation for those he directly spoke to, or that he is the means of salvation for those who read his words. In neither case does this scripture preclude other ways to salvation.

This interpretation seems to be supported by Jesus's statements that we are not to call him good, because no one is good except God, and that of himself Jesus can do nothing. He seems to be saying that the I AM is more than just Jesus the man. The I AM is the saving and healing force behind, above or within the man Jesus; indeed, as it is in all men and women.

In the Gospel of St. James, one of the Gnostic gospels, are recorded these words of Jesus:

> Thus I, the Lord Himself, was a living example for every man, and therefore any human being can now put me on—as I, within a physical body of this earth, put on the Divinity within me—and can independently become completely one with me through love and faith, since as a divine man I am completely one with the Deity in all Its endless fullness (The Holy Order of Mans).

The Gnostic gospels are discussed further in chapter twelve.

Jesus taught mental healing

All the founders of the different groups acknowledge that the method they use in healing is the same method used by Jesus. This method incorporates the next five common concepts about God's creations:

- We are created in God's image and likeness; as such, our nature is good, and we are divine
- It is our birthright to partake of God's goodness
- We are given free agency or free will; thus, we are always at choice
- We are the means by which God expresses into the material world
- Our thoughts, attitudes and beliefs produce our experience

We are created in God's image and likeness; as such, our nature is good and we are divine

This, of course, does not mean that because we have human form, then so does God. This means that we are made in God's likeness, having the same nature, produced from Its imagination. Hence, God *imaged* us. Since God is good, we are good. Since God is divine, we are divine. Our entire selves are not divine, though, for as we discussed in chapter four, matter is not divine. There is within humanity a spark of divinity, a piece of God that partakes of divinity. That part is known by different names—soul, spirit or subconscious. That part of us is the part that remembers our true nature and that chooses to manifest our perfection. It is also the I AM or Christ.

The Book of Genesis tells us that we are created in God's image. That same book also says that when God saw his creations, he pronounced them good. By logical deduction we can see that if God made us in "His" image and "He" is divine and good, then we are divine and good. It also follows that we have these same attributes as God because there is only one substance from which all things are created. Jesus says that we were with him from the beginning (John 15:27), and that we are gods (John 10:34). This seems to confirm our divinity, as well as our immortality.

It is our birthright to partake of God's goodness

God is our Father, and we are the Son of God made in God's likeness. If God is good, then as God's son we have inherited the right to partake of God's goodness. As shown previously, the word *good* incorporates all the universals—love, wisdom, beauty, etc. Therefore, all these, too, are ours.

Jesus tells us that it is God's pleasure to give us his kingdom (Luke 12:32), that all good things will be given to us if we seek the kingdom of God (Luke 12:31) and his righteousness (Matt. 6:33), and that the kingdom of God can be found within (Luke 17:21). He is telling us that all of God's goodness lies within us, and it is up to us to discover it and to partake of it.

While it is our birthright to partake of God's goodness, including an abundance of all things, that is not to be our focus. Jesus plainly tells us that all things will be given us when we seek *God's kingdom and his righteousness.* God's kingdom is the spiritual realm within each of us consisting of God's infinite nature and substance, the abundance of all good. But what does it mean to seek his righteousness? And why will all things be given us if we do so?

Righteousness is defined in New Thought as right thinking; that is, the thinking that leads to truth. Etymologically, the word *right* is formed from the Indo-European base *reg,* "to move in a straight line." From this base come *regulate* and *regent,* words that mean "direct" and "rule," and the English word *rich,* meaning "kingdom" and the Latin word *rex,* meaning "king." *Righteous* is compounded from the Old English *riht,* "right," and *wis,* "way." Thus, *righteous* means "in the right way" (Ayto).

Holmes writes in *Science of Mind* that seeking righteousness is living in peace with spontaneous joy; maintaining a state of thankfulness, for a "thankful heart is in harmony with life"; and embracing "an open and receptive mind" and "a believing heart." Fillmore says righteousness is unselfishness, seeking the good for all not just for the self. Selfishness keeps us in the illusion of separation and away from the truth of the oneness of all. Jesus said that whatever we did to or for another, we did to or for him. Doing an unselfish act for another is being righteous or seeking righteousness. And because we all really are one, what we do for another, we do for ourselves. When our doings are kind (righteous, or in the right way), that same kindness returns to us.

All the abundance of God's kingdom is available equally to everyone because God is impartial, but it must be sought for and then accepted into our experience. Which leads to the next concept.

We are given free agency or free will; thus we are always at choice

We are given free will, which means that God has granted us the right to make decisions for ourselves. God does not force us to do anything nor does It punish us for our choices. By law, each choice carries within it the resulting "reward" or "punishment." Because God does not force, if we wish to participate in our birthright—unlimited blessings of good—*we must choose to do so.*

Jesus said that he came so that we "might have life, and have *it* abundantly" (John 10:10). Notice that he says we *might* have life, not we *will* have life. It is our choice whether or not we have an abundant life. Notice also that *it* is a pronoun referring to the noun *life*. Jesus is saying that *life* and *it* are the same thing. We have seen that both of these words are synonyms for God. Thus, if we have life, we have God. We also have good, love, happiness, joy, and all the other words that mean God or good. Jesus came to bring us this life-changing message. We can have an abundance of all this good if we so choose. How do we choose? Through our thoughts, attitudes and beliefs.

Our thoughts, attitudes and beliefs produce our experience; We are the means by which God expresses into the material world

Everything is available for our use. All the good that exists in the universe is ours. But, as Jesus repeatedly teaches, we must ask for it, *believing that it will be given*, and then accepting it into our experience. (See Matt. 7:7-8, 8:13, 9:22, 9:29, 17:20, 21:22; Mark 5:34-36, 9:23, 10:52, 11:23; Luke 11:9-10, 13:19; and John 11:40, 14:14, 15:7, 15:16, 16:24.) Since God is good, whenever we experience good, we are experiencing God. By allowing good to flow through us we allow God to express into the world. Jesus said he did nothing of himself; all that he accomplished was a result of God working through him (John 14:10). This is one of the reasons for our creation. God wants to experience both through Its act (creation) and through the result of Its act (the acts of Its creations).

We are also told in the Bible that what we are is a result of what we think (Prov. 23:7). Because God works in this world through us, by the use we make of our minds, it follows that our life is the result of the processes of our minds—our thoughts, attitudes and beliefs.

Jesus speaks of the effect our words have on our experience. He says the words that come out of the mouth either corrupt or bless depending on the words, for our words come from our hearts. If the heart is filled with good, then our words illicit that which is good, but if the heart is filled with evil, our words result in sickness and corruption. It is by our words that we are judged, and by them we are either justified or condemned (Matt. 12:33-37, 15:17-20; Mark 7:15; Luke 6:45). At the spiritual level of interpretation this means that our positive words, which are the result of positive thoughts, produce positive results. Likewise, negative thoughts and words produce negative results. By our thoughts and the resulting words we either reap treasure or trash, health or illness, happiness or gloom, joy or anguish.

Jesus tells us not to worry, that we are more precious than the lilies of the field and the birds of the air, and that God will provide everything we need (Matt. 6:25-34; Luke 12:6-7, 27-32). In fact, God knows what we need before we even ask (Matt. 6:8). But we must ask, and we must believe. He also tells us that we will experience more good when we put our focus on spiritual things rather than worrying about material things. In the sixth chapter of Matthew, Jesus says:

> [19]Do not lay up for yourselves treasures upon earth, where moth and rust destroy, and where thieves break in and steal. [20]But lay up for yourselves treasures in heaven, where neither moth nor rust destroys, and where thieves do not break in or steal; [21]for where your treasure is, there will your heart be also. . . . [25]For this reason I say to you, do not be anxious for your life, as to what you shall eat, or what you shall drink; nor for your body, as to what you shall put on. Is not life more than food, and the body [more] than clothing? [26]Look at the birds of the air, that they do not sow, neither do they reap, nor gather into barns, and yet your heavenly Father feeds them. Are you not worth much more than they? [27]And which of you by being anxious can add a single cubit

to his life's span? [28]And why are you anxious about clothing? Observe how the lilies of the field grow; they do not toil nor do they spin, [29]yet I say to you that even Solomon in all his glory did not clothe himself like one of these. [30]But if God so arrays the grass of the field, which is alive today and tomorrow is thrown into the furnace, will He not much more do so for you, O men of little faith? [31]Do not be anxious then, saying, "What shall we eat?" or "What shall we drink" or "With what shall we clothe ourselves" [32]For all these things the Gentiles eagerly seek, for your heavenly Father knows that you need all these things. [33]But seek first His kingdom and His righteousness, and all these things shall be added to you. [34]Therefore, do not be anxious for tomorrow, for tomorrow will care for itself. Each day has trouble enough of its own.

Jesus also teaches that we are to develop an attitude of gratitude. As Jesus stood in the tomb over the body of Lazarus he said, "Father, I thank thee that thou heardest me" (John 11:41). Then he commanded Lazarus to arise. Jesus knew that the Christ within could and would heal, he thanked the Father, the portion of the Absolute that resides within us all, and then spoke the word. First belief, then thankfulness and finally the manifestation. That is the order that Jesus taught.

The Mental Healing Connection

The members of the Road to Well-Being all taught that Jesus was the greatest of all healers and used his teachings as a basis for their mental healing systems.

Quimby, the man credited with beginning the mental science movement, considers Jesus to be the actual founder of mental science. He speaks highly of Jesus in his manuscripts, though he has no use for organized religion. He feels that the churches purposely distort Jesus's message in order to conserve their power over the people. He writes that because the people have accepted false beliefs given them by the priests and doctors, they must die to these beliefs. He paraphrases Jesus's words in Matthew 16:25 and Luke 9:56 in saying,

Disease is a belief: health is in wisdom. So, as man dies to his belief, he lives in wisdom. My theory is to destroy death, or belief, and bring life and wisdom into the world. Therefore, I come to the sick, not to save their beliefs, or life in disease, but to destroy it. And he that loseth his life for wisdom will find his health, or life.

Quimby understands the difference between Jesus and Christ. He writes that the Christ is the healing principle or law which Jesus used —the higher power which was in him and worked through him. This same power is in us and can be used by us. *If* we change our beliefs.

Quimby calls his healing method the "Science of the Christ." This Science is Truth and is the same Truth that Jesus taught. We cannot serve two masters. These masters are ignorance and Truth. We must pick one to follow. If we follow ignorance, we follow the world of matter, bodies, illness, and error. Jesus says, "Out of the heart proceedeth all kinds of evil thoughts" (Matt. 15:19), which are the result of error, superstition and ignorance. In following Truth, we follow the world of spirit, life and light.

Jesus did not perform miracles; he healed using Science. He knew the truth of our being and appealed to that truth in saying "Your faith hath made you well." He did no "doctoring, nor offered up prayers, nor creeds . . . nor talked about any kind of religion." He taught us to pray in secret, asking that our needs be met, believing that God listens, and thanking Him for providing. He condemned those who offered up prayers and sacrifices. Quimby says Jesus's teachings could have healed nations if they had not been misconstrued. To the world Jesus's truth was a mystery, but "Jesus labored to convince the people that it was a science, that the fruits of it were seen in His practice, and that it could be taught."

Quimby's students also emphasize the words of Jesus and recognize them as truth. As to her own healing, Eddy states her recovery was due to the Word of God as taught by Jesus, "a spiritual illumination from the divine Mind" (McCracken). Throughout her writings she teaches that we can heal our bodies of all illness and disease through the power of God working through the mind. In *Science and Health* she writes, "Jesus beheld in Science the perfect man, who appeared to him where sinning mortal man appears to mortals. In this perfect man the Saviour saw God's own likeness, and this correct view of man healed the sick."

Jesus tells us that all we need do is believe. By believing first that a divine power resides in our minds and second that this power can and will heal, we can rid ourselves of all illness. Because of the great power of words, we can create all manner of outcomes depending on the words we use.

Hopkins says Jesus teaches of the power in a name, saying that in his name or God's name resides omnipotent power (John 14:14, 15:16, 16:24). This is where the concept of name is nature comes in. Why do the names of Jesus and God have power? Because the names of Jesus and God correlate with their natures. Jesus's name means "he who will save." God means truth, love, wisdom, peace, etc. There is saving power in Jesus's name. By invoking his name we may be saved from sickness, poverty, depression, etc. Likewise, invoking God's name brings to us a whole bevy of positive, uplifting, healing energies. If we will simply believe.

In Greek the word for believe is *pisteuo* and includes among its meanings the concepts of trust, commitment and obedience. This is the word used in John 3:16, "For God so loved the world that He gave His only begotten Son, that whoever *believes* in Him should not perish, but have eternal life," and in John 14:12, "Verily, verily, I say unto you, He that *believeth* on me, the works that I do shall he do also; and greater works than these shall he do; because I go unto my Father." In both instances we are promised salvation or eternal life and the ability to do the things Jesus did, if we trust and are obedient to his words.

John also says of Jesus, "In him was life; and the life was the light of men" (1:4). This light is that part of us that, as Holmes writes, "partakes of the nature of the Universal Wholeness and . . . is God. That is the meaning of the world *Emmanuel*, the meaning of the word *Christ*. There is that within us which partakes of the nature of the Divine Being, and *since it partakes of the nature of the Divine Being, we are divine"* (*Science of Mind*, emphasis in original).

When we do something in Jesus's name, we are doing it in his nature, his divine Christ nature. When we heal in the name of Jesus Christ, we heal with the divine Christ nature. When the Apostle Peter healed a paralytic named Aeneas, he said, "Jesus Christ heals you" (Acts 9:34). When the disciples commanded people "In the name of

Jesus Christ the Nazarene— walk!" (Acts 3:6), they were stating that the divine Christ nature of Jesus could heal. When the people were healed, it was because they believed in the healing nature of the Christ in Jesus and they accepted that good into their experience.

Evans writes that Deity manifested in Jesus so that we can know about our true selves. Through listening to Jesus's teachings we can recognize ourselves as sons of God and say with Jesus, "I and my Father are one." This realization results in true freedom, for when we realize the self as a son of God it is no longer possible for us to accept anything less than perfection. The truth is that divinity lies within each of us. Jesus declares that truth when he says that the kingdom of God is at hand. But because most of us are unaware of this truth, we cause ourselves a great deal of trouble. Evans says the antagonism between this divine essence and the "disorderly activity of the mind" is the source of all mental and physical unhappiness. The more aware we become of this divine essence the more we can control the thoughts that result in limitation of any sort. This is what Jesus did. Being totally aware of the divinity within him, he was able to perform so-called miracles—events that viewed with proper understanding can be seen to be the logical outcome of thought, belief or word.

Evans also equates disease with selfishness. The universal and immutable law is that what we give we receive. If we do not have what we want in our lives or if we have in our lives what we do not want, the remedy is to give unselfishly to the world. If we want more love, be more loving. If we want more money, share what we already have. If we want health, give out healthy thoughts and words to ourselves and to others. By sending out into the world unselfish thoughts, words and deeds, we are seeking righteousness. And as Jesus said, all good things will be given us.

In the early years of the New Thought movement, the books promulgating the "new" healing method state that the method was taught by Jesus. Henry Wood writes, "No language could be plainer than that which is contained in the recorded words of Jesus as to the power of faith and the validity and permanency of the 'works' and demonstrations which should characterize those who believe."

John Murray, an early Divine Science Minister, writes that Jesus recognized the relationship between sin and disease. The literal definition of *sin* is missing the mark or making a mistake and is induced through the process of thinking. Jesus shows that we can be healed of all disease, and even death, by the type of thoughts we allow in our minds. By thinking or believing correctly, we can be healed.

Jesus cared not whether the sick "deserved" to be cured; neither did he sympathize with pain. He did not view sickness as punishment from God for sin, as a test or as character-building. He knew the only way to evolve is by overcoming weakness and healing all sickness (Harnack, *Das Wesen des Christenthums*; qtd. in James, W.).

The founders all spoke about Jesus's teachings and how to use them for healing.

Fannie James says that Jesus used a power not of his own in healing the sick. He healed by knowing that he was one with God and by trusting fully that the power of Good was within him and would manifest whatever he asked. This same Power dwells in us. When we let this Power work through us, we can also heal "all that seems sick" and "cast out all that seems evil."

Fillmore writes that the way we heal is by changing the mind from thoughts of error to those of Truth. We do this by first realizing our relationship to God, and second, by showing our belief and faith in this relationship in everything we think and do. Jesus demonstrated this kind of faith and belief. When we place ourselves in the same consciousness that Jesus displayed, we will experience "limitless life, strength, power, wisdom, love, and substance that are everywhere present, always present" (*Atom-Smashing Power*).

Holmes speaks of the plainness of Jesus's teachings. Jesus clearly states that it pleases God to give of His kingdom. He gives us the means by which we can receive all of God's goodness. He tells us the truth of our origins and our nature. He teaches of the unlimited supply available to us. So, Holmes asks, why are we suffering? Because we choose not to believe or to accept. We are immersed in an Infinite Creative Medium which creates for us whatever we believe. What we place into this Creative Mind is returned to us. Jesus understood this law in telling those he healed "[L]et it be done to you as you have believed. Your faith has made you well." If we understood and accepted Jesus's words, we could remove false conditions just as he did. "It is done unto you as you believe." This is the law Jesus taught. Holmes says that Jesus's method was to "first realize that Divine Power is, then unify with it, and then speak the word as 'one having authority.'"

Jesus tells us that we are to be perfect, just as our Father in heaven is perfect" (Matt. 5:48). He is telling us that as a child of the Divine Father we are perfect. and we should conduct ourselves accordingly. We have the capacity to see all illness, poverty, or limitation of any sort as untruth and to change what we see. We suffer bondage to various afflictions and difficulties because of ignorance. We have forgotten who we really are. When we accept the Truth—that we are unlimited, divine beings—we will be set free (John 8:32).

Even along the Intellectual Road with its emphasis on science and law, where normally we would not expect to find Jesus, we encounter this master healer. Troward says that Jesus is "the greatest Teacher of Mental Science the world has ever seen." Jesus sees God as Universal Mind and asks his listeners to see this Mind "as a benign Father, tenderly compassionate of all and sending the common bounties of Nature alike on the evil and the good," as caring so much that He numbers the hairs on our head, and values us more than all other things. He teaches us to go to the Unseen in prayer "with the absolute assurance of a certain answer," and to not limit "its power or willingness to work for us." Jesus, "the Master," emphasizes an "exact correspondence" between "the attitude of this unseen Power towards [us] with [our] own attitude towards it." Troward sees these teachings of Jesus as "the very deepest truths of what we now call Mental Science." Jesus's statement "Ask and ye shall receive, seek and ye shall find, knock and it shall be opened unto you" is the "summing-up of the natural law of the relation between us and the Divine Mind."

The final two common concepts among the groups address the concepts of heaven, hell, evil, and sin.

Heaven and hell are states of mind or consciousness

Heaven and hell are not places. No one spends his or her time on earth earning a slot in a postmortem realm. If God is good, then God is heaven. And if God is everywhere, then so is heaven. Heaven is all around us and within us, if we but choose to experience it.

Jesus repeatedly stresses that heaven is not a particular place. He tells us to lay up for ourselves "treasures in heaven, . . . for where your treasure is, there will your heart be also" (Matt. 6:20-21). He says that the kingdom of God is "like a mustard seed, which a man took and threw into his own garden; and it grew and became a tree; and the birds of heaven nested in its branches," and "like leaven, which a woman took and hid in three pecks of meal, until it was all leavened" (Luke 13:19, 21). In all of these cases, Jesus is not speaking of a future place but of an inner state.

Fillmore explains that the last two verses refer to heaven growing from small beginnings, like the leaven and the mustard seed. As our awareness increases and as we seek for righteousness, our experience of heaven increases. If we are diligent in our search, heaven can be the state in which we dwell right here on earth.

Jesus also says that the kingdom of God is within, and the kingdom of heaven is at hand. Therefore, it is impossible for heaven to be a place outside of ourselves.

Just as heaven is within, so is hell. Fillmore writes that the word *hell* is derived from Sheol, which means "the unseen state," and Hades, "the unseen world." Hell, obviously, is not a place. Says Fillmore, the hell of fire Jesus refers to "means simply a state in which purification is taking place. Hell is a figure of speech that represents a corrective state of mind." (*Christian Healing*).

We are in control of whether we achieve heaven or condemn ourselves to hell. The decision is determined by our thoughts and our attitudes, and is experienced in the present moment.

Evil and sin are simply mistakes resulting from ignorance and wrong thinking

It follows logically that since all is God and God is good, there can be no ultimately real evil. God created no Satan nor any other evil being or force. It is impossible for absolute good to create anything not-good.

Holmes says we experience both good and evil rather than just good because we believe in duality rather than unity. In reality, there is only one, and It is good. What appears as evil is simply error of thought. We must learn to say with St. Paul that God—all existence—is for us not against us. For "Law is a Law of Liberty and not of bondage," but "until we learn to use the Law affirmatively, to cooperate with It, and thus to enjoy Its full benefits, . . . *[W]e must expect to experience the logical result of our thought and act, be it good or what we call evil*" (*Science of Mind*, emphasis in original).

As we saw previously, sin is simply an error. We sin when we think wrongly. Believing that an all-good universe could possibly be evil in any way, that divine beings can suffer from ill-health, poverty, or depression is wrong thinking. Jesus urges those he heals, through their faith and the power of God within him, to "sin no more." He is telling them to stop believing wrongly, to cease believing in illness and death, to understand that they have erred in their thinking.

I think it safe to state that while New Thought accepts the words of Jesus as truth, and it accepts Jesus as Christ, it cannot, in the orthodox sense of the word, be considered Christian. New Thought places a different interpretation on the words of Jesus. Jesus as Christ also has a different meaning. Says Holmes, "Mental Science does not deny the divinity of Jesus; but it does affirm the divinity of all people. It does not deny Jesus was the son of God; but it affirms that all men are the sons of God. It does not deny that the kingdom of God was revealed through Jesus, but it says that the kingdom of God is also revealed through you and me" (*Science of Mind*). So, New Thought is not Christian in the orthodox sense, but it is Christian in the sense that it believes that Jesus embodied the Christ and that Jesus came to earth to show us the way to freedom, to deliver us from the consequences of wrong thinking. In this sense he *is* our savior.

We have seen that all the roads New Thought followed in developing its philosophy led to the important teachings of Jesus. All these roads, too, touched upon the doctrines found in Eastern philosophy, as does the road we just explored. I purposely did not include in this chapter the numerous correspondences between the Eastern philosophies, Jesus's teachings and the sixteen common concepts found among the New Thought groups. These topics are covered in chapters eleven and twelve.

X.

THE END OF THE ROAD

It is the secret of the world that all things subsist and do not die, but only
retire from sight and afterwards return again.
Ralph Waldo Emerson (1803–1882), U.S. essayist, poet and philosopher
"Nominalist and Realist" (1844)

As time advances either we become the prey
or masters of our own past deeds.
William Wordsworth, *The Borderers*

In our exploration of the roads followed by New Thought we have found that all of the roads include ideas gleaned from the teachings of Jesus and the Eastern philosophies of Hinduism, Buddhism and Taoism.

As shown in the last chapter, New Thought's concept of God is different from that of orthodox Judaism and Christianity. In New Thought there is nothing but an infinite and eternal God in which everything exists. This is a monistic view. As we discussed in chapters four and six in connection with the mind/matter debate and pantheism, monism is the belief that there is only one substance in the universe and everything is made out of that substance. In monistic theism that substance is God or Divine Reality.

In our discussion of pantheism we saw that there are several kinds of pantheists: those who negate the world of matter, those who deny the very existence of matter, and those who affirm matter. In the Eastern philosophies can be found systems that negate and affirm matter. Within matter-affirming pantheism are found monists (the universe and God as essentially the same thing) and dualists (the universe is God, but God is more than the universe). Whether they negate the world (it is *maya*, or mere illusion) or affirm it (God is all, and all is God), all Eastern philosophies are pantheistic. The only reality is God.

The Ancient World

To assist our understanding of these philosophies and the world to which they were born, a quick trip through the ancient world is in order.

The first homo sapiens, literally "wise man," appear around 100,000 B.C.E. and subsist as hunter gatherers until around 10,000 when they shift to growing their food. At around 5000 the Yangshao culture develops in China, and settlements are established in Egypt along the Nile River and in India along the Indus River. By around 3750 mangoes are being cultivated in Southeast Asia and methods for weaving cotton are developed in Mohenjo-Daro, India. Three centuries later wheel-made pottery is produced in Sumeria.

During these early centuries religions are tribal rather than personal and most are fertility cults. Ceremonies are designed to generate a sense of oneness between tribal members. The earth is considered female, the sun, male. Across western Asia the Great Mother or Goddess is worshiped. She is known by various names, the most well known to the Western world are the Hellenized versions—Artemis and Diana.

The first kings begin to rule around 3200 in Upper (Southern) Egypt, hieroglyphic writing is developed and cloth is woven from flax. In Mesopotamia the lunar calendar and wheeled transportation are developed. Cuneiform writing evolves in Sumeria.

During the next five centuries Upper and Lower Egypt are unified, and Memphis is established as the capital. Memphis reigns for thousands of years as one of the ancient world's greatest cities. A form of writing is invented in the Tigris, Euphrates and Nile regions. The first Sumerian cities appear, and surprisingly modern cities, containing multilevel dwellings with indoor plumbing, develop in the area along the Indus river that is now Pakistan. In China, silk is manufactured, Fu Hsi invents the first form of Chinese writing, fishing and trapping are employed for the first time as a means of subsistence, and Shen Nung formulates the first methods of agriculture and commerce.

Between 2700 and 2100 a cultural exchange develops between the Indus Valley and Mesopotamian (Iraqi) civilizations. The Mesopotamians develop a place-value mathematical system. The Yellow Emperor, one of the Sage Kings, begins his reign in China. The Sage Kings continue their rule until 2205 when Yu founds the first Chinese dynasty. During this period Egypt enjoys a Golden Age. The king is considered to be the incarnation of the god Horus and the son of Re, the sun god. The Step Pyramid, the first major stone building in the world, is constructed at Saqqara, followed by a number of pyramids, including Khufu's (Cheops) Great Pyramid at Giza. Basic forms for furniture and wind instruments are constructed. The Early Vedic period of Indian civilization evolves resulting in the writing of the first Vedic scripture, the *Rig Veda* (some believe this dating is incorrect). At the end of this period a natural disaster alters the course of the Indus River destroying the entire Indus Valley civilization.

Commencing in 2100 the Minoans on Crete begin worshiping the Mother Goddess. In Old Babylonia, the great city of Babylon is founded. Mesopotamian mathematicians solve quadratic equations, and hundreds of mathematical tables are created, including tables of multiplication, reciprocals, squares, square and cube roots, coefficient lists, and conversion factors for problems involving weights and measures. Horses are introduced to western Asia. Personal religion develops throughout the area. In Egypt, terra cotta pottery is produced, a solar calendar is in use, and religion includes the belief in personal immortality. In China, the first historical Taoist text is written.

Around 1790 the Code of Hammurabi is established. Hammurabi, the ruler of Babylon, the world's first metropolis, is considered to be a wise lawgiver. His code is carved upon an eight-foot high black stone monument that clearly sets out the long-standing rules to which the people are expected to adhere.

During the years 1782 to 1570 the Hyksos, invaders from Asia, move into the Egyptian Delta bringing with them horse-drawn chariots, composite bows, and bronze weapons. An ideographic script (pictures or symbols) develops in China, and an alphabet made up of consonants is invented in Syria. Sacred animals are killed and eaten as part of religious ceremony, for it is believed by the worshipers of Bacchus, symbolized by the bull, that in eating the god they imbibe a spark of divinity.

Beginning in 1500 Egypt develops great wealth as a result of trade and foreign conquests. Massive temples are built to honor the state god Amun-Re, and the capital is moved from Thebes (modern-day Luxor), where it had been for centuries, north to Tell-el Amarna. For a short period of time, around 1400, King Amenhotep IV changes the object of worship to Aten, a universal god, thus introducing monotheism. He and his wife Nefertiti, the most famous Queen of Egypt except perhaps for Cleopatra, are murdered by priests who wish to return to the worship of the old gods, goddesses and stone idols. After the king's death his son Tutankhaten becomes king. Tutankhaten changes his name to Tutankhamun, the famed King Tut. Around this time transparent glass is invented and papyrus, pen and ink are used for writing. Many of the pharaohs' tombs are moved to the Valley of the Kings. Tuthmosis III, the Napoleon of ancient Egypt, comes to power. His kingdom encompasses ancient Nubia (south of modern Aswan and northern Sudan) and much of the present Middle East. Ramesses the Great comes to the throne around 1100. He receives this moniker because of his building program and his success at establishing peace. He signs the world's first recorded peace treaty. By the end of this millennia, the pharaoh's power is almost nonexistent, and so is peace. Upper Egypt is controlled by the Theban priesthood. Moses unites the Hebrews enslaved in Egypt in worship of Yahweh and leads them from Egypt.

In other parts of the world the alphabet is developed by Phoenicians, the city of Troy falls to the Greeks, Crete's Minoan civilization ends, and in China the influential Chou Dynasty begins its reign. Israel splits into two countries in 1000. The north country retains the name Israel, and the south country calls itself Judah. In India, the caste system emerges, giving rise to the priestly caste of the Brahmans.

India uses a symbol for zero for the first time in 876. Greek city-states begin operating around 800, the first recorded Olympic games are held in 776, and writing is brought to Greece by the Phoenicians. The Greeks later add vowels to the existing alphabet. Around 750 Homer writes *The Iliad* and *The Odyssey*, Rome is founded, and the first alphabet based on a Semitic script (Hebrew, Aramaic and Arabic) is developed. During this time period the Assyrian Empire reaches its pinnacle, and the *Upanishads* are written in India.

Between 750 and 400 the New Babylonians make significant astronomical observations of the sun, moon and planets and discover the cycle of eclipses. They develop a sophisticated system of calculation and of keeping records. They divide the day into 24 hours and the circle into 360 degrees. Magic, divination and astrology are common practices.

In 722 the Assyrians conquer Israel, driving the Israelites from their homeland, and over the next 80 years gain control of Mesopotamia, Asia Minor, Syria, Palestine, and Egypt.

Around 700, the Chou dynasty collapses and with it the order that China has experienced for several centuries. Over the next five centuries various groups compete for power, and for that reason this era is called the Period of the Warring States.

Between the seventh and fifth centuries several religious leaders are born: Zarathustra (founder of Zoroastrianism), Confucius, Lao Tzu (founder of Taoism), and Siddhartha Gautama (founder of Buddhism).

During the sixth century, the iron plow is used in China, and in Persia Cyrus the Great begins his conquests, greatly enlarging his empire. Greece achieves its Golden Age. Philosophy, which at this time includes all the disciplines, is born. The philosophers/scientists/mathematicians/theologians writing and teaching during this century are Anaximander, Anaximenes, Thales, Xenophanes, Heraclitus, Parmenides, and Pythagorus, many of whom we have come across in our journey. Pythagorus, whom the philosopher Bertrand Russell calls "a combination of Einstein and Mrs. Eddy," formulates his theorem for use with right triangles. Though it is the Pythagorean Theorem that geometers use today, it is believed that other right triangle theorems had been developed previous to Pythagorus by mathematicians in China, Mesopotamia and Egypt.

The worshipers of Bacchus, who is known in this time period as Dionysus, are now called Orphics. The Orphics embrace beliefs in the transmigration of souls and the Wheel of Birth, beliefs that parallel those of Hinduism, though it is believed that no contact between the groups occurred during this time. Nebuchadrezzar captures Jerusalem, destroys the Temple, and removes a large portion of the population to Babylon. Irrational numbers (numbers that cannot be expressed as a fraction) are discovered by Hipparcos of Metapontum.

Much fighting takes place between Assyria, Persia, Athens, and Sparta during the next two centuries. The Persians conquer the Indus Valley, which becomes a province of the Persian Empire. They also invade Egypt, and are later defeated at Marathon by the Greeks. The Egyptians take advantage of this distraction and revolt against the Persians who retaliate with constant invasions. (Interestingly, beginning in 343 Egypt does not see an Egyptian ruler for almost two thousand years.) The Parthenon is built, and Socrates and Plato teach in Greece. In India, the *Mahabharata*, which contains *The Bhagavad Gita* and *Ramayana*, is put into final form, and Panini's *Sutra* is composed.

During the fourth century the worship of Pan, the All-God we encountered in chapter six, comes to Greece and Aristotle founds his school, the Lyceum, in Athens. In China, Chuang Tzu pens the book of the same name which later joins with the *Tao Te Ching* as the recognized scriptures of Taoism. Alexander the Great invades India, Asia, Persia, Persepolis, Samarkand, and Egypt. He orders that all the Egyptian temples sacked by the Persians be restored. The city of Alexandria is constructed and flourishes as the Jewel of the Ancient World. Its great library and famous lighthouse are built. The first Indian empire is founded. Upon Alexander's death in 323 peace is finally achieved, and within two decades the Persian Empire ceases to exist.

In India during the third century, Ashoka establishes the Buddha's *Dharma* as the national code of morality; the canon of Buddhist scriptures is selected; and the Mahayana branch of Buddhism is founded. In Greece Euclid writes *Elements of Geometry*, and 70 years later Eratosthenes develops the means for finding prime numbers.

The second century brings the banning of Dionysus worship, the Hellenization of Roman myth and religion, and the canon of the Theravada School of Buddhism is written on palm leaves in the Pali language.

The religious philosophies considered in this chapter began flourishing several centuries before the birth of Jesus and the subsequent founding of Christianity and more than two millennia before the history outlined in the introduction to this book. It is interesting to note how many current ideas were present in these ancient cultures.

Hinduism

As can be seen in the history just presented, Hinduism is the oldest religion for which we have records, though some claim that the extant writings of Hermes Trismegistus, whom we encountered in chapter seven, are older. It is also under debate as to whether the civilizations of India, China or Egypt are the most ancient.

Of Hinduism's numerous scriptures, the *Vedas* are the oldest. In fact, the *Rig Veda* is the oldest book in existence. The exact date of its origin is uncertain and has been assigned between 12,000 and 4000 B.C.E. based on the astronomical events the book refers to and at around 1500 B.C.E. by modern Western scholars following their Christian precursors, though that date is being nudged back by recent archeological discoveries ("Hinduism"). According to David Frawley, two of the *Vedas* speak of astronomical events that occurred about 2400 B.C.E.—the vernal equinox in the Krittikas (the Pleiades) in Taurus and the summer solstice in Magha (the 11th month in the Hindu calendar) in Leo. John Playfair, a Scottish mathematician, suggested in 1790 that based on Hindu astrological tables the astronomical events mentioned in the *Rig Veda* occurred in 4300 B.C.E. Therefore, he feels the traditional dating of all the Hindu scriptures must be pushed back. He sets the date of the core text of the *Mahabharata* at about 4000 B.C.E. and the *Brahmanas* and *Sutras* about two thousand years later (Elst).

The reasons that the ages of these different cultures keep changing are due to the increasingly accurate methods of science used to date the numerous artifacts that are being found, and the fact that many past scientists were Christian. Traditionally, Christianity has held that our world has existed for only six thousand years; thus, regardless of the age indicated by scientific means, the age of any civilization necessarily had to have been less than that.

Regardless of the exact dating, it is indisputable that the *Vedas* are ancient and predate all other extant literature.

The Hindu scriptures were written in Sanskrit, the sacred language of India. Scholars studying this previously unknown language discovered that it derives from the same source as the Persian, Greek, Latin, Celtic, Germanic, and Slavonic languages. This ancient source is thought to be Aryan, though there is no definitive proof for that claim.

The term *veda* means "knowledge" but it is not the kind of knowledge that can be gained from books; rather, it refers to knowledge of the true self. The *Vedas* consist of more than one thousand hymns in ten books which set out the basic philosophy of Hinduism and the means for discovering knowledge of the self. These hymns are addressed to the various aspects of the Divine, which are referred to as Gods and Goddesses. This is why Hinduism has been mistakenly called a polytheistic religion. Hinduism is, however, monistic. The *Vedas* clearly proclaim that God is one. The Divine is the universe but it is also more than the universe. It is both One and Many.

In Hinduism every male aspect of God has its female counterpart. For instance, Shiva is paired with Parvati, Vishnu with Lakshmi, and Krishna with Radha. Each of the many Vedic Gods and Goddesses have different levels of meaning, much like the biblical stories about God and Its creations. At the spiritual or intuitive level they represent the way we gain knowledge of our true self. The more important Gods are Indra, the God of the awakened life-force, symbolizing the consciousness of the seer; Agni, the God of consciousness, awareness and mindfulness, representing the higher awareness within us; Soma, the Moon and ruler of the waters, symbolizing bliss; Surya, the Sun, the presence of Deity, symbolizing the enlightened mind and creative intelligence; Usha, the Goddess of the Dawn, representing spiritual aspiration; and Saraswati, the Goddess of the Divine Word, symbolizing wisdom and inspiration ("Hinduism").

Some of the *Rig Veda*'s hymns are in the form of prayers. They ask for protection, forgiveness of sins, removal of fear and the deities' love. They ask the deities to allow them to stay in the light and away from darkness. Others state that "God gives wisdom to the simple; and leadeth the wise unto the path of good" (VII.86.7). They speak of the time before creation when "[t]here was not then what is nor what is not. . . . There was neither death nor immortality then. . . . The ONE was breathing by its own power, in deep peace. Only the ONE was: there was nothing beyond" (X.129.1-2, emphasis in original). They speak of how the sages sought and found "the bond of union between being and non-being" (X.129.4).

Most of the practices of Vedic Hinduism; i.e., yoga, meditation, mantra, and the medical system of Ayurveda are found in the *Rig Veda*.

Vedanta is the form of Hinduism based on the *Vedas*, and means "the end or the goal of knowledge," both the knowledge of God and the knowledge of our divine nature. God is infinite existence, infinite consciousness, infinite bliss, impersonal, and transcendent. God as Brahman is the divine ground of all being. As Atman, God is the perfect, divine Self that dwells in the hearts of all humans. Atman is also infinite and eternal.

Our inevitable goal is to realize and then manifest our divine Self. We all will at some point realize our inherent divinity, whether it is in this life or a subsequent one. We cannot *not* achieve this goal, because it is the truth of our being.

The unity of all existence is one of the most important messages of Vedanta.

> Unity is the song of life; it is the grand theme underlying the rich variations that exist throughout the cosmos. Whatever we see, whatever we experience, is only a manifestation of this eternal oneness. The divinity at the core of our being is the same divinity that illumines the sun, the moon, and the stars. There is no place where we, infinite in nature, do not exist" ("What is Vedanta?").

The *Upanishads* are among the most recent of the Hindu scriptures and are traditionally dated at 600 to 400 B.C.E. The word *upanishad* means "secret and sacred knowledge" and "texts incorporating such knowledge." There are ten primary *Upanishads* that teach that the ultimate reality lying behind or above the visible world is Brahman — transcendent, pure consciousness. The Atman, the essence of a human being, is also pure consciousness. Brahman and Atman are one.

These texts have been interpreted two different, yet similar, ways. In one, the world is an unreal projection, and Brahman is without attributes—a monistic and idealistic philosophy. Another of the Hindu scriptures, *The Bhagavad Gita*, which means "The Lord's Song," or "The Song of the Blessed," written sometime between 500 and 200 B.C.E., seems to support this interpretation in saying that Brahman cannot be defined because It is beyond thought and imagination and outside time and space. The most we can say is that It is a state of consciousness.

The other interpretation holds the *Upanishads* to teach monotheism or immanence—the concept of one all-pervasive, transcendent, supreme being containing numerous attributes. In this interpretation Brahman is the ultimate principle of reality, the one source of the many, the creator and guide of the universe, imperishable, inexhaustible, and unbounded. In gaining knowledge of Brahman we gain knowledge of the self. The second interpretation seems to be supported by the *Chandogya Upanishad*, which says that Brahman is "The formed and the unformed, the mortal and the immortal, the abiding and the fleeting, the being and the beyond" (qtd. in McGreal).

As we shall see, both views are supported by the *Upanishads* and the *Bhagavad Gita*.

The *Chandogya Upanishad* also speaks of Brahman as Spirit and says that it is "mind and life, light and truth" and "enfolds the whole universe, and in silence is loving to all." This Spirit is in our hearts, "smaller than a grain of rice, or a grain of barley, or a grain of mustard seed, or a grain of canary seed, or the kernel of a grain of canary seed." This Spirit that is in our hearts is also "greater than the earth, greater than the sky, greater than heaven itself, greater than all these worlds." This Spirit is Brahman.

The Truth or Ultimate Reality of the Universe is Brahman. Our own inner truth is atman. And they are one. This concept is known as *Tat Tvam Asi*—Thou art that or That art thou. This phrase can be interpreted as I am Brahman, I am Atman, I am God, but One in all things, God within and without, or Only Thou art, meaning only God is. In all these interpretations, our sense of an individual, separate personality disappears and the I AM becomes preeminent.

The *Viveka-Chudamani*, "The Crest-Jewel of Wisdom," says:

> Brahman has neither name nor form, transcends merit and demerit, is beyond time, space and the objects of sense-experience. Such is Brahman, and "thou are That." . . . Pure, absolute and eternal Reality–such is Brahman, and "thou are That." . . . Though One, Brahman is the cause of the many. There is no other cause. And yet Brahman is independent of the law of causation. Such is Brahman, and "thou are That" (qtd. in Huxley).

Since Brahman is absolute truth, when we know truth we know ourselves as divinity. This self-knowledge brings us closer to experiencing the Absolute, for Atman is Brahman. In this realization unity becomes the reality. This is the same as the mystical experience discussed in chapter seven. We understand that the macrocosm is the microcosm. All is One. There is no difference between nature, humanity and divinity. Spirit is the reality and matter and all its conditions are *maya*—they are real, yet illusory, because matter is limited and ever changing. We think matter is real in the same sense as spirit is real because of our ignorance of the truth, much like confusing the map with the land it represents. Realizing this truth is the inevitable goal of life; it is our birthright. If we don't achieve this realization in this life, then we will have another chance in our next life.

The *Isha Upanishad* also addresses this concept in saying "Whoever sees all beings in the Self, and the Self in all beings, hates none. For one who sees oneness everywhere, how can there be delusion or grief?" All our fears and suffering are the result of seeing all objects of the world as separate. The *Brihadaranyaka Upanishad* states that this duality implies that something exists besides God, but "There can be no other" (qtd. in "What is Vedanta?").

The *Bhagavad Gita* speaks of God in all things and of all things in God. "And Arjuna saw in that radiance [of a thousand suns] the whole universe in its variety, standing in a vast unity in the body of the God of gods" (11.13). It describes Krishna, the Love aspect of God and the aspect that indwells all things, as everlasting, omnipresent, never-changing, never-moving, ever One, invisible to the mortal eyes, beyond thought and beyond change. It is never born and never dies. It is the Father and the Mother of the universe and brings forth all creation. It is Eternity. It is the I AM. It is immanent in all. It is.

There are eight visible forms of God's nature: earth, water, fire, air, ether, the mind, reason, and the sense of "I." Beyond God's visible nature is the invisible Spirit. In the words of Krishna, "This is the fountain of life whereby this universe has its being. All things have their life in this Life, and I am their beginning and end" (7.5-6).

According to Juan Mascaro, translator of the *Bhagavad Gita*, the Hindu scriptures show the evolution of the One to the Many and back again to the One. The *Vedas*, the oldest scriptures, speak of the One, the action of the outer world of the many, and the dawning of spiritual insight. The storyline of the *Mahabharata*, the longest poem in the world and the next oldest of the scriptures, revolves around the forces of good and evil and speaks of a great war. While this war is likely based on historical fact, the war in the *Bhagavad Gita*, which is a later addition to the *Mahabharata,* is symbolic. "The vision of action with a consciousness of its meaning is interwoven . . . with the idea of love." The *Upanishads*, the most recent of the scriptures, illustrate the magnificence of inner vision. "From nature outside in the *Vedas*, man goes in the *Upanishads* into his own inner nature: and from the many he goes to the ONE."

The preferred name for Hinduism by Hindus is *Sanathana Dharma*, which means "the eternal essence of life, which unites all beings, and the teaching which leads one to realize that essence." As can be seen, this is an extremely appropriate name.

Buddhism

Buddhism was founded by Siddhartha Gautama, the son of a king. The date of Gautama's birth is thought to be sometime between 566 and 490 B.C.E. in what is today Nepal. Raised in the privileged world of royalty, he married a princess and was blessed with a son.

According to legend, Gautama's father sought out fortunetellers for information about his heir. He was told that his son would face challenges in his life choices. He could choose to focus on worldly matters and become the leader of his country or he could focus on spiritual matters and become the redeemer of the world. His father preferred his son be leader of his nation and arranged Siddhartha's life so that he was shielded from the seedy side of existence. Whenever Gautama left the palace, he was guided into areas in which all trace of poverty, crime and sickness had been removed.

But on four different occasions Gautama encountered the things from which his father wished to protect him—an old man leaning on a staff, a visibly diseased body, a corpse, and a monk. From these encounters Gautama learned about old age, illness, death, and living in spiritual retreat from the world.

These encounters affected him deeply. No longer able to enjoy the comfort in which he had lived, he shaved his head, dressed himself in rags, and left his family and his life of luxury in search of truth. He was but 28 years old.

He first sought Hindu masters from whom he could learn the wisdom they taught. After exhausting their knowledge he joined with a group of ascetics to learn their ways. Throwing himself fully into the austere life he became so weak that he almost died. At this point he realized that neither a life of luxury nor a life of privation was the correct kind of life. The Middle Way was the proper path. He then embarked upon the final portion of his six-year quest for truth.

One evening toward the end of that period near the current town of Patna in northeast India, Gautama sat down under a Bo tree (short for Bodhi, which means enlightenment or the correct perception of reality) and vowed not to arise until he had attained enlightenment. He remained under the Bo tree for 49 days during which Mara, the Evil One tempted him with desire, death, his right to seek illumination, and finally, with reason. Throughout, Buddha remained unfazed, the efforts of Mara only deepening his meditative state. Upon arising, filled with the bliss of enlightenment he immediately began imparting the philosophy that Huston Smith calls scientific, pragmatic, therapeutic, psychological, and democratic.

Having learned the importance of silent retreat, he spent nine months teaching among the people and three months in retreat with his monks. Each day he also spent time in silent meditation in order to center himself with his spiritual source. Gautama died at the age of 80 after accidentally eating poisoned mushrooms.

Siddhartha Gautama is known by various names: Sakyamuni, the "silent sage (*muni*) of the Sakya clan," Tathagata, the "Thus-Come" or the "Truth-winner," and Buddha, the "Enlightened One." *Budh* in Sanskrit means "to wake up" and "to know." He is best known as the Buddha, a name received when asked if he was a god, an angel or a saint. To his reply of "No," he was then asked, "Then what are you?" Buddha answered, "I am awake."

Buddha's vow to impart the knowledge he received under the Bo tree resulted in what many have called a religion of infinite compassion. He understood that all people flow from one source and deserve honor and respect. He lived simply and happily and devoted his life to his mission. Like Jesus, Buddha did not write down any of his teachings. In fact, his teachings were not put into written form until nearly 150 years after his death.

He tended not to discuss metaphysics for he felt that "Greed for views tend not to edification." He was pragmatic and felt it more important to teach the ways we can rise above the suffering that permeates our lives. Thus, his teachings were more aligned with psychotherapy than with metaphysics. He did speak, though, of the One. "There is, O monks, an Unborn, neither become nor created nor formed" (qtd. in Burtt).

The ultimate goal of life is the state known as Nirvana, which means "to blow out" or "to extinguish," as in putting out a fire. In this state we extinguish the awareness of separation. We see that we do not consist of a finite self but are one with the All, that it is "power, bliss and happiness, the secure refuge, the shelter, and the place of unassailable safety; that it is the real Truth and the supreme Reality" (Conze, *Buddhism: Its Essence and Development*; qtd. in Burtt).

The state of Nirvana is "incomprehensible, indescribable, inconceivable [and] unutterable," for in the words of Edwin Burtt, "after we eliminate every aspect of the only consciousness we now know, how can we speak of what is left?"

Buddha taught the Hindu concept of karma. He also taught that we all experience free will, that the most basic human component is mind, that all manifest things are finite and transient, and that all things are constantly changing.

He taught us to think for ourselves and to seek out truth. "Do not accept what you hear by report, do not accept tradition, do not accept a statement because it is found in your books, nor because it is in accord with your belief, nor because it is the saying of your teacher. . . . Be ye lamps unto yourselves" (qtd. in Woodward).

Buddha says there are two ways of experiencing life. In one, we live randomly, at the whim of life's circumstances, unconscious as to our actions or their purpose, what he called "wandering about." The second way of living is intentional and is what he called "the Path." In order to follow the Path we must associate with those who embody the highest ideals and values. We must "converse with them, serve them, observe their ways, and imbibe by osmosis their spirit of love and compassion" (Smith).

The entire teaching of Buddha is summarized in his Four Nobel Truths.

The First Nobel Truth is *dukkha*, "suffering" or "pain that seeps at some level into all finite existence." This term is used in reference to a dislocated bone, a bone that has slid out of its socket. The life the majority of the world experiences is dukkha—dislocation from truth.

The Second Noble Truth states that the cause of this dislocation is *tanha*, "desire." This type of desire is selfish desire, desire that in no way considers other life forms. In that all life is composed of various aspects of the one Reality, such selfish desire results in separation and suffering.

The Third Nobel Truth instructs that since the cause of the dislocation we experience in life is our selfish desires, the remedy is to overcome these desires.

The Fourth Nobel Truth teaches that these desires can be dissolved by following the Eightfold Path, which consists of eight right thoughts, actions or behaviors:

1. *Right Knowledge or Understanding.* We must have certain beliefs or convictions in order to follow the Path. These are the Four Nobel Truths. We must understand that the causes of our suffering are our selfish desires and our belief in separation and that the remedy for this suffering is the Eightfold Path.

2. *Right Purpose or Aspiration.* We must understand that the world does not consist of separate beings but that we are all aspects of the same One. We must set our intentions so that our goals include all others, but do not harm others. We are all One and all our efforts must reflect this single-mindedness.

3. *Right Speech.* We are to become aware of the reasons we say what we say. There is always a motive for the words we speak. When we become aware of these motives, we can easily see which of our words need to be changed.

4. *Right Behavior.* In contemplating the motives for our behavior we can determine which of our actions are motivated by selfish desire. We can then consciously work to

change such behavior. The Buddha sets forth five behaviors that absolutely are to be avoided: lying, killing, stealing, immorality, and consumption of intoxicants.

5. *Right Livelihood.* Our occupations should edify life rather than demean it. If we feel satisfied and fulfilled at the end of our workday, if we have done nothing in our work that would contribute to the harm of any living thing, if at the end of our day even one life has been made better through our efforts, we have participated in right livelihood. It is good to remember that our life's work is simply a means, not an end.

6. *Right Effort.* We cannot help another turn away from the beliefs that result in suffering until we have helped ourselves. We must first develop the proper thoughts that lead to proper words and actions. We must learn to always include others in our desires and make sure our motives are pure.

7. *Right Mindfulness or Concentration.* It is important to remember that our thoughts make our self and our experience what they are. If our thoughts are creating misery, then we must change our thoughts. We must keep our thoughts loving. We need not worry about trivial matters, but must focus on Reality.

8. *Right Absorption.* As with Right Mindfulness, we must focus on the higher and loving aspects of life. Our goal is to live in the spiritual realm, not the physical or material. We can actually transmute ourselves into another type of being, one who lives in the world but is not of it. This is the path to enlightenment.

After Buddha's death his teachings spread throughout the Eastern world, modifying, morphing and combining with other philosophies as it went. The two main schools of Buddhism are Theraveda and Mahayana, the form that is considered to be the closest to Buddha's actual teachings and also to the teachings of New Thought.

According to Mahayana Buddhism, life is one. All life is connected because "a boundless power, grounded in Nirvana, regards and dwells without exception in every soul" (Smith). This "boundless power" is Mind, and all the phenomena in the universe are manifestations of this mind. As such, the phenomenal world is illusory and impermanent. This concept is similar to the Hermetic concept discussed in chapter seven.

All human beings have the Buddha-nature (Universal Mind or Nonbeing), but most are not aware of its existence. Such ignorance keeps us tied to the Wheel of Birth and Death. When we understand that we possess the Buddha-nature, we can, with practice, "see" it. This "seeing" is a "sudden enlightenment" (though some consider enlightenment to come gradually) and is an awareness that each individual is really one with the Buddha-nature, which, in turn, is one with all that is.

When we truly understand the illusion of phenomena, that we are nothing but manifestations of the mind and "see" with the Buddha-nature, it becomes possible to return to the Ultimate, and attain the Original or Nirvana. This is known as *moksha*.

There are no particular acts to be performed in achieving Nirvana. Since all deeds are impermanent, they are linked to the Wheel of Birth and Death. Thus, deeds do not lead directly to Nirvana, but to karma. The only "doing" required in achieving Nirvana is the doing that rids us of our old karma and doesn't create new karma.

This is the goal of the follower of Mahayana. A person who has attained such enlightenment is called a *Bodhisattva*, one whose essence (sattva) is perfected wisdom (bodhi), and one who voluntarily leaves the state of Nirvana and devotes his or her life to guiding others to this state.

Within the Mahayana philosophy are found several schools, the main ones being Madhyamika (Doctrine of the Middle Position) and the Vijnanavada (Doctrine of Consciousness) or Yogacara (The Way of Yoga). The Madhyamika school, founded sometime during the first two centuries of the common era, taught of the qualified reality of the phenomenal world and of the reality of *Sunyata*, Emptiness or the Void, or *Tathata*, Suchness—all equivalent concepts to Nirvana. These terms are often misunderstood as indicating a state of nothingness; however, the meaning is just the opposite—the very source and essence of all life. And since the Ultimate Emptiness is here now (everywhere and always), the phenomenal world *is* the Emptiness. All is One. We already are the Buddha-nature and are in Nirvana. We only need to recognize it.

The Vijnanavada school holds a concept of sense-impressions that is similar to the theosophical concept of grooves discussed in chapter seven. The Buddhist grooves are called *samskaras*. All of our thoughts and actions leave an imprint or groove upon the mind. The more we perform the same act or think the same thought the deeper the grooves become. This is great if our thoughts and acts are positive, but if they are not, things get much worse. Since our minds continue beyond death, these imprints go with us into the next life. If the *samskaras* are negative, it makes it harder to gain the realization of truth that will lead to liberation.

From the Yogacara school of Buddhism come the various forms of yoga. In the *Yoga Sutras*, Patanjali, who combined elements of Hinduism as well as Buddhism, sets out the four themes of yoga: *samadhi* (concentration), *sadhana* (practice), *vibhuti* (empowerment*)*, and *kaivalyam* (isolation). The purpose of yoga is to gain control over the mind and to understand the difference between the seer (the true self or atman) and the seen (the manifest world). Such understanding leads to the state of isolation and freedom from karma. The ultimate goal of yoga is the state of *jivanmukta* (living liberation) and the removal of the self from the Wheel of Birth and Death (Moyer).

The various forms of meditation and yoga have the same purpose: the realization that all the things we see in the world as external to ourselves are actually manifestations of our minds. In actuality, there is no independent world outside of mind. All is one and is unified in Mind.

Reincarnation

Hinduism and Buddhism accept the concept of reincarnation—rebirth into new bodies. Reincarnation and karma help explain the apparent inconsistencies in the world. We alone are responsible for our thoughts and acts, and thus the results, be they positive or negative. We alone determine the circumstances of our future in this life and the next. If we experience unpleasant circumstances, it is because an atmosphere of negativity has built up in our minds and in our past attitudes and behaviors.

In Buddhism this chain of causation is known as *samsara*, which literally means "incessantly in motion." Because of our ignorance concerning things and their nature, we crave for them and become attached to them. This is the basis for the suffering we experience in our lives (the Four Noble Truths). In order to eliminate any future karma, thus any future effects, we must remove ourselves from samsara—the Wheel of Birth and Death. This can occur only when all the effects of previously accumulated karma are depleted, when we "see" from our Buddha-nature, when we act "spontaneously, without any deliberate discrimination, choice, or effort" (Yu-lan), when we replace ignorance with enlightenment as to our true selves, and when we follow the principles of "no mind" and "no activity." Thus, because there is no yearning for or cleaving to things, retribution is avoided. We can then attain Nirvana, the state in which the human condition has been transcended.

The concept of reincarnation is not unique to these Eastern philosophies. It has been taught in many traditions throughout the world, including Judaism and Christianity, and was not excluded from Christian teachings until the sixth century C.E. Many of the ancient Greek philosophers, including Anaximander, Plato and Pythagorus and many of their followers, accepted the concept of reincarnation or what is sometimes called *the transmigration of souls*. The concept was common among the transcendentalists, spiritualists and theosophists as well.

There is and was widespread belief in reincarnation among adherents of New Thought. The Fillmores accepted the concept and believed that it was taught by Jesus:

> When man loses his body by death, the law of expression works within him for reembodiment. He takes advantage of the Adam method of generation to regain a body. . . . We teach, and our doctrine is sustained by the teachings of Jesus, that rebirth is the unifying force of nature at work in its effect to restore man to his original deathless estate. Man, through his disregard of the law of life, brought death upon soul and body."

During Jesus's lifetime, the world was engaged in trade and war. Traveling caravans brought tales and ideas to Palestine, located at the crossroads of the trade routes from Rome, Greece, Egypt, Syria, Persia, Babylon, Assyria, and many points East. It is believed that the beliefs of these many cultures, including the belief in reincarnation, became mingled with those of the Jews.

Teachings about reincarnation can be found in the New Testament, though most references were removed in the early centuries of the Christian church. The clearest reference is in the book of John. Jesus is asked whether a certain man's affliction of blindness at birth resulted from his own sin or that of his parents. The assumption of the question is that consequences of sin (karma) are carried over into one life from another. There is no way a newly-born baby could be blind because of its own sin if it had not previously lived. Many believe that Jesus spoke of his own previous life in John 8:58: "Before Abraham was, I am," and of John the Baptist's in Matthew 11:13-15, 17:10-13 and Mark 9:11-13, wherein he calls John the returning Elijah.

According to the authors of *The Original Jesus*, several of the scriptures that originally referred to reincarnation have been incorrectly translated. The correct translation of John 3:1-4 reads, "Verily, verily, I say unto thee: except a man be born again and again, he cannot be (re)admitted into the Kingdom of God. . . . Ye must be born again and again." And the retranslated Matthew 18:3 states, "If ye be not reborn, ye shall not enter into the Kingdom of Heaven."

The Gnostic Gospel of Thomas says, "Blest is he who was before he came into being" (verse 19), and "lest are the solitary and chosen–for you shall find the Kingdom. You have come from it, and you shall return unto it" (verse 49).

The Epistle of James 3:6 speaks of the tongue as defiling the body and setting it on "the course of its existence." Correctly understood, this passage is a reference to the "circle of births" or "wheel of existence." Right speech is one of the conditions of removal from the Wheel of Rebirths.

The Gospel of the Holy Twelve, which is also known as *The Essene New Testament*, quotes Jesus as saying, "The soul is purified through many births and experiences."

Officially, none of the New Thought groups either encourage or discourage the belief in reincarnation. Along with the Fillmores, prominent New Thought writers Ralph Waldo Trine, Emmet Fox and Ella Wheeler Wilcox supported the concept. Since the goal is to realize the oneness of life and to manifest this understanding in our lives, it is understood that it might take more than one lifetime to achieve this realization. Ernest Holmes did not accept reincarnation as a valid proposition but never discouraged it in others, and many adherents to the Religious Science philosophy accept reincarnation as a true principle or at least as a potentially-true principle. Holmes writes:

> I do not believe in the return of the souls to another life on this plane. The spiral of life is upward. Evolution carries us forward, not backward. Eternal and progressive expansion is its law and there are no breaks in its continuity. It seems to me that our evolution is the result of an unfolding consciousness of that which already is, and needs but to be realized to become a fact of everyday life. I can believe in planes beyond this one without number, in eternal progress. I cannot believe that nature is limited to one sphere of action.

There are numerous writers who brought knowledge of these Eastern philosophies to the Western world. Of particular importance to New Thought are the teachings of Sri Aurobindo.

Sri Aurobindo

Aurobindo Ghosh (1872-1950), whose writings were studied by Holmes, was born in the West Bengal district of Calcutta in East India. His father, the first Bengali Indian to study in Britain, was so impressed by the education he received that he sent Aurobindo and his three brothers to a convent school in Darjeeling run by an Irish nun.

Aurobindo taught that the Absolute is Brahman and is a Consciousness of limitless bliss. The Absolute is unmanifest but makes itself manifest by a process of involution. The involution of the One results in the evolution of the many. All things are actually united in that One, but because of ignorance we see everything as separate, separate from each other as well as separate from the One. We can regain the knowledge that all is One by first going into the mind and realizing that we have mental will. We can choose or will our minds to focus on the higher plane of spirituality rather than the lower plane of materiality. But our minds can only go so far, as they are limited to the finite plane. To free our minds so that we can realize the truth of our being, we must use processes that do not involve the mind, but use the part of the self that is higher than the mind. This process is yoga, which means "to yoke" or "to join," and refers to the joining of the individual soul to Brahman. In practicing yoga, the mind is silenced and the inner self—the true divine self—is allowed expression.

Aurobindo describes the effects he experienced from practicing Pranayama Yoga. He says that he had many visions and felt some kind of electric power around his head. His writing ability increased greatly and he gained in health. He also was able to feel the living presence of God. He realized that he had the ability to change what he perceived was about to happen. One day while traveling along the road to Baroda he discovered that he had the will to prevent an impending accident. There "appeared a Being of Light in him who was there, as it were, to master the situation and to control the details" (Sri Aurobindo").

We travel now to China to explore its contribution to New Thought.

XI.

SIDE TRIP TO CHINA

So meet extremes in this mysterious world,
And opposites thus melt into each other.
William Wordsworth
The Borderers

As we saw from our short visit to the ancient world in the last chapter, civilization in China flourished during the same time as that in India, in which arose Hinduism and later, Buddhism. It is not thought that India and China had any contact during the time that the earliest Hindu and Taoist texts were written. Taoism arose from a completely separate, yet similar, line of thought.

Taoism

Even though there is evidence of Taoist texts dating back to the eighteenth century B.C.E., Lao Tzu, born sometime between 604 and 550 B.C.E., is considered the traditional founder of Taoism. Few factual writings exist concerning Lao Tzu and whether or not such a man actually lived is merely conjecture. The name Lao Tzu is translated as the Old Boy, the Old Fellow or the Grand Old Master.

According to legend, a frustrated Lao Tzu mounted a water buffalo and rode west toward the land we know as Tibet leaving his people behind, for he felt that they did not have the proper regard for the natural and simple life he advocated. At the Hankao Pass a gatekeeper, who apparently appreciated Lao Tzu's message, stopped Lao Tzu and attempted to persuade him not to abandon his people. After considerable discussion, the gatekeeper convinced Lao Tzu to commit his beliefs to writing. Three days later Lao Tzu returned to the gate-keeper and presented him with a small volume of approximately five thousand characters that has come to be known as the *Lao Tzu* or more commonly the *Tao Te Ching*.

Traditionally, *tao* has been translated to mean "path" or "way," *te* to mean "virtue" or "power," and *ching* refers to a classic or funda-mental text. The *Tao Te Ching*, then, is a classic text often translated to mean "The Way and Its Power" or "The Way of Virtue." However, according to Thomas Cleary, a prominent translator of Chinese, *tao* can also refer to a principle, a method, a doctrine, or a system of order, or it can also refer to the matrix, structure and reality of the universe itself; thus, *Tao Te Ching* can mean "The Way of Heaven" or "The Way of Nature." Additionally, in classical Chinese the same words can be used as nouns, adjectives or verbs, so their order is determined by the emotional content and intended meaning rather than by rules of grammar. Because pictorial characters rather than alphabetic letters are used to describe words, they are suggestive and capable of evoking strong mental pictures and emotions. Therefore, the translation of character words into alphabetic words is highly subjective.

A second Taoist text is the *I Ching*, supposedly written by the founders of the Chou dynasty, Kings Wen and Wu, sometime between 1100 and 400 B.C.E. The *I* in the title has been translated as "change" or "changes," thus its Westernized title—the *Book of Changes*. The *I Ching* has been used for centuries as a book of wisdom and as an oracle that converts a problem or question into a language of images and symbols. These images change the way we perceive a situation and lead to an understanding of the inner beliefs that are causing the problem or question. This understanding is known as *shen ming*, "the light of the gods," or an intuitive clarity.

The other main book of Taoist thought is attributed to Chuang Tzu, or Master Chuang, who lived during the latter part of the Chou Dynasty (ca. 370-300 B.C.E.) known as the Warring States Period, when China was devastated by civil wars. As with Lao Tzu, little is known about Chuang Tzu. The book is called the *Chuang Tzu*, for while it is thought to consist of the words of several writers, the mystical and skeptical core is attributed to Chuang Tzu himself. The central theme of the *Chuang Tzu* is freedom, specifically the freedom that comes from living outside the world of chaos and suffering.

Chuang Tzu teaches that all our suffering is of our own creation and occurs as a result of our fears.

All the differing strains of Chinese philosophy studied the *Tao Te Ching*. In fact, in the second century B.C.E., it was one of the imperial court's favorite books of practical wisdom. The *Chuang Tzu*'s teachings, however, remained known mainly to groups of mystical Taoists and even was banned during the Han dynasty when Confucianism became the state philosophy. Outside of Confucius's teachings only the *Tao Te Ching* was allowed. When the Han dynasty fell during the first century C.E. and with it Confucian philosophy, the *Chuang Tzu* reappeared in public and gained popularity with Chinese intellectuals, poets and artists.

Over the next several centuries Buddhist masters studied the *Tao Te Ching* in order to explain through Taoist concepts the Buddhist philosophy moving across China. In fact, the influence of the three Taoist texts increased as Buddhism gained in popularity. To this day in China, Buddhism is sometimes called Neo-Taoism because of the mixing of the two philosophies.

In the seventh century under the control of the T'ang dynasty, Taoism became the state religion, the *Tao Te Ching* and the *Chuang Tzu* became the sanctioned Taoist canon, and official mystic colleges opened in which to study these books. Ten centuries later China's Mongol ruler ordered all Taoist books burned, with the exception of the *Tao Te Ching*. China's numerous rulers obviously recognized the wisdom of this small book.

These influential Taoist texts teach that the Tao is everywhere, always. It is an inexhaustible supply of life-giving and life-sustaining forces and is entirely responsible for the way things are.

The Tao has two aspects: being and Nonbeing. Being is the Tao's visible and nameable aspect and is responsible for producing the myriad creatures, the earth, the order of the universe, and all that can be seen. Nonbeing is the Tao's indescribable and invisible aspect, the "Eternal, Unvarying, Absolute Tao, the all-embracing first principle for all things" (Welch), and the Something Else behind the universe's order and upon which it is dependent.

The Tao is manifested in many ways, one being its ceaseless motion and its cyclical pattern of change. "Unvaryingly the wheel turns; what goes up must come down. Victories lead in the end to defeat, force to weakness, laws to lawlessness, good to evil" (Welch). This is because any extreme movement in one direction brings about a corresponding but opposite result, somewhat like the movement of a pendulum, as discussed in chapter seven.

The *Tao Te Ching* refers to this cyclical pattern: "Turning back is how the way moves; Weakness is the means the way employs. The myriad creatures in the world are born from being, and being from Nonbeing" (40.88-89)*. *Turning back* is a reference to the cycle of human events, to the notion that all things in the universe eventually return to nonbeing, to the return of the Taoist to his natural state, and to Nonbeing itself.

It is this return to Nonbeing and the process involved in doing so that makes Taoism such a mystical philosophy. In returning to our natural state, we return to our original nature. In this state we perceive the oneness of all things, and the nonexistence of absolutes, polarity and material objects. In this state, there is simply consciousness or Nonbeing. This sort of experience is experiential rather than intellectual or sensory and tends to be indescribable. It is felt or perceived in the inner realm rather than seen, touched, thought, or spoken about.

The indescribable nature of this experience is true also of the Tao itself. "The way that can be spoken of [is not the constant way" (1.1), for "the way is for ever nameless" (32.72). Though the Tao is nameless, we give it names so that we can speak about it. In the *Tao Te Ching*, we find such names for the Tao as great, silent, void, indistinct, shadowy, evanescent, rarefied, the shape that has no shape, the image that is without substance, the one, the way, and the mother of the world. These names do not say what the Tao is but only say what it is like, for ultimately it is beyond or above description.

The ideas presented in the Taoist canon attempt to make known the two aspects of the Tao: being, the changing universe, and Nonbeing, the unchanging laws that underlie it. These two aspects are exemplified by the Two Great Powers—the *yin* and the *yang*, the means by which the creative force of the Tao manifests in the world. Originally, yin and yang referred, respectively, to the shady and sunny sides of a mountain. The yin/yang symbol is called *T'ai-chi Tzu* which translates as "Diagram of the Supreme Ultimate."

---

* All references to the *Tao Te Ching* are from D.C. Lau's translation.

The symbol indicates a rotational symmetry indicative of continuous cyclic movement. Thus, the changes in nature are simply the interaction between the polar opposites.

Reminiscent of the Hermetic principle of polarity discussed in chapter seven, the yin and yang are two aspects of the same power. They represent the basic oppositions; e.g., active and passive, light and dark, positive and negative, dry and moist, male and female. These opposites interact in such a way that we perceive them as dualistic, thus giving rise to inner conflict. It is an important function of life to understand these opposites and to keep them balanced. Such harmony is achieved only when we are able to adapt and adjust to all the circumstances we face in life. This is the first attitude we must incorporate in following the Tao.

The *Chuang Tzu* says, "life and death are the same story, . . . acceptable and unacceptable are on a single string" (Sec. 5).* This book contends that such concepts as good and bad or right and wrong are based on nothing more than each individual's distinct point of view. All views are thus relative.

Since there are as many views as there are people to hold them, acknowledging that there is no single "right" view allows for the acceptance of a higher viewpoint. Seeing from this higher viewpoint is seeing from "the light of Heaven" (Yu-lan), which means that things are seen from a point of view which transcends the finite and is the point of view of the Tao. From this viewpoint, things do not have subjective meanings; rather, they just are what they are.

The *Chuang Tzu* is filled with humorous anecdotes, the purpose being somewhat analogous to Jesus's parables—teaching through storytelling. One such story is called "Three in the Morning" and illustrates the relativity or subjectivity of all judgments.

* All references to the *Chuang Tzu* are from Burton Watson's translation.

When the monkey trainer was handing out acorns, he said, "You get three in the morning and four at night." This made all the monkeys furious. "Well, then," he said, "you get four in the morning and three at night." The monkeys were all delighted. There was no change in the reality behind the words, and yet the monkeys responded with joy and anger. Let them, if they want to . . . (Sec. 2).

As Chuang Tzu's monkeys show us, keeping to a certain viewpoint at the expense of another has nothing to do with the reality of any situation. Things are how they are whether we see them that way or not. When we have Tao at our center, we can see things in perspective, for our view is based on *what is*.

The one who is following the Tao also incorporates an attitude of accepting or yielding to what is, rather than wishing for what is not, or how it is thought it ought to be. The *Tao Te Ching* uses the analogy of water to illustrate the concept of yielding. Water remains clear as long as nothing is mixed with it and smooth if nothing agitates it. Water always takes the path of least resistance but if it is blocked, it loses its natural tendency to flow. And though it is unresisting, it is one of the strongest elements on earth. It can erode great canyons in the earth, and when it freezes, it can crack large boulders.

In the world there is nothing more submissive and weak than water. Yet for attacking that which is hard and strong nothing can surpass it. This is because there is nothing that can take its place (78.186).

The highest motive is to be like water: water is essential to all life, yet it does not demand a fee or proclaim its importance. Rather, it flows humbly to the lowest level, and in so doing it is much like Tao (8.20).

The reason why the River and the Sea are able to be king of the hundred valleys is that they excel in taking the lower position (66.159).

Though the analogy for yielding used in the *Tao Te Ching* is physical, the lesson to be learned is psychological. That is, yielding is a behavior, an attitude, or an acceptance. The Taoist accepts that there are unchangeable laws in Nature and unchangeable traits in human nature, and does not try to change what is unchangeable. He or she understands that "force defeats itself, [e]very action produces a re-action, every challenge a response" (Welch). Lao Tzu offers wise advice. He tells us that "[t]o yield is to be preserved whole . . . Because the wise man does not contend no one can contend against him" (22.50c). And that it is best to ignore challenges, for "[t]he soft over-comes the hard and the weak the strong" (36.79a).

The next sentiment to incorporate in following the Tao is the attitude of doing nothing. This "doing nothing" can be taken as doing less and as thinking less.

Taken in the sense of doing less, "doing nothing" is activity that is necessary and natural. *Necessary* means doing what must be done in order to attain the Tao. *Natural* means going about the business of living with simplicity, spontaneity and genuineness. This necessary and natural activity is known as *wu wei*. Because too much of anything can be harmful; e.g., too much food often results in an abundance of body fat, too much exercise can result in sore muscles and damaged ligaments, too much dependence on other people results in laziness and hostility, the Tao teaches a sort of moderation in all things.

This natural activity of doing less is symbolized by *p'u*—the uncarved block. P'u refers to wood in its natural, uncarved and un-painted condition and is the Taoist symbol for man's natural state, the state of innocence, plainness and simplicity, "when his inborn powers [*te*] have not been tampered with by knowledge or circumscribed by morality." The uncarved block is a state of pure consciousness in which you "see without looking, hear without listening, know without thinking" (Waley).

The uncarved block is simple and natural. It "is in a state as yet untouched by the artificial interference of human ingenuity and so is a symbol of the original state of man before desire is produced in him by artificial means" (Lau). It is an internal state, a state achieved by stilling the mind and contemplating the obscure, the "secrets" of the Tao. Unencumbered by desires, possessions, judgments, and limits, the uncarved block represents a state of freedom or heaven, the ulti-mate goal of all practitioners of Taoism. As can be seen, the Taoist's heaven is not a place nor is it a post-mortem experience; rather, it is, or can be, our life in the present. Experiencing heaven depends on whether we are following the Tao. The path of life can be free (heaven) or it can remain bound by limits, judgments and suffering (a Western term would be "hell").

The Taoist heaven—the secret, simple and natural inner nature exemplified by the uncarved block—is an extension of the nature of the universe. Since there is harmony in the universe, when we are in touch with our inner nature, we are in harmony with our own self and everything else.

The other sense of "doing nothing" has to do with the inactivity of the mind. Wu wei means that not only do we do things in a natural and necessary manner, but that we restrict our thinking. Wu wei involves letting go of the noise in the conscious mind. We stop thinking and open up to the quiet of the intuitive or obscure and listen. This type of "doing nothing" is exemplified by the practice of meditation.

When the mind is quiet, when it is emptied of all thoughts and distractions, when we become empty, we are able to "see" our inner nature, become aware of our self, and really know our self. We discover that we are part of the whole, that our inner nature flows from the nature of the Universe. So, inasmuch as the Universe is part of the Tao, we, too, are part of the Tao.

Often when we first attempt the second sense of doing nothing, "sitting but racing around" occurs. This phrase refers to the sitting of the body and the racing of the mind. Anyone who has practiced meditation knows of this situation. It is not always easy to turn off the noise in our minds. But it is the sitting of the mind as well as the body that results in wu wei. Lao Tzu says, "One who knows does not speak; one who speaks does not know" (56.128), and "Without stirring abroad One can know the whole world; Without looking out of the window One can see the way of heaven. The further one goes, The less one knows" (47.106). "Knowing the whole world without stirring" and "knowing less the further one goes" are references to the thinking less aspect of wu wei. We do not have to go outside of ourselves to know nor to know *more*. We simply have to listen to our inner self, to get in touch with our inner nature. It is through such introspection or contemplation of the inner self that we gain an understanding of the simple principles of the Tao.

Blending of the Philosophies

In Chinese Buddhism, Sudden Enlightenment is known as the "vision of the Tao," and is an awareness of being one with the Tao. But since the Tao cannot be known, Sudden Enlightenment involves an awareness of the unknowable, or emptiness. This emptiness is not a void, however. It is a state without distinctions, without any sense of separateness.

It is from the Madhyamika school of Buddhism that the intuitive or mystical branches developed. The word that means "the meditation that leads to insight" in Sanskrit is *dhyana,* in Chinese is *ch'an,* and in Japanese is *zen.* The blending of India's Mahayana Buddhism with China's Taoism resulted in Ch'anism, more popularly known by its Japanese transliteration—Zen Buddhism.

Ch'anism was founded in the sixth century C.E. by Bodhi-dharma, an Indian Buddhist born near Madras who traveled to China, met the emperor Wu, and joined the Shao-lin monastery.

Ch'anism or Zen is simply our common daily thoughts, though those thoughts work under different principles than normally understood. They are "more satisfying, more peaceful, more full of joy than anything you ever experienced before. The tone of life [is] altered" (Suzuki).

The goal of Zen is knowledge of one's own nature. It is a search for self. This kind of knowledge is not intellectual, it is spiritual and mystical. It is the knowledge in which the knower and the known are the same. It is, quite literally, an inside job.

Zen consciousness is all around us waiting to be seen. It is we who are blind to it. This is why the actual attainment of Zen can only be accomplished from within. "All the causes, all the conditions of *satori* are in the mind; they are merely waiting for the maturing." Satori is awakening to the truth of our self and is comparable to the mystical experience of Western traditions.

One of the methods used in Zen to bring about satori is the *koan.* Koans are apparently nonsensical riddles or questions, the answers to which cannot be comprehended by analytical thought. For example, Alan Watts quotes the following three questions and answers, known as "Huang-lung's Three Barriers," submitted by Huang-lung (1002-1069) to his prospective students:

Q: Everybody has a place of birth. Where is your place of birth?
A: Early this morning I ate white rice gruel. Now I'm hungry again.

Q: How is my hand like the Buddha's hand?
A: Playing the lute under the moon.

Q: How is my foot like a donkey's foot?
A: When the white heron stands in the snow it has a different color.

At first glance the answers seem totally unrelated to the questions. However, one who has developed Zen consciousness will see the relationship. Evan Harris Walker provides an excellent interpretation of this relationship. As to the answer to the first question, Walker says that regardless of the actual physical location of our birth, each morning upon awakening our consciousness comes into being. Further, we are constantly being born "in each moment's hunger, each moment's joy, each moment's sight of the visions around [us]."

To the second question he explains that playing the lute under the moon refers to doingness. Our hand is like Buddha's hand when we are conscious of our experience each moment and of our hand as an experience, not as an object.

The third answer is similar to the second. Our foot is like a donkey's foot in seeing the foot as a part of the experience.

Walker further explains:

The answer does not lie in the words, it lies in the experience that is the totality of being. The consciousness that is the true reality is the same thing whether it looks upon a foot that looks like another form or looks upon a colorless bird that becomes another experience when it stands in the colorless field of snow. The idea of Zen and the reality that is consciousness being are simple. It is an immediate part of you.

Thus, Zen is totally experiential.

Paradox

The Hindu, Buddhist and Taoist classics set forth the same paradoxes found in all mystical writings. Tao, Brahman, or the One is nowhere yet everywhere, is nothing yet everything, has names but cannot be named.

Paradox also can be found in the two types of truth theorized by the Middle Path of Chinese Buddhism (also known as the School of Emptiness): truth in the common sense and truth in the higher sense. This theory of double truth is divided into three levels.

On the first level, the common sense truth is the understanding that all things are *yu* (they have being and are existent), and the higher sense truth is understanding that all things are *wu* (have no being and are nonexistent).

On the second level, awareness of things as yu is seen as one-sided, as is awareness of things as wu. Since they are both one-sided, people are left thinking that wu (nonexistence) occurs only when there is no yu (existence), when in reality, yu is coincident with wu. So, on this level, common sense truth is understanding that all things are both yu and wu (existence and nonexistence), and higher sense truth is the understanding that things are neither yu nor wu.

On the third level, there is an understanding that claiming things are neither yu nor wu means that distinctions must be made, and since all distinctions are one-sided, nothing can be said at all. This is the higher sense truth.

This kind of logic is called *paradoxical logic*. In paradoxical logic it is possible for A to be non-A at the same moment. Paradoxical logic is Eastern in origin and is found mainly in Chinese and Indian philosophy, though Heraclitus uses it in portions of his philosophy, and Hegel and Marx use it in their dialectics.

Most of us in the West are educated with Aristotelian logic, consisting of three basic laws. The law of identity says that A is A. The law of contradiction holds that A is not non-A. The law of the excluded middle says that A is not both A and non-A, neither A nor non-A. Thus, the same thing (A) cannot both be and not be (A and non-A) nor neither A nor non-A at the same time. Our minds have not been conditioned to accept A and non-A as valid for the same subject at the same time. Such is not the case, however, in the logic of the East.

We have seen that in Hinduism, Brahman is the ultimate supreme God. Walter T. Stace sets forth the three aspects of the paradox surrounding Brahman. The first aspect is that Brahman has qualities yet doesn't have qualities. The *Upanishads* state that "Self is to be described as not this, not that." An early translation states that "Self is to be described by 'No! No!'" So, no matter what quality is suggested, the answer always is "No." Is he matter? No. Is he spirit? No. Is he infinite? No. Is he eternal? No. Is he good? No. Is he evil? No.

The second aspect of the paradox is that Brahman is both personal and impersonal. He is the self. Both *he* and *self* imply personalness. Brahman is also referred to as "It" and is impersonal and mindless.

The third aspect of the paradox is that Brahman is both active and inactive in creating, guiding and controlling the world. It also is silent and unmoving. "That One, though never stirring, is swifter than thought; though standing still, it overtakes those who run. It moves and it moves not" (*Upanishads*, qtd. in Stace).

The *Bhagavad Gita* sums up these three aspects of Hindu paradox: "He is beyond all, and yet he supports all. He is invisible: he cannot be seen. He is far and he is near, he moves and he moves not, he is within all and he is outside all" (13.15).

The *Mandukya Upanishad* explains the paradoxes concerning Brahman.

> OM. The eternal Word is all: what was, what is, and what shall be, and what beyond is in eternity. All is OM. Brahman is all and Atman is Brahman. . . . Atman in His own pure state [is] the awakened life of supreme consciousness. It is neither outer nor inner consciousness, neither semiconsciousness nor sleeping consciousness, neither mere consciousness nor unconsciousness. He is Atman, the Spirit Himself, that cannot be seen or touched, that is above all distinctions, beyond thought and ineffable. In the union with Him is the supreme proof of His reality. He is peace and love (qtd. in *Bhagavad Gita*).

So, Brahman is Atman, both the mindless and the self. Brahman is "the eternal Word," or OM (the combination of the sounds symbolic of the Hindu Trimurti, more accurately written as *aum*). Atman is outward-moving consciousness and inner-moving consciousness, silent consciousness, and none of these.

We saw that the Tao is one and not-one, Being and Nonbeing, active and passive, male and female, yin and yang. The *Tao Te Ching* tells us that "in order to observe the Tao's secrets, desire must be eliminated, yet in order to observe the Tao's manifestations, desires are necessary" (1.3), and in following the Tao, "the closer one gets, the further away they seem to be" (47.106).

In Buddhism, we saw that there are common sense truth and higher sense truth, and these truths are found on three levels. On the first level, we see that all things have being and are existent, and are nonbeing and nonexistent. On the second level, we see that things either exist or don't exist, or they neither exist nor don't exist. On the third level, we see that nothing can be said about the existence or nonexistence of things.

Paradox cannot be understood at the thinking level. It can only be understood on an intuitive or experiential level. Such understanding comes as a flash of insight, a "Zen moment" or an "A-ha! I get it!" experience that leaves consciousness as quickly as it enters. For one brief moment all apparent paradoxes are understood. Thinking about it and trying to analyze it does not work. Only by letting the mind flow freely and by allowing the space for intuitions and thoughts from the inner self to pass in and out can an understanding be gained.

From the previous discussions it can be seen that while Hinduism, Buddhism and Taoism are highly intellectual, they are concerned with intuitive wisdom rather than rational knowledge. All three philosophies, in fact all mystical philosophies, view the intellect as a means to an end. Its role is simply to release all concepts and ideas and make room for the mystical experience, for the Tao can only be comprehended in the silence, when the undisciplined mind has ceased its incessant chatter.

Parallels With New Thought

The common concepts about God that are held by the New Thought groups are:

- God is Spirit, Mind or Intelligence
- God is Good, Wise, Loving, etc.
- There is only God and God is always present
- God is the Creator of all that exists and creates from within Itself
- God is a Triune Being
- God is impersonal and impartial

What do Hinduism, Buddhism and Taoism say about these concepts? These three philosophies teach of a monistic Absolute or Ultimate Reality. In Hinduism it is called *Brahman* (The Supreme) or *Tat* (That One). In Buddhism it is *Sunyata* (Emptiness) or *Tathata* (Suchness). And in Taoism it is the *Tao* (the Way). As we have seen, the word Emptiness does not mean "nothing" but relates to the sense of self-abandonment or of going beyond the finite self and realizing the oneness of all.

The methods for achieving this sense of oneness vary among the groups, but going into the silence is integral to all. The One or the Tao is the creator of the ten thousand things (the universe). It resides within all humans and in nature; indeed it is the laws of nature. It is not a person but is a mystical, undefinable, unknowable, underlying principle behind all things. The Buddhist *Lankavatara Sutra* tells us that the visible world is Mind or Universal Mind. The One thinks or contemplates all things into existence. Later forms of Hinduism and Buddhism speak of three aspects of the One. In Hinduism the Trimurti consists of Brahma—the uncreated creator, Vishnu—the maintainer or preserver of the universe, and Shiva—the destroyer of evil. In Buddhism the trinity consists of the Three Treasures: Buddha—the Ultimate Being ever present in all living things; Dharma or Dhamma—the Law of Righteousness; and Sañgha—the monastic orders, though Mahayana Buddhism includes all believers in the third treasure.

Is God good, wise and loving? In Taoism we cannot distinguish between good and not-good. But the *Tao Te Ching* tells us that the Tao gives life to all things, "rears them; Brings them up and nurses them; Brings them to fruition and maturity; Feeds and shelters them" (51.115). That certainly sounds like goodness and love. The *Tao Te Ching* also states that the one who is following the Tao is wise, so by implication, the Tao is also wise. The *Rig Veda* says "God gives wisdom to the simple; and leadeth the wise unto the path of good" (VII.86.7). Buddha spoke much of wisdom and love. In fact, he was called the Compassionate Buddha.

Two of the common concepts held by the New Thought groups concerning humanity parallel the teachings of these Eastern philosophies—the concepts that we are created in God's image and likeness, imparting to us a divine and good nature; and that our thoughts, attitudes and beliefs produce our experience. The Buddha taught that we all contain the buddha-nature, the divine nature of the One and that our rightful state is one of pure bliss. He taught eight right thoughts, actions or behaviors that lead to the realization of this state. The seventh, right mindfulness, states that our thoughts create what we are and what we experience. Hinduism teaches that Brahman and Atman are one, that we are all inherently divine and that by the law of karma all we experience is a result of our thoughts and behaviors. Taoism teaches that our natural inner state is that of freedom or heaven, words synonymous with divinity and goodness. Chuang Tzu teaches that we make our own suffering and bondage, and that we can choose heaven instead. All three philosophies emphasize that as long as we believe that we are other than divine and that we are all separate, we will experience a world of pain and suffering.

The final two parallels involve the concepts concerning heaven, hell, evil, and sin. These three philosophies consider these terms in the same manner as New Thought. Neither heaven nor hell are places, but are states of mind and attitudes that are experienced in the present life. Evil and sin are merely results of human actions on the temporal plane, and are thus maya—the illusions or effects of our ignorance.

The vedantist considers sin as any act that alienates or separates us from the Reality within us. For both the vedantist and the Buddhist, sin (ignorance of our true self) results in continuous rebirths. And because we are reborn as many times as needed to reach nirvana, there is nowhere in these philosophies for hell except in our minds and our experiences in the present life.

The *Bhagavad Gita* describes hell as the experience of our having been "[l]ed astray by many wrong thoughts, entangled in the net of delusion, [and] enchained to the pleasures of their cravings" (16. 16). When we are not bound by external things and are experiencing everlasting joy and gladness because our soul is united with Brahman, we experience heaven.

We have seen that Taoism teaches that freedom is heaven and is our natural state, a state that can be attained during our earthly life. Taoism also emphasizes that considerations of things as being good or evil are merely relative attitudes and beliefs. But there is a moral law that governs the entire universe. This law is cause and effect or karma—what we think, say and do today affects us tomorrow and may also affect our next life. The pesky problem of evil discussed in philosophical circles is resolved by this law, for God is not responsible for the evil we experience in the world. We are. The *Bhagavad Gita* says, "It is greedy desire and wrath, born of passion, the great evil, the sum of destruction: this is the enemy of the soul" (3.37).

Aldous Huxley writes:

> Pain and evil are inseparable from individual existence in a world of time; and, for human beings, there is an intensification of this inevitable pain and evil when the desire is turned towards the self and the man, rather than towards the divine Ground.... [G]ood is the separate self's conformity to, and finally annihilation in, the divine Ground which gives it being; evil [is] the intensification of separateness, the refusal to know that the Ground exists. The crimes which are everywhere forbidden proceed from states of mind.

Mohandas Gandhi (1869-1948), one of the most well-known practitioners of Hinduism, also provides a solution for the problem of evil. He says that because all is One and One is good, we consist of inherent goodness, as does everything. Therefore, evil must be unreal and illusory. The movie based on his life quotes Gandhi as saying that the only devils in this world are the ones running around in our own mind. Thus, evil is not real of itself but is the result of the kind of thoughts that reside in our mind.

So, we can see that most, but not all, of the sixteen common concepts held among the New Thought groups are taught by the Eastern philosophies of Hinduism, Buddhism and Taoism. Our next excursion takes us to the numerous parallels between these philosophies and the teachings of Jesus.

XII.

MERGING ROADS

The painful secret of gods and kings is that men are free, Aegistheus.
You know it and they do not.
Jean-Paul Sartre (1905–1980)
French novelist, philosopher, dramatist, and political activist
Jupiter in The Flies

There are numerous correlations between the teachings of Jesus and those of the three Eastern philosophies presented in the last two chapters. The following chart comparing the sayings of these four philosophies is not meant to be exhaustive, but sets forth only a sampling of the parallel teachings that I discovered during my studies.

The sayings of Jesus are from the *Holy Bible* and the Gnostic gospels.

The Hindu sayings are from the *Bhagavad Gita* (BG), *Brihadaranyaka Upanishad* (BU), *Rig Veda* (RV), *Katha Upanishad* (KU), *Chandogya Upanishad* (CU), *Yuddha Kanda* (YK), *Aranya Kanda* (AK), *Tandya Maha Brahmana* (TMB), *Srimad Bhagavatam* (SB), *Laws of Manu* (LM), *Apastamba Dharma Sutra* (AD), *Garuda Purana* (GP), and *Anusasana Parva* (AP).

Buddha's sayings are from the *Gandhari Dharmapada* (GDh), *Udanavarga* (Ud), *Dhammapada* (Dh), *Digha Nikaya* (DN), *Vinaya Mahavagga* (VM), *Majihima Nikaya* (MN), *Mahaparinirvana Sutra* (MS), *Itivuttaka* (It), *Sutta Nipata* (SuN), *Perfection of Wisdom in Eight Thousand Lines* (PW), *Guide to the Bodhisattva' s Way of Life* (GBW), *Sutra of Hui Neng* (HN), and *Mahaparinibhanasutta* (MB).

The Taoist sayings are from the *Tao Te Ching* (TTC), *Chuang Tzu* (CT), *I Ching* (IC), *Tract of the Quiet Way* (TQW), and the *Treatise on Response and Retribution* (TR).

Jesus	Hinduism
Do not lay up for yourselves treasures upon earth, where moth and rust destroy, and where thieves break in and steal. But lay up for yourselves treasures in heaven, where neither moth nor rust destroys, and where thieves do not break in or steal; for where your treasure is, there will your heart be also. (Matt. 6:19-21)	The man who sees Brahman abides in Brahman: his reason is steady, gone is his delusion. . . . He is not bound by things without, and within he finds inner gladness. His soul is one in Brahman and he attains everlasting joy. For the pleasures that come from the world bear in them sorrows to come. They come and they go, they are transient: not in them do the wise find joy. (BG 5.20-22)
I am telling you, love your enemies, bless those who curse you, pray for those who mistreat you. (Matt. 5:44)	The man whose love is the same for his enemies or his friends, he is dear to me. (BG 12.17-18)
Truly I say to you, to the extent that you did it to one of these brothers of Mine, *even the least of them*, you did it to Me. (Matt. 25:40)	When a man sees that the God in himself is the same God in all that is, he hurts not himself by hurting others. (BG 13.28) When a person responds to the joys and sorrows of others as if they were his own, he has attained th highest state of spiritual union. (BG 32)
You shall love your neighbor as yourself. (Matt. 22:39)	Let your aims be common, and your hearts of one accord, and all of you be of one mind, so you may live well together. (RV 10.191.4

Buddhism	Taoism
In this world the wise man holds onto faith and wisdom. Those are his greatest treasures; all other riches he pushes aside. (Ud 10:9)	He who is attached to things will suffer much. He who saves will suffer heavy loss. (TTC 44.100) Fill your bowl to the brim and it will spill. Keep sharpening your knife and it will blunt. Chase after money and security and your heart will never unclench. Care about people's approval and you will be their prisoner. Do your work, then step back. This is the only path to serenity. (TTC 9.23)
Happily shall I live without hostility among the hostile; among the hostile live without hostility. (GDh 167)	[D]o good to him who has done you an injury. (TTC 63.148)
Whosoever does no harm to living creatures, whosoever does not kill or participate in killing, is to be called a holy man. (Ud 33.45) If you do not tend to one another, then who is there to tend you? Whoever would tend me, he should tend the sick. (VM 8.26.3)	
O let us live in joy, free of hatred, among the spiteful; among the spiteful let us live without hatred. (Dh 15.1)	Love the world as your self; then you can care for all things. (TTC 13.31)

Jesus	Hinduism
The lamp of the body is the eye. If your eye is good your whole body will be full of light. But if it is bad your whole body will be full of darkness. If the light in you is darkness, how great is that darkness. (Matt. 6:22-23) Your eye is the lamp of your body; when your eye is sound, your whole body is full of light; but when it is not sound, your body is full of darkness. Therefore be careful lest the light in you be darkness. If then your whole body is full of light, having no part dark, it will be wholly bright, as when a lamp with its rays gives you light. (Luke 11:34-36)	Out of compassion for them, I, dwelling in their hearts, destroy with the shining lamp of knowledge the darkness born of ignorance. (BG 10.11) As one not knowing that a golden treasure lies buried beneath his feet may walk over it again and again, yet never find it, so all beings live every moment in the city of Brahman, yet never find him because of the veil of illusion by which he is concealed. (CU 8.3.2)
I am the door; if anyone enters through Me, he will be saved, and will go in and out and find pasture. (John 10:9)	Leave all things behind, and come to me for thy salvation. I will make thee free from the bondage of sins. Fear no more. (BG 18.66)
If anyone loves Me, he will keep my word; and My Father will love him, and We will come to him, and make Our abode with him. (John 14:23)	He who in oneness of love, loves me in whatever he sees, wherever this man may live, in truth this man lives in me. (BG 6.31) Only by love can men see me, and know me, and come unto me. (BG 11.54)

Buddhism	Taoism
Just as a lotus blossom, scented and beautiful, can blossom on a dunghill at the side of a road, so too radiates the wisdom of the Buddha's pupils who have realized the Dharma, while normal mortals are blind. (GDh 303-304) Every being has the Buddha Nature. This is the self. Such a self is, since the very beginning, under cover of innumerable illusions. That is why a man cannot see it. (MS 214)	My light is the light of sun and moon. My life is the life of Heaven and Earth. Before me all is nebulous; behind me all is dark, unknown. Men may all die, but I endure for ever. (CT, "On Tolerance")
Thus, O monks, is the Doctrine well taught by me . . . all those who have merely faith and love toward me are sure of Paradise hereafter. (MN, Sutta 22)	Nowadays, all living things spring from the dust and to the dust return. But I will lead you through the portals of Eternity to wander in the great wilds of Infinity. (CT, "On Tolerance")
	To those who have conformed themselves to the Way, the Way readily lends its power. To those who have conformed themselves to the power, the power readily lends more power. (TTC 23)

Jesus	Hinduism
Give, and it will be given to you... for the measure you give will be the measure you get back. (Luke 6:38) . . . freely you received, freely give. (Matt. 10:8)	He who gives liberally goes straight to the gods; on the high ridge of heaven he stands exalted. (RV 1.125.5)
Do not judge lest you be judged. For in the way you judge, you will be judged; and by your standard of measure, it will be measured to you. (Matt. 7:1-2)	
For if you love those who love you what reward have you? (Matt. 5:46) And as you would that men would do to you, do you also to them likewise. . . . Love your enemies and do good, and lend, hoping for nothing again. (Luke 6:31, 35)	A superior being does not render evil for evil; this is a maxim one should observe; the ornament of virtuous persons is their conduct. One should never harm the wicked or the good or even criminals meriting death. A noble soul will ever exercise compassion even towards those who enjoy injuring others or those of cruel deeds when they are actually committing them—for who is without fault? (YK 115)

Buddhism	Taoism
Conquer anger by love. Conquer evil by good. Conquer the stingy by giving. Conquer the liar by truth. (Dh 223) If beings knew, as I know, the fruit of sharing gifts, they would not enjoy their use without sharing them, nor would the taint of stinginess obsess the heart and stay there. Even if it were their last bit, their last morsel of food, they would not enjoy its use without sharing it, if there were anyone to receive it. (It 18)	The Way of heaven is like drawing a bow; the high is lowered, the low is raised, excess is reduced, need is fulfilled. The Way of heaven reduces excess and fills need, but the way of humans is not so; they strip the needy to serve those who have too much. (TTC 77)
Judge not the mistakes of others, neither what they do or leave undone, but judge your own deeds, that just and the unjust. (GDh 271-272)	
Surmount hatred by not hating, surmount evil with good; surmount greed through generosity, surmount lies with truth; speak what is true, do not succumb to anger, give when you are asked. Through those three steps you will come close to the gods. (GDh 280-281)	I treat those who are good with goodness, And I also treat those who are not good with goodness. (TTC 49.111) Do good to him who has done you an injury. (TTC 63) It is only when one does not have enough faith in others that others will have no faith in him. (TTC 17)

Jesus	Hinduism
In the beginning was the Word, and the Word was with God, and the Word was God. All things came into being by Him and apart from Him nothing came into being that has come into being. (John 1:1, 3)	I go for refuge to that Eternal Spirit from whom the stream of creation came at the beginning. (BG 15.4) I am the beginning, the middle and the end of all beings. (BG 10.20) This, [in the beginning] was the only Lord of the Universe. His Word was with him. This Word was his second. He contemplated. He said, "I will deliver this Word so that she will produce and bring into being all this world. (TMB 20.14.2)
[Evil] is powerful because we have not recognized it. . . . Ignorance is the mother of all evil. . . . The word said, "If you know the truth, the truth will make you free." Ignorance is a slave. Knowledge is freedom. (Gospel of Philip) You will know the truth, and the truth will make you free. (John 8:32)	O son of Bharata, the mode of ignorance causes the delusion of all living entities. The result of this mode is madness, indolence and sleep, which bind the conditioned soul. (BG 14.8) That disciplined man with joy and light within, becomes one with God and reaches the freedom that is God's. (BG 5.24)
Do to others as you would have them do to you. (Luke 6:31)	One should not behave towards others in a way which is disagreeable to oneself. This is the essence of morality. All other activities are due to selfish desire. (AP 113.8)

Buddhism	Taoism
	In the beginning was the Tao. All things issue from it; all things return to it. (TTC 52.117)
When a man is free from all sense pleasures and depends on nothingness he is free in the supreme freedom from perception. He will stay there and not return again. (SuN 1072)	
Consider others as yourself. (Dh 10:1)	The sage does not distinguish between himself and the world; the needs of other people are as his own. (TTC 49)

Jesus	Hinduism
Truly, truly, I say to you, he who hears My word, and believes Him who sent Me, has eternal life, and does not come into judgment, but has passed out of death into life. (John 5:24)	For this is my word of promise, that he who loves me shall not perish. (BG 9.31) The supreme Lord who pervades all existence, the true Self of all creatures, may be realized through undivided love. (BG 8.22)
He who believes in the son has eternal life. (John 3:36)	But even dearer to me are those . . . who come to the waters of Everlasting Life. (BG 12.20)
He who believes to know the All but not himself falls completely short. (Gospel of Thomas)	To anyone who leaves behind this world without having recognized his own real world, that is of as little use as the Veda he has not studied or some work he has avoided. (BU)
I and the Father are One. (John 10:30)	The man of vision and I are one. (BG 7.18)

Buddhism	Taoism
By faith you shall be free and go beyond the world of death. (SuN 1146)	Men flow into life, and ebb into death. Some are filled with life; some are empty with death; some hold fast to life, and thereby perish, For life is an abstraction. Those who are filled with life Need not fear tigers and rhinos in the wilds, Nor wear armour and shields in battle; The rhinoceros finds no place in them for its horn, The tiger no place for its claw, The soldier no place for a weapon, For death finds no place in them. (TTC 50)
	Being in accord with Tao, he is everlasting. (TTC 16)
	Those that live their full life in Tao achieve realization of their nature in inaction. Hence the saying 'Fish lose themselves (are happy) in water; man loses himself (is happy) in Tao.' (CT, "The Great Supreme")
Every being has the Buddha Nature. This is the self. The nature of self is nothing but the undis-closed storehouse of the Tathagata.(MS 214, 220)

Tathagata [is] . . . Suchness. There is no division within Suchness. Just simply one single is this Suchness, not two, nor three. (PW 31.1) | Tung-kuo Tzu asked Chuang Tzu, "What is called Tao – where is it?" "It is everywhere," replied Chuang Tzu. . . . Nothing escapes from Tao. (CT 22) |

Jesus	Hinduism
Jesus saith unto him, I am the way, the truth, and the life. (John 14:6) I have come as Light into the world. (John 12:46) Jesus spoke to them, saying "I am the light of the world; he who follows me will not walk in darkness, but will have the light of life." (John 8.12)	I am the Way (BG 9.18), Life (BG 7.6) and Light. (BG 11.47, 13.17)) Whenever truth is forgotten in the world, and wickedness prevails, the Lord of Love becomes flesh to show the way, the truth, and the life to humanity. Such an incarnation is an avatar, an embodiment of God on earth. (SB 1.1) I [Krishna] am the goal of the wise man, and I am the way. I am his prosperity. I am his heaven. There is nothing dearer to him than I. (SB 11.12)
Come to Me, all who are weary and heavy-laden, and I will give you rest. Take My yoke upon you and learn from Me, for I am gentle and humble in heart; and you shall find rest for your souls. (Matt. 11:28-29)	I am the goal, the sustainer, the master, the witness, the abode, the refuge and the most dear friend. I am the creation and the annihilation, the basis of everything, the resting place and the eternal seed. (BG 9.18)

Buddhism	Taoism
It is wonderful, Lord! It is wonderful, Lord! It is as if, Lord, one might set upright that which had been upturned, or might reveal what was hidden, or might point out the path to one who had gone astray, or might bring an oil lamp into the darkness so that those with eyes might see material shapes. (Ud 49)	
Just as a deep lake is clear and still, even so, on hearing the teachings and realizing them, the wise become exceedingly peaceful. (Dh 82) He who has gone for refuge to the Buddha [the teacher], the Dhamma [the teaching], and the Sangha [the taught], sees with right knowledge the Four Noble Truths . . . This, indeed, is refuge secure. By seeking such refuge one is released from all sorrow. (Dh 188-192)	The Tao is the refuge for the myriad creatures. It is that by which the good man protects, and that by which the bad is protected. (TTC 62)

Jesus	Hinduism
Do you not know me, Philip? He who has seen me has seen the Father; how can you say, "Show us the Father?" Do you not believe that I am in the Father and the Father in me? (John 14:9-10)	To love is to know Me, My innermost nature, The truth that I am. (BG 18.55)
But many who are first will be last; and the last, first. (Matt. 19:30) Whoever exalts himself will be humbled, and whoever humbles himself will be exalted. (Matt. 23:12, Luke 18:14) But it shall not be so among you; but whosoever will be great among you, let him be your minister; And whosoever will be chief among you, let him be your servant: Even as the Son of man came not to be ministered unto, but to minister. (Matt. 20:26-28)	A brahmin should ever shrink from honor as from poison, and should always be desirous of disrespect as if of ambrosia. (LM 2.162)
Think not that I have come to abolish the law and the prophets; I have not come to abolish them but to fulfil them. For truly, I say to you, till heaven and earth pass away, not an iota, not a dot, will pass from the law until all is accomplished. (Matt. 5.17-18)	Whenever the Law declines and the purpose of life is forgotten, I manifest myself on earth. I am born in every age to protect the good, to destroy evil, and to reestablish the Law. (BG 4.7-8)

Buddhism	Taoism
The fool who knows that he is a fool is for that very reason a wise man; the fool who thinks he is wise is called a fool indeed. (Dh 63)	[T]he Sage puts his person last and it comes first. (TTC 7) To know when one does not know is best. To think one knows when one does not know is a dire disease. (TTC 71) Therefore, desiring to rule over the people, One must in one's words humble oneself before them; And, desiring to lead the people, One must, in one's person, follow behind them. (TTC 66.160)

Jesus	Hinduism
Do not ye yet understand, that whatsoever entereth in at the mouth goeth into the belly, and is cast out into the draught. But those things which proceed out of the mouth came forth from the heart; and they defile the man. For out of the heart proceed evil thoughts, murders, adulteries, fornications, thefts, false witness, blasphemies. These are the things which defile a man. (Matt. 15:17-20)	All things are determined by speech; speech is their root, and from speech they proceed. Therefore he who is dishonest with respect to speech is dishonest in everything. (LM 4.256)
Everyone who hears my words and does them is like a man who built a house on rock. The rain fell, a torrent broke against the house, and it did not fall, for it had a rock foundation. But everyone who hears my words and does not do them is like a man who built a house on sand. The rain came, the torrent broke against it, and it collapsed. (Matt. 7:24-27)	
Put your sword back into its place; for all those who take the sword will perish by the sword. (Matt. 26:52)	The highest charity is refraining from violence. (SB 11.12)
[F]or he makes his sun rise on the evil and on the good; he sends rain on the just and on the unjust. (Matt. 5:45)	I look upon all creatures equally; none are less dear to me and none more dear. (BG 9.29)

Buddhism	Taoism
Man does not purify himself by washing as most people do in this world Anyone who rejects any sin, larger and small, is a holy man because he rejects sins. (Ud 33:13) Evil is done through the self; man defiles himself through the self. Evil is made good through the self; man purifies himself through the self. (Dh 12:9)	Do not assert with your mouth what your heart denies. (TQW)
Just as rain penetrates a badly-covered house, so passion enters a dispersed mind. Just as rain does not penetrate a well-covered house, so too does passion not enter a well-developed mind. (Dh 1:13-14)	
Abandoning the taking of life, the ascetic Gautama dwells refraining from taking life, without stick or sword. (DN)	Those who wrongfully kill men are only putting their weapons into the hands of others who will in turn kill them (TR 5)
	It is the way of heaven to show no favoritism. (TTC 79.192)

Jesus	Hinduism
If someone slaps you on the cheek, offer your other cheek as well. If anyone grabs your coat, let him have your shirt as well. (Matt. 5:39-40) He who has two coats, let him share with him who has none; and he who has food, let him do likewise. (Luke 3.11)	The husband and wife of the house should not turn away any who comes at eating time and asks for food. If food is not available, a place to rest, water for refreshing one's self, a reed mat to lay one's self on, and pleasing words entertaining the guest–these at least never fail in the houses of the good. (AD 8.2)
Enter by the narrow gate; for the gate is wide and the way is easy that leads to destruction, and those who enter by it are many. For the gate is narrow and the way is hard that leads to life, and those who find it are few. (Matt. 7:13-14)	Arise! Awake! Approach the great and learn. Like the sharp edge of a razor is that path–so the wise say–hard to tread and difficult to cross. (KU 1.3.14)
But it shall not be so among you; but whosoever will be great among you, let him be your minister; And whosoever will be chief among you, let him be your servant: Even as the Son of man came not to be ministered unto, but to minister. (Matt. 20:26-28)	
The wind blows where it wills, and you hear the sound of it, but you do not know whence it comes or whither it goes; so it is with every one who is born of the Spirit. (John 3:8)	As the path of the birds in the air or of fishes in the water is invisible, even so is the path of the possessors of wisdom. (Ma 12.6763)

Buddhism	Taoism
If anyone should give you a blow with his hand, with a stick, or with a knife, you should abandon any desires and utter no evil words. (MN 21:6) One should give even from a scanty store to him who asks. (Dh 224)	Show endurance in humiliation and bear no grudge. (TR) Relieve people in distress as speedily as you must release a fish from a dry rill [lest he die]. Deliver people from danger as quickly as you must free a sparrow from a tight noose. Be compassionate to orphans and relieve widows. Respect the old and help the poor. (TQW)
Surely, the path that leads to worldly gain is one, and the path that leads to Nibbana is another; understanding this, the bhikkhu, the disciple of the Buddha, should not rejoice in worldly favors, but cultivate detachment. (Dh 75)	Were I but possessed of the least knowledge, I would, when walking on the great way, fear only paths that lead astray. The great Way is easy, yet people prefer bypaths. (TTC 53)
	Therefore, desiring to rule over the people, One must in one's words humble oneself before them; And, desiring to lead the people, One must, in one's person, follow behind them. (TTC 66.160)
He whose corruptions are destroyed, he who is not attached to food, he who has Deliverance, which is void and signless, as his object – his path, like that of birds in the air, cannot be traced. (Dh 93)	

Jesus	Hinduism
A good tree does not bear rotten fruit; a rotten tree does not bear good fruit. Are figs gathered from thorns, or grapes from thistles? Every tree is known by its fruit. (Matt. 7:17-18)	Unrighteousness, practiced in this world, does not at once produce its fruit; but, like a cow, advancing slowly, it cuts off the roots of him who committed it. (LM 4.172)

Even if they attain to sovereignty, the wicked, engaged in cruel deeds, condemned by all men, do not enjoy it long, but fall like trees whose roots have been severed. O dweller in darkness, as in its proper season the tree puts forth its flowers, so in the course of time evil actions produce bitter fruit. (AK 29) |
| What man of you, having an hundred sheep, if he loses one of them, does not leave the ninety and nine in the wilderness, and go after that which is lost, until he finds it? (Luke 15:4) | |
| And if your right eye makes you stumble, tear it out, and throw it from you; for it is better for you that one of the parts of your body perish than for your whole body to be thrown into hell. (Matt. 5:29) | When you let your mind follow the call of the senses, they carry away your better judgement as storms drive a boat off its charted course on the sea. Use all of your power to free the senses from attachment and aversion alike, and live in the full wisdom of the Self. (BG 2.62-68) |

Buddhism	Taoism
No matter what a man does, whether his deeds serve virtue or vice, nothing lacks importance. All actions bear a kind of fruit. (Ud 9:8)	
	I have heard the Master say, "He who is good at nourishing life is like a herder of sheep—he watches for stragglers and whips them up." (CT 19)
Whosoever has destroyed the longing for worldly goods, sinfulness, and the chains of the fleshly eye, who has torn out longing at its roots, him I call a holy man. (Ud 22:68)	The five colors make man's eyes blind; the five notes make his ears deaf; the five flavors injure his palate; riding and hunting make his mind go mad. Goods hard to come by serve to hinder his progress. Hence the sage is for the belly and not the eye. Therefore he discards the one and takes the other. (TTC 12)

Jesus	Hinduism
How can you look for the splinter in your brother's eye and not notice the stick in your own eye? How can you say to your brother, "Let me remove the splinter in your eye," when you do not see the stick in your own eye? You hypocrite, first take the stick from your own eye, and then you can see to remove the splinter that is in your brother's eye. (Matt. 7:5)	The vile are ever prone to detect the faults of others, though they be as small as mustard seeds, and persistently shut their eyes against their own, though they be as large as Vilva fruit. (GP 112)
Go therefore and make disciples of all nations, baptizing them in the name of the Father and of the Son and of the Holy Spirit, and teaching them to obey everything that I have commanded you. (Matt. 28:19-20)	
I am telling you, do not worry about your life, what you will eat, or about your body, what you will wear. Isn't life more than food, and the body more than clothing? (Matt. 6:25)	

Buddhism	Taoism
The faults of others are more easily seen than one's own, but seeing one's own failings is difficult. The failings of others are winnowed like chaff in the wind, but one conceals one's own faults like a cheating gambler. (Dh 18:18)	Men do not mirror themselves in running water–they mirror themselves in still water. Only what is still can still the stillness of other things. (CT 5)
Teach the dharma which is lovely at the beginning, lovely in the middle, lovely at the end. Explain with the spirit and the letter in the fashion of Brahma. In this way you will be completely fulfilled and wholly pure. (VM 1:11.1)	
Whosoever is free of worries, holding onto truth and the Dharma, will cross the sea of life, will put an end to suffering. (Ma 3:66)	The people are busy with purpose, Where I am impractical and rough; I do not share the peoples' cares But I am fed at nature's breast. (TTC 20) The Master said, "What need has nature of thought and care? In nature all things return to their common source and are distributed along different paths; through one action, the fruits of a hundred thoughts are realized. What need has nature of thought, of care? (IC, Great Commentary 2.5.1)

Jesus	Hinduism
Jesus answered, "My kingdom is not of this world; if my kingdom were of this world, then would my servants fight, that I should not be delivered to the Jews; but now is my kingdom not from this world." (John 18:36) They are not of the world, even as I am not of the world. Sanctify them in truth; thy word is truth. As thou didst send me into the world, so I have sent them into the world. (John 17:16-18) If you were of the world, the world would love his own; but because you are not of the world, but I have chosen you out of the world, therefore the world hates you. (John 15:19)	Elder Sona Krishna, thou Lord of the senses, though moving amongst the objects of sense, remain unaffected by them. Thou hast indeed shown us the ideal: to live in the world and yet not be of it. (SB 11.1)
No man can serve two masters. Either he hates the one and loves the other, or he is loyal to one and despises the other. You cannot serve God and wealth [Mammon]. (Matt. 6:24) Beware, and be on your guard against every form of greed; for not even when one has an abundance does his life consist of his possessions. (Luke 12:15)	One who is free from illusion, false prestige, and false association, who understands the eternal, who is done with material lust and is freed from the duality of happiness and distress, and who knows how to surrender unto the Supreme Person, attains to that eternal kingdom. (BG 15.5)

Buddhism	Taoism
Just as the mighty ocean consorts not with a dead body; for when a dead body is found in the mighty ocean it quickly wafts it ashore, throws it up on the shore; even so, monks, whatsoever person is immoral, of a wicked nature, impure, of suspicious behavior, of covert deeds, one who is no recluse though claiming to be such, one rotten within, full of lusts, a rubbish-heap of filth—with such the Order consorts not, but gathering together quickly throws him out. Though he be seated in the midst of the Order, yet he is far away from the Order; far away is the Order from him. (Ud 55)	To conserve his stock of virtue, the superior man withdraws into himself and thus escapes from the evil influences around him. He declines all temptations of honor and riches. (IC 12: Stagnation)
One way leads to worldly gain and the other to Nirvana. Let the mendicant monk, the Buddha's pupil, seek wisdom, not worldly honors. (Dh 5:16) If by giving up a lesser happiness one may behold a greater one, let the wise man give up the lesser happiness in consideration of the greater happiness. (Dh 290)	Do not race after riches, do not risk your life for success, or you will let slip the Heaven within you. (CT 29)

Jesus	Hinduism
Be ye therefore perfect, even as your Father which is in Heaven is perfect. (Matt. 5:48) [The perfection of God is impartiality and unconditional love.]	They are completely filled by spiritual wisdom and have realized the Self. Having conquered their senses, they have climbed to the summit of human consciousness. To such people a clod of dirt, a stone, and gold are the same. They are equally disposed to family, enemies, and friends, to those who support them and those who are hostile, to the good and the evil alike. Because they are impartial, they rise to great heights. (BG 6.7-9)
The good man out of his good treasure brings forth what is good; and the evil man out of his evil treasure bings forth what is evil. (Matt. 12:35) You hypocrites, rightly did Isaiah prophecy of you [the Pharisees and scribes], saying. "This people honors me with their lips, but their heart is far away from me. But in vain do they worship me, teaching as doctrines the precepts of men." They are blind guides of the blind. And if a blind man guides a blind man, both will fall into a pit. (Matt. 15:7-9, 14)	The infinite joy of touching the Godhead is easily attained by those who are free from the burden of evil and established within themselves. They see the Self in every creature and all creation in the Self. With consciousness unified through meditation, they see everything with an equal eye. (BG 6.28-30)

Buddhism	Taoism
Whose minds are well perfected in the Factors of Enlightenment, who, without clinging, delight in the giving up of grasping, they, the corruption-free, shining ones, have attained Nibbana even in this world. (Dh 89) The man who is not credulous but truly understands the Uncreated (Nibbana), who has cut off the links, who has put an end to occasion [of good and evil], who has eschewed all desires, he indeed is a supreme man. (Dh 90, 97)	Only the Perfect Man can wander in the world without taking sides, can follow along with men without losing himself. (CT 26) Fire blazing from the earth. The Superior man reflects in his person [Heaven's] virtue. (IC 35: Progress)
If you wish to find the true way, Right action will lead you to it directly; But if you do not strive for Buddha-hood You will grope in the dark and never find it. (HN 2)	Do not try to develop what is natural to man; develop what is natural to Heaven. He who develops Heaven benefits life; he who develops man injures life. (CT 19)

Jesus	Hinduism
. . . Be it done to you according to your faith. (Matt. 9:29) All things are possible to him who believes. (Mark 9:23)	Man is made of faith: as his faith is so he is. (BG 17.3)
Blessed are the poor in spirit, for theirs is the kingdom of heaven. Blessed are those who mourn, for they shall be comforted. Blessed are the meek, for they shall inherit the earth. Blessed are those who hunger and thirst for righteous-ness, for they shall be satisfied. Blessed are the merciful, for they shall obtain mercy. Blessed are the pure in heart, for they shall see God. Blessed are the peacemakers, for they shall be called sons of God. Blessed are those who are persecuted for righteousness' sake, for theirs is the kingdom of heaven. (Matt. 5:3-10)	[Those who live established in wisdom] see themselves in all and all in them, who have renounced every selfish desire and sense craving tormenting the heart. Neither agitated by grief nor hankering after pleasure, they live free from lust and fear and anger. Established in meditation, they are truly wise. Fettered no more by selfish attachments, they are neither elated by good fortune nor depressed by bad. Such are the seers. . . . They live in wisdom who subdue their senses and keep their minds ever absorbed in Me. (BG 2.54-61)

Buddhism	Taoism
People must store up reserves of faith since true merits cannot be taken away and no one need fear thieves. Happy are the disciples who have gained faith, and happy is the wise man when he meets such a believer. (Ud 10:11)	
He whose knowledge is deep, who is wise, who is skilled in the right and wrong way, and who has reached the Highest Goal–him I call a brahmin. He who has no longings pertaining to this world or to the next, who is desireless [for himself] and emancipated–him I call a brahmin. He who has no longings, who, through knowledge, is free from doubts, who has gained a firm footing in the Deathless–him I call a brahmin. Herein he who has transcended both good and evil, and the Ties [lust, hatred, delusions, pride and false views] as well, who is sorrowless, stainless, and pure–him I call a brahmin. He who is spotless as the moon, who is pure, serene, and unperturbed, who has destroyed craving for becoming–him I call a brahmin. . . . The fearless, the noble, the hero, the great sage, the conqueror, the desireless, the cleanser [of defilements], the enlightened–him I call a brahmin. Dh (402-22)	He who tiptoes cannot stand; he who strides cannot walk. He who shows himself is not conspicuous; He who considers himself right is not illustrious; He who brags will have no merit. He who boats will not endure. (TTC 24)

Jesus	Hinduism
Again I say to you, if two of you agree on earth about anything they ask, it will be done for them by my Father in heaven. For where two or three are gathered in my name, there am I in the midst of them. (Matt. 18:19-20) I do not pray for these [my disciples] only, but also for those who believe in me through their word, that they may all be one; even as thou, Father, art in me, and I in thee, that they also may be in us, so that the world may believe that thou hast sent me. (John 17:20-21)	Meet together, speak together, let your minds be of one accord, as the Gods of old, being of one mind, accepted their share of the sacrifice. May your counsel be common, your assembly common, common the mind, and the thoughts of these united. A common purpose do I lay before you, and worship with your common oblation. Let your aims be common, and your hearts of one accord, and all of you be of one mind, so you may live well together. (RV 10.191.2-4)
Jesus said, "You know that the rulers of the gentiles lord it over them, and their great men exercise authority over them. It shall not be so among you; but whoever would be great among you must be your servant, and whoever would be first among you must be your slave; even as the Son of man came not to be served but to serve, and to give his life as a ransom for many." (Matt. 20.25-28)	Strive constantly to serve the welfare of the world; by devotion to selfless work one attains the supreme goal in life. Do your work with the welfare of others always in mind. It was by such work that Janaka attained perfection; others, too, have followed this path. The ignorant work for their own profit, Arjuna; the wise work for the welfare of the world, without thought to themselves. By abstaining from work you will confuse the ignorant, who are engrossed in their actions. Perform all work carefully, guided by compassion. (BG 3.10-26)

Buddhism	Taoism
Happy is the unity of the Sangha [the taught]. Happy is the discipline of the united ones. (Dh 194)	
If, for my own sake, I cause harm to others, I shall be tormented in hellish realms; But if for the sake of others I cause harm to myself, I shall acquire all that is magnificent. By holding myself in high esteem I shall find myself in unpleasant realms, ugly and stupid; But should this [attitude] be shifted to others I shall acquire honors in a joyful realm. If I employ others for my own purposes I myself shall experience servitude, But if I use myself for the sake of others I shall experience only lordliness. (GBW 8.126-128)	The sage does not accumulate for himself. The more he uses for others, the more he has himself. The more he gives to others, the more he possesses of his own. The Way of Heaven is to benefit others and not to injure. The Way of the sage is to act but not to compete. (TTC 81)

In most cases all three philosophies have corresponding sayings with those of Jesus. How can such a close correlation exist?

The Missing Years

Some believe that Jesus spent the eighteen years missing from the account of his life given in the Bible in the East learning of the perennial philosophy and the ways of the Masters and Yogis. Numerous books have been written on this subject.

There is also a legend of a man named Issa who studied with the various sects of Buddhism and Hinduism in India and Tibet, returned to Jerusalem to preach the truth about humanity and its relations with God, and there was crucified. The book, *The Lost Years of Jesus: The Life of Saint Issa*, is based on ancient scrolls written by Brahmin historians who recorded Issa's seventeen-year journey from Jerusalem to Nepal and back again.

According to the scrolls, in his fourteenth year, Issa, blessed of God, went to the other side of Sind (Pakistan) to the Aryas people in "the land beloved of God." He passed through "the country of the five rivers" and Rajputana to Juggernaut in Orissa (India) "where the white priests of Brahma made him a Joyous welcome." The Brahmin priests taught Issa Sanskrit so that he could read and understand the *Vedas*. They taught him how to cure illness using prayer and "to drive out evil spirits from the bodies of men, restoring unto them their sanity." He received instruction in how to teach the holy scriptures to the people. He studied and taught in Juggernaut, Rajagriha, Benares, and in other holy cities of India for six years.

Issa then traveled to the country of Gautamides (Nepal), where Gautama Buddha had been born. He learned the Pali language and studied the sacred writings of the *Sutras*. The scrolls claim that Buddha himself elected Issa to spread Buddha's holy word.

After six years in Nepal, Issa descended the Himalayan mountains returning to the valley of Rajputana before continuing west, preaching "the supreme perfection of man," and doing good to our neighbors—the most certain way in which to merge rapidly with the Eternal Spirit. "He who shall have regained his original purity will die having obtained remission for his sins, and he will have the right to contemplate the majesty of God." During his twenty-ninth year Issa arrived in the land of Israel and embarked on his holy calling to "remind a depraved humanity of the true God."

Upon his return he discovered the Israelites in the depths of despair. Many had abandoned the laws of Mossa and their God hoping to appease their cruel conquerors.

Saint Issa taught the people of Israel for three years, and everything he predicted came to pass. Having stirred up fear among the chiefs of the cities, Issa was taken before Pilate, governor of Jerusalem. The priests and wise elders told Pilate, "We have seen the man whom thou accusest of inciting our people to rebellion; we have heard his discourses, and we know him to be our compatriot." They charged the leaders of the cities with making false reports, "for [Issa] is a just man who teaches the people the word of God." But Pilate ordered soldiers to seize Issa and two thieves whom they led to crosses erected on the ground. There they were hanged.

Soldiers guarded the bodies of Issa and the two thieves while their families prayed and wept. At sunset Issa lost consciousness, and his soul left his body and was "absorbed in the Divinity." His parents buried his body nearby. Crowds prayed, groaned and lamented over his tomb.

Three days later, upon fear of insurrection, Pilate sent his soldiers to take the body of Issa and to bury it in an unknown location. When the crowd returned to the tomb, they found it open and empty. "At once the rumor spread that the supreme Judge had sent his angels to carry away the mortal remains of the saint in whom dwelt on earth a part of the Divine Spirit."

It is claimed that the people in Benares, India to this day revere Jesus as St. Issa, their "Buddha."

Many parallels can be seen in this rendering of Issa and that of the biblical Jesus. Note, however, that in Issa's story, he was not resurrected with his body, but rather was "absorbed in the Divinity." The latter narrative thus adheres to classical Hindu/Buddhist doctrine.

Historians of religion have written that during the early *antenicene* period of the Christian Church—the period prior to 324 C.E., the date of the Council of Nicaea—the Church Fathers were aware of the many similarities between Indian philosophy, the Gnostic texts discussed later in this chapter, and those canonized as the New Testament. Though the Indian teachings had been in existence for centuries prior to the birth of Jesus, the Fathers claimed Jesus's teachings as unique. As God's only incarnate son, Jesus taught the Word of God, the substance of which simply could not be compared to other philosophies or religions.

Jesus and the Essenes

It is thought that before commencing his three-year mission to the people of Palestine, Jesus spent a period of time with the Essenes, a Jewish religious group that lived near the Dead Sea. It is also thought that his parents, as well as John the Baptist, were members of the group. While the word *Essene* is not found in the Bible nor is any mention of Jesus's association with the group, neither is there anything to contradict such a claim. Hebrew youth commonly spent a period of time with the Essenes in order to increase their level of spiritual understanding.

Some scholars believe that the Dead Sea Scrolls discovered in 1947 at Qumran are the library of the Essene community. Some of the teachings on the scrolls are comparable to those of the New Testament Gospels; however, most are considered to be of Gnostic origin. Written between about 200 B.C.E. and 100 C.E. the scrolls were placed in clay jars and hidden in caves when the Romans began destroying the Jewish and Christian scriptures.

The noncanonical scrolls describe various esoteric visions and experiences of their authors and are believed to contain an inner, hidden meaning. Members of the Christian clergy, who found the contents of the scrolls disconcerting, were the first to analyze the scrolls. According to many historians, this is the reason the scrolls were not disclosed to the public for several decades after their discovery.

In the Dead Sea Scrolls the Essenes refer to themselves by several names: *Zadokim*, the Just; *Ebionim*, the Poor; *Nazoreans,* the Pure; and *Hasideans*, Zealous for the law (Mizrach). The word *essene* derives from a Syrian root meaning "physician," and the traditional view of the Essenes as living a peaceful, simple and health-producing lifestyle for body, mind and soul is supported by the scrolls.

The Essenes lived in a completely self-sufficient commune. They held all things in common and performed the labor that best suited them. Most members joined the group in order to avoid the worldliness of society, preferring a simple life of service and gratitude.

Typically, they arose at dawn and spent time in prayer before beginning their chosen duties. At midday they bathed, offered prayers and thanksgiving, ate a light lunch, and then returned to their work until dusk.

They held all living things in high regard; therefore, they abhorred slavery even though it was sanctioned by their scriptures—the Old Testament. Neither did they sacrifice animals in the temple as was the Jewish custom nor did they use them for food. According to *The Gospel of the Holy Twelve* which is also known as *The Essene New Testament*, the Essenes were primarily vegetarian. Jesus is quoted as saying, "Ye shall not eat the flesh of any creature, nor yet anything which bringeth disorder to your health or senses."

The book also quotes Jesus's teachings concerning God as both Father and Mother: "Therefore shall the name of the Father God and Mother God be equally praised, for they are the great aspects of God, and the one is not without the other."

The Essenes considered learning of great importance, and their skills at teaching, tutoring, and counseling were in demand. Besides scholarly subjects, they taught their pupils the virtues that lead to high moral character, such as honesty, integrity and respect.

The community was known as a place of refuge, and anyone in need was welcome to abide for a time in the peaceful society.

The Formative Years

In the decades following Jesus's death, the disciples spread the gospel (from the Greek for "good news") across Palestine to Syria to India, focusing on differing aspects and interpretations of Jesus's message, which they saw as a reformed Judaism rather than a new religion. The Church body consisted of various groups identified by the leader to whom they looked for inspiration. There were Peter Christians, Johannine Christians, Pauline Christians, Arian Christians, and Thomas Christians, among others. In fact, Thomas Christians can be found in India to this day. At first, though, the Greek Jews preached the good news only to other Jews. St. Paul, however, perhaps because he was not Jewish, wanted gentiles also to receive the Christian message.

Much debate occurred between the many Christian factions concerning which of the numerous texts written during the centuries after Jesus's death were true renderings of his message. It is rather incongruous that so much dissension arose among the disciples, and later among the Church Fathers, in disseminating the peaceful and loving message of Jesus. The New Testament book of Galatians records the friction between Peter and Paul, and secular historians record the discord among the many Christian groups.

The book of John, the last of the four New Testament Gospels, was one of the texts under debate, for John's gospel differs significantly from the other three gospels. Elaine Pagels writes that there are several deviations, but the main one is the manner in which Jesus is viewed. Matthew, Mark and Luke see Jesus as human while John portrays him as divine. For Matthew, Jesus is the messiah, Israel's future king. Mark sees him as "the son of man," which in the book of Ezekiel is translated as "mortal." Luke's Jesus is a man who acts by divine will. John alone declares Jesus as the divine incarnation of God. Interestingly, it is this claim that caused the debate.

Eventually, John's depiction of Jesus became the accepted view. His gospel, along with the other three gospels, some of the writings of the disciples, and the letters of Paul, became the New Testament canon. This canonization process took over two hundred years to complete, during which time Jesus's followers advanced many different interpretations of Christian doctrine.

The philosophical doctrines espoused by the early Church Fathers were actually based upon fundamental concepts of Hellenic thought, much of which derived from Plato, and were taught by Philo (c.20 B.C.E.-50 C.E.), one of the leading figures of the Jewish community in Alexandria. Two of his students, Clement (c.150-220) and Origen (c.185-254), attempted to reconcile Christianity with Platonic philosophy. Following their teacher, they interpreted the Bible allegorically rather than literally, and they accepted the Platonic doctrines that the sensible world is an illusion, that the eternal world is the only reality, and that we are able to live in this eternal world during our earthly existence by means of intellectual and moral discipline. Both proclaimed an immanent and universal God indwelling in man.

Origen, the first to systematically integrate Christian thought, is considered by some historians to be the founder of Christian philosophy. Origen taught four doctrines accepted as truth in the early centuries of Christianity, but later condemned as heresy: 1) The Platonic concept of the preexistence of souls; 2) Jesus being both human and divine, and both natures existing prior to his incarnation; 3) Our material bodies being transformed into ethereal bodies upon resurrection; and 4) The eventual salvation of all humanity, even the evil and unrepentant.

Actually, many of the Church Fathers accepted these as well as several other heretical concepts: 1) An immanent God indwelling all of Nature; 2) Humans created in the spiritual image of God and actually containing the divine presence; 3) God's law and kingdom found within the consciousness of each person not in rigid, external commandments; and 4) Humans are not saved by grace from without, but by coming "into a harmonious and conscious relationship with God" (Allen). They also considered Jesus the "normal man," the one who revealed to us our divine nature and whose example we should follow.

Much of the debate centered around the substance and unity of God. Sabellius (c. 215) taught that the Father and Son were different aspects of the same Being. Arius (250-336), on the other hand, held to the doctrine that no one, not even Jesus, is equal to the Father. Many decades later, the Council of Nicaea condemned and labeled heretical both of these doctrines and upheld the view that the Father and the Son are equal, distinct Persons consisting of the same substance.

Constantinople and most of Asia continued to endorse the doctrines of Arius until the Nicene Creed became the official Christian doctrine in 325. Constantine tried, but failed, to make unlawful membership in the "heretical sects," which some historians estimate included about half the Christians in the empire.

None of the so-called heretics taught of the Fall, of a separation from God, or that God is offended by our conduct. Neither did they teach many of the doctrines that became part of orthodoxy; e.g., the doctrines of total depravity, vicarious atonement, endless punishment, infant damnation without baptism, divine election, and Purgatory. The responsibility for the addition of these doctrines rests with Church Fathers Tertullian (165-220), Athanasius (c. 297-373), and especially St. Augustine (c. 354-430).

St. Augustine, an astrologer and Manichaean (Manichaeanism is discussed in the next section), both of which he condemned after converting to what later became known as Catholicism, did his best to quash Platonism and Neo-Platonism. Augustine's theology dominated the post-nicene period. He made the fallen Adam, not Jesus, the "normal man," which, coupled with Athanasius's view of a humanity hopelessly flawed by sin, resulted in the concept of original sin.

Athanasius, the bishop of Alexandria from 361-373 and the vigilante of the Nicene doctrine, declared that all reading of the newly canonized scriptures must be done with *dianoia*—discernment of the implicit meaning or intention of the text, rather than *epinoia*—spiritual intuition as to the meaning, for the subjectivity of thought allowed by epinoia leads to error. This view is still held by many mainstream Christian churches.

Interestingly, over his lifetime, Athanasius's thoughts seem to have completely reversed, for earlier in his career he wrote:

> The revelation of God is written in the human consciousness; the ground of all certitude is within man, not in any authority external to his nature. In order to know the way that leads to God and to take it with certainty, we have no need of foreign aid, but of ourselves alone. As God is above all, the way which leads to him is neither distant nor outside of us, nor difficult to find. Since we have in us the kingdom of God, we are able easily to contemplate and conceive the King of the Universe, the salutary reason of the universal Father. If anyone asks of me what is the way, I answer that it is the soul of each and the intelligence which it encloses (qtd. in Allen).

Thus, the Council at Nicaea condemned as heresy the concept of God taught by Jesus in the New Testament and the Gnostic Gospels and transformed Jesus from Israel's future mortal king to an equal, yet distinct, member of a Divine Trinity, a concept not taught anywhere in the Bible.

The Gnostic Jesus

Gnosticism is another system for which we have no certain date of origin. There are two theories for its inception. One holds that Gnosticism is extremely ancient and that its doctrines have filtered over time into many religions and philosophies, including those of the Quakers, the early Christians, the Kabbala, Zen Buddhism, Taoism, Sufism, Baha'i, and several Greek philosophies. Some believe that the biblical Abraham brought Kabbalistic Gnosticism or its precursor to Palestine from Ur of the Chaldees.

The other theory says that Gnosticism developed in the first or second century C.E. in response to early Christianity. There were two separate Gnostic groups, one in Syria and the other in Alexandria. Simon Magus, a Samaritan whose name translates to "Simon the Magician," directed the Syrian group. He is mentioned in the Acts of the Apostles in the New Testament, though because he was considered a heretic some believe the biblical account has been distorted. According to the New Testament account, Simon listened to the sermons of Philip, who baptized him as a believer in Christ. Later, after having been condemned by Peter for blasphemy, he repented and was reconciled with the Christianity of that time. The Alexandrian group was led by Basilides, who included elements of Egyptian Hermeticism, Oriental occultism, Chaldean astrology, Persian and early Christian philosophy, and pagan mysteries in his gnostic teachings.

These two groups greatly influenced the doctrine and the structure of the early Christian church, even though some of their teachings later were labeled heretical. Gnosticism's popularity threatened the Church's authority. So the Church took measures to bar it and saw that the most threatening of the Gnostic gospels were excluded from the official canon.

Under the leadership of Mani, a Jewish Christian, Gnosticism became a world religion in the third century. His Christian church, called Manichaeanism, gave the people an alternative to the traditional Church. Quite powerful, it existed for more than a thousand years until Roman Catholicism became the state church in the Middle Ages. At that time, under terrible persecution, the Gnostics buried their writings and went into hiding.

The knowledge of the Gnostics, however, was not lost. The writings of Jacob Boehme in the early 1600s, the poetry of William Blake in the late 1700s, and the discovery in Egypt of the Gospel of Mary Magdalene in 1896 kept the philosophy alive. Interest further increased in 1945 when two peasants in Nag Hammadi, Egypt unearthed clay jars containing thirteen papyrus codices containing gnostic and other texts. Included in these codices were texts thought to have been destroyed during the early years of Christianity. Much of the information contained in these codices was not released to the

250 ~ The Roads to Truth

general public until 1977, for the same reasons translators held back the Dead Sea Scrolls.

Gnosticism is considered to be a mystical religion that combines elements from numerous philosophies. Besides those listed above, Gnosticism includes Hellenism, Neo-Platonism, esoteric Judaism, and Zoroastrianism.

Gnosis is a Greek word that means "knowledge," specifically the knowledge of God inspired by God. Thus, Gnostics consider their doctrine to reflect the truth about God. God can be found within the self and in the world. The goal, as with all mystical doctrines, is to attain an experience of God during life. When this gnosis is achieved, it is to be shared with others. Upon death those who have gnosis rise to the spiritual plane—the *pleroma*. Those who have not, return to earth for as many succeeding lifetimes as is required until gnosis is achieved.

These texts provide a picture of God much like those of the idealists, the esoteric philosophies and the East. The Apocryphon of John tells us that the Supreme God is ineffable, unnameable, and composed of "immeasurable light which is pure, holy and immaculate." The Gospel of Truth adds that God is both the Father and the Mother, unchangeable, unity and perfection, kind and good, knows the beginning and the ending of all things, and emanates all things from within Itself by means of thought. Both the Oxyrhinchus Logia of Jesus and the Gospel of Thomas declare God is in everything: "Lift the stone and you will find me. Cleave the wood, and I am there."

Human beings consist of two parts: the physical and the spiritual. The spiritual part is made of the divine essence and is called the divine spark. Most of us are unaware of this divinity residing within. Over time, though, the human race will gradually evolve from a material focus to one of a more spiritual nature.

A number of messengers have come to earth to help us in our evolution. Three of these messengers are believed to have been Seth—one of Adam's sons—Jesus and Mani, the third century Gnostic leader discussed earlier in this section.

The Nag Hammadi codices use the words blindness, sleep, ignorance, dreams, darkness, and night to describe the unconscious state in which most humans dwell. Once gnosis is achieved we awaken from the dream, see the truth, darkness becomes light, and night becomes day. Speaking of the pre-gnosis state of humans, the Gospel of

Truth says: "Thus they were ignorant of the Father, he being the one whom they did not see. . . . [T]here were many illusions . . . as well as empty fictions, as if they were fast asleep and found themselves a prey to disturbing dreams."

Within Gnosticism is found the concept of stillness and silence within which we return to our source. Through meditation we are able to learn the truth of the inner self, a specific type of knowledge called *gnois*, or "illuminated Logos." Jesus is considered to be the primary teacher of the attainment of gnois and is therefore seen more as an emancipator than as a savior, in the orthodox sense of the term, or as a judge.

Jesus communicated his private or secret knowledge to a specific group of his followers. It is recorded in the biblical gospels at Matthew 13:10-11, 34; Mark 4:10-12, 33-34; and Luke 8:9-10 that Jesus spoke to the people in parables but to his disciples he gave the secret teachings, some of which can be found in the biblical records.

Jesus taught the disciples that the Kingdom of God is not a physical place or a future consequence, but is a spiritual event that is found within and can be experienced in a state of heightened consciousness. This particular secret teaching is found both in the gnostic and the biblical Gospels.

His disciples said to Him: "When will the Kingdom come?" Jesus said: "It does not come by expecting it. It will not be a matter of saying: 'See, it is here!' or: 'Look, it is there! Rather, the Kingdom of the Father is spread over the earth, but men do not see it" (The Gospel of Thomas 113).

Beware that no one lead you astray saying Lo here or lo there! For the Son of Man is within you (Gospel of Mary).

And when he was demanded of the Pharisees when the kingdom of God should come, he answered them and said, The kingdom of God cometh not with observation: Neither shall they say, Lo here!, lo there! for, behold, the kingdom of God is within you (Luke 17:20-21).

Even the Spirit of truth; whom the world cannot receive, because it seeth him not, neither knoweth him: but ye know him; for he dwelleth with you, and shall be in you (John 14:17).

I am thou and thou art I (Gospel of Eve).

It seems clear that Jesus is saying that heaven (the Kingdom of God) and all the happiness, peace and joy we expect to find there can be found within us. Thus, we must step out of worldliness, turn inside, learn the truth of ourselves and this Kingdom, and liberate this divine light from the darkness in which it has been confined. According to the Gospel of Thomas:

> But the Kingdom is inside You and outside You. When You know Yourselves, then You will be known, and You will know that You are the children of the Living Father. But if You do not know Yourselves, then You dwell in poverty; then You are that poverty (3).

> There is light within a man of light, and he lights up the whole world. If he does not shine, there is darkness (24).

> If You do not fast as regards the world, You will not find the Kingdom (27).

> He who believes to know the All but not himself falls completely short (67).

Note that the pronoun "you" in verse three is capitalized just as "he" and "him" in other verses referring to Jesus are capitalized, indicating that, with Jesus, we are divine.

The importance of knowing this truth is paramount and is key to attaining the gnosis that releases us from the world of materiality. In the Gnostic work Pistis Sophia, Jesus charges his disciples to search day and night for this knowledge. In Dialogue of the Savior, he advises: "Bring in your guide and your teacher. The mind is the guide, but reason is the teacher. . . . Live according to the mind. . . . Acquire strength, for the mind is strong. . . . Enlighten the mind. . . . Light the lamp within you."

Gnosticism teaches nonattachment and nonconformity, a "being in the world, but not of the world" attitude toward life. We are to be "passers-by." It also teaches that all those who believe in the teachings of Jesus are transformed and are no longer Christians, but are Christs.

Gnostics do not view God as an angry judge who casts sinners or unbelievers into the everlasting fires of hell. Neither do they baptize nor do they partake of the Eucharist. They view sin as resulting from ignorance rather than a thing for which salvation is required. They also do not accept the doctrine of the virgin birth.

Several of these Gnostic texts are attributed to women and indicate the importance of women in Jesus's teachings. Elaine Pagels writes that the Church Father Tertullian expressed shock when learning that women participated with men in teaching, preaching and baptizing. From this and other writings, it is thought that in Gnostic communities women held an equal, or almost equal, status to men.

Many of these teachings did not set well with the Church, and it is not difficult to understand why the Church labeled the Gnostics heretics and why it removed many Gnostic teachings from the canon.

We see in the merging of these various roads that all the different groups accepted many of the same ideas. We might even say that Jesus's teachings rest at the junction between the philosophies of the East and those of the West.

In chapters nine and eleven we saw how the common concepts of the New Thought groups parallel Jesus's teachings and the philosophies of the East. We can see in this chapter the many correlations between the teachings of Jesus, the Essenes, the Gnostics, and New Thought. Many of the sixteen common concepts can be found in these "heretical" teachings. The connections between these sixteen concepts and philosophy-at-large are discussed in chapter fourteen.

During several of the stops we made along the way, we encountered many laws which, for ease of maneuverability, were put off for a later visit. It is now time to learn the rules of the roads.

XIII.

THE RULES OF THE ROADS

The thing always happens that you really believe in;
and the belief in a thing makes it happen.
Frank Lloyd Wright (1869–1959), U.S. architect

They can conquer who believe they can.
Virgil (70 BC–19 BC), Roman epic poet

No matter what road we follow, we find rules. These rules are of great consequence not only for navigating our way but also for providing us with an enjoyable experience.

In our journey we have seen that the rules, or laws, of the roads are extremely important to New Thought and to many of the minds that influenced New Thought philosophy. After visiting each of the three main New Thought groups, we found sixteen common concepts held by these groups. We discussed in chapter nine what Jesus had to say about these concepts, and chapter fourteen explores what the rest of the world says about them. All, that is, except for one: God works by use of Divine laws. That is the topic of this chapter.

We discovered that all of the minds we met along the Road to Well-Being—Hopkins, Eddy, Quimby, Evans, and Swedenborg—spoke of the spiritual, natural and Divine laws that are part of Reality. It is, in part, because of Divine law that mental healing is possible. This connection is discussed later in this chapter.

The members of the Rebellious Road also taught about law, though Calvin's concept of law was different from the Unitarians and the Transcendentalists. Emerson spoke of innate universal laws that apply to everyone and everything across all time. He, and Thoreau, too, spoke of the laws enacted by humans and showed how these laws cannot compare to the perfection of Divine Law.

Along the Esoteric Road we encountered Spiritualism and Theosophy and their concept of natural law being the same as spiritual law. Blavatsky also spoke of cyclic and karmic laws that work in response to our level of consciousness. In support of such practices as telepathy and clairvoyance, Troward wrote that these activities follow laws as accurate as those that govern our normal faculties. He also said that we progress to higher states of being by consciously cooperating with the universal laws. The Rosicrucians taught of the natural laws that when applied, will produce an experience of Divine unity.

We met Troward again on the Intellectual Road. His teachings about Divine Law influenced Holmes's Science of Mind, in which God as the Thing-Itself manifests by using Divine Law. We learned that the One Mind is Subjective Law and is the creative medium in which Spirit works. This is also where we learned that Law is neutral. We found Drummond's concept of the same Divine laws running through both the natural and spiritual worlds, and we found that the authority of law is the authority of God. We saw that Browning and Holmes equate Love with Law. We discovered that Larson and Trine both posited laws that govern our thought forces and showed us how we can make use of these laws to create the things and experiences we desire. We also discovered that Newton referred to God as Universal Law or Principle and that James understood the psychological law of mental equivalents.

Along the important Road to Jesus we found that Jesus taught that he had come to fulfill the law, meaning that he showed mastery of the universal laws of God's kingdom through his many so-called miracles. He commanded the winds, changed the elements of water into those of wine, and returned the dead to the living. Most important of all, he taught that we all could do what he did. Why? Because he worked by using the law, the same law that we can use if we place ourselves in the same consciousness as he did. It is done unto us as we believe. This is the law that Jesus understood, taught and used.

Upon reaching the end of the road we again discovered Divine Law being taught by the philosophies of the East. In Hinduism and Buddhism, we found the law of karma or the law of cause and effect. In Taoism, we found the unvarying laws that underlie the changing universe, the understanding of which leads to a life of harmony and freedom. Embedded in these laws is the important concept of the yin and the yang—the polarity of opposites—which forms the basis for paradoxical logic and allows for a thing to be and not be at the same time.

The Eastern world has known about and has applied to life for thousands of years the universal laws that permeate nature on all levels. It was not until the doctrines of the East became well known to the West that these divine laws were accepted into our unorthodox religions. This makes sense, for the unorthodox religions, New Thought among them, see God in nature or God as nature.

It appears that orthodox clerics in the Western world did not entertain the notion of spiritual law until the late 1800s when Henry Drummond wrote *Natural Law in the Spiritual World*. Prior to that time it was accepted in religious circles that the only laws that applied to religion were the moral and social laws presented in the Bible, in spite of the fact that the spiritual laws were taught by Jesus. Outside orthodoxy, though, the existence of spiritual law was well known. Emerson, Swedenborg, Blavatsky, Davis, and many mystics mention these laws in their writings.

We speak of Divine Law in the singular sense, and in one respect it is, for Divine Law is the One. However, within Unity is multiplicity, and within the One Mind are numerous Divine Laws. All of the laws, both spiritual and natural, flow from the same source and, in actuality, are the same laws. As Drummond points out, the invisible and visible realms are simply aspects of the same Reality and are governed by the same laws. Berkeley puts it this way: "Laws of nature are simply the habitual ways in which God wills things to behave." Spinoza, too, says that the "ultimate universe is one infinitely enormous integrated logical structure" governed by "unavoidable, irreversible laws" (Sahakian).

All of the founders of New Thought had much to say about these laws, and they all refer to God as Principle and Law.

Holmes writes that Spirit creates through law, and law is mind in action. Every time we think we set mind into action. It creates for us whatever thought it is given, for law is immutable. Therefore, law works for us only as it works through us. By being conscious in our thinking we can determine the outcome of the law.

Myrtle Fillmore comments that few among the orthodoxy have ever suggested that Jesus used universal law to heal. Charles Fillmore contends that when we obey our inner guide, the laws established by infinite Mind automatically accomplish whatever we desire. He also says that Divine Mind creates by use of mental law. He speaks of "the divine creative law," "the law of expression and form," "the law of mind," and a "higher law."

Brooks writes, "Law is the unchanging method by which God is expressing; it is always true to Divine Being. Law is the basis upon which truth rests. . . . God in action is law as well as love. . . . God expresses by law."

It is important to remember that Divine Law is not vindictive, though sometimes it may seem that way. Divine Law is corrective and instructive. It teaches us that we are responsible for the events of our lives, for the up times and the down times, for the so-called punishments as well as the rewards.

We look now at the most important of these Divine Laws.

Law of Cause and Effect

The most important of all the laws is the Law of Cause and Effect. A common expression for this law is "What goes around, comes around." In biblical terms this law states "As you sow, so shall you reap." Nothing happens by accident. What we send out into the world, returns to us. Someone once said, "Speak kind words and you will hear kind echoes." This works with thoughts, too. A positive thought results in a positive effect. A negative thought results in a negative effect. If we are unhappy with the effects we experience, then we must change what we think, for every action is the result of a thought. Holmes says, "Change your thinking, change your life."

Emerson describes cause and effect as the "absolute balance of Give and Take." Expressed in terms of compensation this law states that everything has its price. In order to receive the thing desired (the effect) the proper price must be paid (the cause). If we want health, we must live a healthy lifestyle and think healthy thoughts. If we want a certain job, we must educate ourselves. If we want loving relationships, we must be the kind of person who says and does the kind of things that attract loving people.

This law is also known as the Law of Karma. As we saw in chapter ten, karma is the concept of reaping the consequences of our actions either in the present lifetime or in a future one. There is a consequence for every act we perform. These consequences can be positive or negative, depending upon the act. If we do a good deed, a good deed will be done to us. If we do harm, harm will be returned. It's that simple. And when we understand that all things are connected, that truly there is no separation, what we do to others, we do to ourselves. The great Suquamish Chief Seattle says, "Man did not weave the Web of Life, he is merely a strand in it. Whatever he does to the Web, he does to himself." The understanding of this law is extremely important, for it is our thoughts and deeds that either keep us in the world of suffering (hell) or release us into Nirvana (heaven).

Scientists, from physical to psychological to metaphysical, understand this law as absolute and unvarying. While physicists observe cause-effect relationships among objects or forces only in the physical world, psychologists understand that the mental plane can affect the physical body. Metaphysicians, however, see cause-effect relationships occurring on all levels and view them as God in action. A thought on the mental plane can affect that same plane as well as the spiritual and the physical planes. Our thoughts determine the state of our mind and our body. They also determine whether or not we experience peace and contentment in the soul.

Emmet Fox, probably the most well-known New Thought writer in modern times, explains Jesus's teaching on this law. Jesus, the master metaphysician, said, "For unto every one that hath shall be given, and he shall have abundance: but from him that hath not shall be taken away even that which he hath" (Matt. 25:29).

This most-misunderstood saying appears on the surface to be cruel and unjust. However, when coupled with Jesus's teaching that we reap what we sow and when we look at his words on the spiritual level, its meaning becomes clear. Inasmuch as our thoughts and our states of consciousness become the world we experience, positive thoughts or a high state of consciousness show up as well-being. The world looks rosy, everything works out perfectly, we feel good, and look good. But when our thoughts or our state of consciousness is low or negative, everything looks black. Nothing goes right, things continue to get worse, we feel poorly, we suffer depression, and the world is out to get us. A positive state produces an even more favorable state. A negative state produces one even worse than the one we started with. In Jesus's terms, "one that hath" refers to those who have a positive state of mind, and "him that hath not" refers to those who have a negative state of mind. Therefore, everyone that hath (those who think rightly) shall have abundance (their positive thoughts produce even more of the things they desire), and those that hath not (have not right thinking) lose the abundance they had prior to moving into negative thinking.

Law of Subconscious Activity

The Law of Subconscious Activity works in conjunction with the Law of Cause and Effect. The subconscious mind takes any idea placed into it and puts it into effect. It uses every resource available—all the knowledge we have ever collected, all of our many mental powers, the unlimited energy of the collective consciousness, and the laws of nature.

Depending upon how deeply the idea is held, the effect may manifest immediately, next week, or next year. It matters not whether the idea is beneficial to our well-being. If the idea is given to the subconscious as truth, it will act on it.

Law of Belief

This law is similar to the Law of Cause and Effect and is one of the laws that has been known throughout recorded history. The Bible says, "As you believe, so shall it be done unto you," and "As a man thinketh in his heart, so is he." The *Brihadaranyaka Upanishad* says, "Now as a man is like this or like that, according as he acts and according as he behaves, so will he be," and "as is his desire, so is his will; and as is his will, so is his deed; and whatever deed he does, that he will reap." Marcus Aurelius, the second century Roman emperor, writes, "Our life is what our thoughts make it." Aristotle notes, "We are what we repeatedly do. Excellence, then, is not an act, but a habit."

Our beliefs become our reality. We literally create our experience by the thoughts we think and the words we speak.

This law is also similar to the Law of Attraction. In fact, these first laws basically state the same principle: The universe brings to us exactly those things that match the state of our consciousness.

Law of Attraction

This law says we draw into our lives exactly what we expect. Everything that happens to us is a result of our expectations, our attitudes, our beliefs, our words, and our thoughts. What we see and experience in the outside world is built from our internal states. Self-fulfilling prophecy ("I knew that was going to happen!") and Murphy's Law ("If something can go badly, it will.") are good examples of how the Law of Belief and the Law of Attraction work.

The Law of Attraction works on all planes of existence throughout the universe. As with all Divine Laws, the Law of Attraction is unceasing and unbending. Like attracts like. Always. By being tuned in to this law, by aligning our thoughts with this great power, by expecting that our desires will be manifested, we allow this great law to actualize the conditions we desire.

This law is a kind of tattletale law with shades of clairvoyance, for an observant person can know exactly what another person has been thinking about. Since what we focus on in our minds manifests into the outer world, the conditions of our own or someone else's outer experiences say a lot about what is going on in the inner realm. Especially when the outer experience is ongoing or repetitive.

Many New Thought writers have explained the process by which this law works.

Troward states the Law of Attraction in scientific terms. The law is a train of causation, and by use of focus and intention, we can make this law work for any desired outcome. First comes a thought or emotion which results in a desire. Next we decide whether we will externalize the desire. If we decide in the affirmative, then the will directs the imagination to form a mental picture (a spiritual prototype). The focus of the imagination on the desired object sets the forces of attraction into motion. The more mental effort given, the faster the law of attraction draws to us the desired outcome.

Holmes writes of the law in terms of consciousness. We are always either drawing things to us or pushing them away, and most of the time this process is an unconscious one. The key to achieving the things we desire is to use the law consciously. It is important that we keep our thoughts focused on the things we desire. But it is not just positive thinking. It is positive seeing, tasting, smelling, and touching.

It is also intention. It is feeling the desire so strongly that it becomes a part of us.

In the words of Napoleon Hill, we must *burn* for what we want. Trine concurs. We must own and live our desires, feel them in our bones. We must surround ourselves with them. We must keep always in mind the car, the house, the partner, the vacation, the peace of mind, whatever is desired. We must never allow the mind to go into longing, pining, or any negative state whatsoever. We must never become discouraged if the desired object does not manifest immediately, for such negativity attracts more negativity. We must "establish in ourselves a center so strong that instead of running hither and thither for this or that, we can stay at home and draw to us the conditions we desire."

Atkinson wrote an entire book concerning this law: *Thought Vibration or the Law of Attraction in the Thought World*. He writes that thought is an attractive force and works much as a magnet does. The positive and negative poles of a magnet draw to it in kind. Positive attracts positive. Negative attracts negative.

Our thoughts vibrate out into the world just as do waves of light, sound, heat, and electricity, some of the known waves of the electromagnetic spectrum. These waves move at incredible speed (186,000 miles per second), vibrate at various frequencies (the number of times a wave completes a full cycle in a period of time), and are measured in Hertz (Hz). At the top of the spectrum are cosmic waves with frequencies of 10^{28} Hz (that's the number one followed by 29 zeros). Next come gamma rays, x-rays, and ultraviolet rays, then the only visible waves—light waves at 10^{14}— followed by infrared, radar, TV, and radio waves—FM at just 10^8 (one billion) and AM at 10^6 (ten million) Hz. The more cycles per second the higher the energy carried by the wave.

It is important to remember than thought waves are not the same thing as brain waves. The brain is made of matter and is part of the body, which is electrical and basically energy (more on that in the next chapter). Our thoughts are immaterial and are part of our consciousness. The brain's electroneurological activity can be measured, while thoughts and consciousness cannot. (The various measurable brain waves vibrate at extremely low frequencies—under 30 Hz.) Therefore, it is not known where exactly on the electromagnetic scale of frequencies thought waves fall. They probably incorporate a wide range, since passionate thoughts carry much more energy than do depressing thoughts. We do know that thought waves move fast, for all electromagnetic waves travel at the speed of light. (Light waves emitted by our Sun take a mere eight minutes to travel the 93 million miles to Earth.) Those who have had an almost immediate response to a thought, know just how quickly our thoughts can attract.

In order for these various waves to be of use, there must be a receiver that picks up the vibrations, and the receiver must be tuned to the correct wavelength or frequency. This is how television and radio receivers work. It is also the means for telepathic communication. All of us are able to pick up thought waves from others, but most of us are not tuned in. Often the best times to pick up thought waves are when we are asleep and the busyness of the conscious mind is turned off.

Unlike these other forms of waves, though, thought waves attract, and they reproduce. They draw to us the thoughts of others, objects, circumstances, people, "luck," and fortune according to the types of thoughts that occupy our minds. The stronger the thought or the longer the thought has been in mind, the more attractive and reproductive it is. If the thought is of love, then love is what will be seen everywhere. If it is of visiting a certain place, advertisements, movies and songs having to do with that place will proliferate. A couple of years ago, I began thinking of purchasing a truck. Suddenly, it seemed that trucks were everywhere. I noticed all the different kinds of trucks and how many there were wherever I went. Now, the numbers of trucks did not increase just because I began thinking about them. They seemed to increase because I had become aware of them. My tuner had been set to "truck wavelength."

This notion of being tuned in is an important one, for if we allow our thoughts to dwell at longer wavelengths, where energies are low (the negative end of the spectrum), those are the thoughts we attract. So, it is imperative that we keep our thoughts in the shorter ranges, where energies are higher, so that we attract only the good—health, wealth, success, friends, love, etc.

Atkinson says that more people transmit thoughts on the negative plane than on the positive plane. If this is true, it provides an explanation for war, and for all forms of conflict. If there seems to be an overabundance of discord and friction in our lives, the solution is two-fold: make sure our attitude is compatible with higher levels of thought and then set our tuners to receive at that level. We cannot attract high-level thought waves if our receivers are calibrated to a lower setting.

One way we can keep our receivers at a high level is by using affirmations—affirming that we already are or have what we desire. Simply repeatedly stating an affirmation is not enough, though doing so does tend to establish new mental attitudes within us. We must develop a belief in the words we are affirming and a confident expectancy of receiving the desired results. We must strongly desire a thing, intend to obtain it, and concentrate all our thought power toward that end. Belief, expectancy, intention, strong desire, and concentration are the magnets that attract.

Atkinson points out the importance of being a mental monogamist rather than a mental polygamist. It is best to focus all of our thought power on one desired outcome at a time, rather than scattering it over several desires. This way we can more quickly bring the desired effect into our experience.

Law of Mental Equivalents

The Law of Mental Equivalents works in conjunction with the Law of Attraction and is taught by all motivational and positive thinking teachers. This law states that what we picture in thought manifests into our lives. The more consciously aware we are of this law, the more positive become our manifestations. And the more specific we are, and the greater our ability to visualize and hold a picture of our desires in mind, the sooner will they manifest. So-called undesirable events manifest into our experience, too. This is because the law *always* works. If we hold negative ideas and pictures in our minds, either at the conscious or unconscious level, we will manifest negativity. William James writes, "There is a law in psychology that if you form a picture in your mind of what you would like to be, and you keep and hold that picture there long enough, you will soon become exactly as you have been thinking."

This process of forming a picture in our minds is often referred to as visualization, and is based on the biblical idea "As you think, so shall ye be." But the Law of Mental Equivalents goes well beyond positive thinking. When the passion is there, and we refuse to allow any interference from any external sources, nothing can stop us. This is the law!

Law of Correspondence

This law, along with the old Hermetic Law, says "As within, so without. As above, so below." In biblical terms it is, "By their fruits shall ye know them." Every external effect corresponds to an internal belief. Physical illness corresponds to sick or negative thoughts. Lack of money corresponds to a poverty-consciousness. Loneliness and depression correspond to negative feelings or beliefs about our self and our worthiness.

Metaphysicians such as Jesus and Emanuel Swedenborg knew of this law as did physical scientists such as Henry Drummond and Isaac Newton, the sixteenth century British mathematician and physicist whose theories helped to propel the scientific view into dominance during the Renaissance. J. Stillson Judah writes that Newton said there are a spiritual world and a natural world that correspond to one another. The natural world is produced and sustained by a spiritual force lying behind it.

This is the concept that Swedenborg called *the Doctrine of Correspondence*. In this doctrine our inner spiritual world of thoughts, feelings, and responses corresponds to our outer natural or physical world. And both worlds operate by the same laws. This doctrine, in the words of Swedenborg, is "a living relationship in which natural forms are symbols and images of our spiritual life" (Dresser, J.).

Two centuries later, Drummond writes, "As in the natural, so in the spiritual, there is a Principle of Life" (*Natural Law*) and this Life manifests itself in correspondences. Troward added two decades later that this law of correspondence cannot be bypassed. Our external results will always match our internal intentions. Further, this law is unlimited. "What it can do for us today it can do tomorrow, and through all that procession of tomorrows that loses itself in the dim vistas of eternity."

Since our outer world is based on the consciousness of our inner world, how do we develop the consciousness that corresponds only to positive outcomes? It is the same process used in the Law of Mental Equivalents and the Law of Attraction. The Law or Higher Principle is Perfect and Complete. It needs nothing, wants nothing and knows everything. So, according to Holmes, aligning our lives with the Higher Principle and meditating daily upon the Indwelling God raises our consciousness. We align ourselves with this Higher Principle and incorporate its truths into our experience through daily meditation, visualizing our desires as already having been achieved, focusing constantly on positive thoughts, and developing an "attitude of gratitude."

This verse written by Samuel Smiles more than a century ago sums up the preceding six laws:

> *Sow a thought and you reap an act.*
> *Sow an act and you reap a habit.*
> *Sow a habit and you reap a character.*
> *Sow a character and you reap a destiny.*

Law of Circulation

The Law of Circulation has to do with movement and is often thought of in terms of money or energy. Money comes in and it goes out. Energy levels ebb and flow. It is important to keep money circulating and to keep energy flowing. Blessing everything and everyone that comes into our lives keeps positive energy circulating and brings to us the things we desire.

Congestion and blockage are the enemies of this law. Congestion results in illness, depression, poverty, war, contention, and conflict. Circulation can be blocked on all planes. Being closed to new ideas and different ways of doing things creates blocks on the mental level. And because the mind influences the body, mental blockages can result in physical effects. This is true on the spiritual plane, as well. Regret, envy, jealousy, and hatred block spiritual energy, which is healing energy, and physical illness is the result.

The law of tithing is a law of circulation. We give, and then we receive. We receive from someone else's giving, and we pass it on in our own tithing and in paying our creditors. When we hang tightfistedly onto our money, it stops the flow.

Deepak Chopra writes that giving and receiving are just different aspects of the universal flow of energy. In our willingness to give, we keep the abundance of the universe circulating in our lives.

Law of Polarity

We discussed this law in chapter seven in the section dealing with the Hermetic principles. This law or principle says that all things can be characterized by two opposite pairs, which in reality are just two aspects of the same thing. The Taoist concept of yin and yang provide the best example of this law. Yin is feminine, moist and dark. Yang is masculine, dry and light. The Taoists believe that all pairs of opposites are dynamically linked. "Everything has its 'that,' everything has its 'this.' . . . So I say, 'that' comes out of 'this' and 'this' depends on 'that'—which is to say that 'this' and 'that' give birth to each other" (*Chuang Tzu*). The Tao, which is both being and Non-being, contains all these characteristics. We can see from our journey that many metaphysical systems accept the concept that God contains all possible ideas and their contradictions or opposites.

A stunning example of this concept is provided by a sculpture of Shiva in the Hindu temple of Elephanta. The sculpture, as beautifully described by Fritjof Capra, "shows three faces of the god: on the right, his male profile displaying virility and willpower; on the left, his female aspect—gentle, charming, seductive—and in the center the sublime union of the two aspects in the magnificent head of Shiva Mahesvara, the Great Lord, radiating serene tranquility and transcendental aloofness." This same temple also displays Shiva in androgynous form, as half male and half female. Again, in Capra's words, "the flowing movement of the god's body and the serene detachment of his /her face symboliz[e] the dynamic unification of the male and female."

Though the Taoists knew of and emphasized the polarity of the opposites long before the Greeks, the Greeks first suggested in writing the interplay between the opposites. Anaximander (c. 547 B.C.E.) observed the opposites in the changing of the seasons. He contrasted the heat and drought of summer with the cold and snow of winter. Together he noted these opposites form a whole—the year. A few years later Parmenides posited that creation is the result of the harmonious interaction of opposite powers.

Heraclitus (c. 480 B.C.E.), sometimes called The Greek Taoist (though it is thought that India influenced Greek philosophy rather than China), stated that all things are one, that this one is unity and multiplicity at the same time, and that this one exists only because of the tension of the opposites contained within. He refers to this one as the *Logos*, which is "day night, winter summer, war peace, satiety hunger" (Kirk, qtd. in Capra). The whole is dependent upon its parts, since one of a pair of opposites cannot exist without the other. As examples he says that sea water is both pure and polluted; fishes can drink it, but humans cannot. The path both up and down the mountain is one and the same path. Disease makes health pleasant, hunger makes fullness gratifying, and weariness makes rest most welcome. Further, within all things there is a portion of the opposite thing. This appears to be the same exact concept of the yin and yang. The yin/yang symbol shows this in having a small dot of white within the black and a small dot of black within the white. (See yin/yang symbol on page 199.) Anaxagorus (499-427 B.C.E.) also held this view. He said that there is a portion of the black in snow and that hot and cold cannot be cut off from one another into separate pieces but rather exist in a continuum we call temperature.

Law of Synthesis

The Law of Synthesis states that the synthesis of two opposing or conflicting ideas produces a new idea that is not a compromise of the original two.

The Laws of Polarity and Synthesis often work together. Hegel's dialectic, which consists of a series of triads—thesis, antithesis and synthesis—epitomizes the combining of these laws. In Hegelian dialectic, things can only be known in relation to their opposites. So, a set of opposites (thesis and antithesis) is synthesized. Then that synthesis becomes a thesis and is combined with its antithesis to form a completely new synthesis. This new synthesis is combined with its antithesis to form yet another synthesis. This series continues as long as necessary until truth is reached.

Hegel used this process in formulating his philosophy. He took Aristotle's *Nous* (reason) as thesis and Kant's transcendental reality as antithesis and synthesized them into his God or Absolute, which contains all opposites and is both rational and real. Hegel also synthesized objectivity (awareness only of the object) and subjectivity (awareness only of the self) into self-knowledge or self-consciousness (in which self and object are no longer separate). He saw this as the highest form of knowledge, thus it is the knowledge possessed by the Absolute.

Though Hegel was the first to set out a formal system of dialectic, synthesis had been employed in formulating various different philosophies for centuries prior to Hegel. The earliest synthesizer was Plato who synthesized Parmenides's permanent One and Heraclitus's changeable plurality into his concept of God as Ideas or Forms and the world as Its shadow. Plotinus synthesized Anaxagorus's *Nous* and Plato's Forms to produce his concept of God as a suprasensible object. Continental Rationalism (positing a conceptual or rational world of ideas) as thesis and British Empiricism (positing a phenomenal world of perception) as antithesis were synthesized by Kant into his Transcendental Idealism, in which the world of experience is dependent upon reason or the mind. Fichte took Kant's Thing-of-Itself as thesis and Spinoza's Absolute as an abstract universal substance as antithesis and synthesized them into his Subjective Idealism, in which spiritual substance is both mind and matter. Leibniz's theory that everything works according to God's purpose is an attempt to synthesize Cartesian mechanistic views of nature with Aristotelian views of potentiality. Lotze's Teleological Idealism, in which the physical world relies on physical and chemical laws for direction while humanity relies on the mind, is a synthesis of both Mechanism with Teleology and Realism with Idealism (Sahakian).

In New Thought, Evans synthesized Quimby and Swedenborg, the Fillmores synthesized numerous systems into their Practical Christianity, and Holmes synthesized many more into his Science of Mind.

Law of Growth

The Law of Growth states that everything grows in its own time. A seed planted and given water and light will grow according to the inherent knowledge or intelligence in the seed itself. We cannot make it grow faster than it is intended.

This law works in the world of thought in exactly the same way it does in the physical world. We plant our thoughts and provide nourishment for them. Then, we must let the Law of Growth take over.

Abel Allen, an early New Thought writer, explains that we have evolved and are continuing to evolve on all levels. "Change and growth are the silent mandates of divinity. . . . Back of all, unseen yet all powerful, is the one universal law or cosmic urge, forever pushing and projecting man forward into higher physical, mental, and spiritual development."

Law of Tendency

This law states that Spirit is committed to guiding us into an environment conducive to well-being. However, because of Spirit's intelligence and impersonalness and our free will, it will not oppose us in any way. Rather, it uses its power to manifest exactly what we intend. This law, then, is similar to the Law of Attraction, which states that the law provides for us exactly as we intend. Intention works both ways, though. In the Law of Attraction, the intention was that of the human. In the Law of Tendency, it is the intention of Spirit. According to Jesus, Spirit's intention is that we might have life, and have it more abundantly.

Law of Influence

According to this law, we become like those with whom we surround ourselves. These people can be friends, acquaintances, co-workers, and family or they can be television and movie personalities, musical artists and literary characters. It is very important to surround ourselves with those whose words and attitudes benefit our consciousness, not degrade it.

Law of Substitution

This law states that once a thought has been placed into mind the only way to remove it is to replace it with another thought. This law works on thoughts much like it works on habits. To overcome a bad habit, we replace it with a good habit. To override the effects of negative thoughts, we must substitute positive thoughts. But replacing thoughts one-on-one doesn't move us upwards, for replacing a negative thought with a positive one only erases the old one. It does nothing toward moving us forward. So every negative thought must be replaced with at least two positive thoughts. The more positive thoughts we place into mind, the better.

Law of Nonresistance

The Law of Nonresistance is somewhat of a pacifist law, for in this law we support an attitude of peace and love rather than one of aggressive action. The biblical ideal of this law is to love our enemies. Adherence to this law results in a boomerang effect. When we send love to our enemies, they are no longer enemies. Our love transforms them into coequals, at least in our minds. The ones who receive our love may or may not know that they had been previously perceived as enemies. They also may or may not perceive the love that is sent. It matters not. For it is our mind and body that are being affected, not theirs. It is our body that suffers the effects of our envy and hatred, not theirs. And it is our body that will be healed by the love we express. This, however, is not to say that others cannot be affected or healed by our thoughts. They can, if they are sensitive to, or in tune with, our thoughts.

This lengthy discussion of law can be summed up by these words of Holmes: "The road to freedom lies . . . through the intelligent use of Nature's forces and laws."

Divine Law and Mental Healing

All of the above laws play roles in the process of mental healing. Since we are what we think, it is extremely important to monitor our thoughts. It is also important to have the correct beliefs. As taught by Jesus, it is done to us as we believe. If we accept the concept that there is only One, that the only One is Divine, and that this One Divine is the only substance from which all things are created, then we, too, are one and divine. If Divinity is perfection, then we are perfect. If we are perfect, then we cannot suffer from illness or limitation of any sort. If we believe this is true, then by holding these beliefs in mind and by seeing and knowing ourselves as perfect, we can heal any imperfection. This is how the Fillmores and the co-founders of Divine Science healed themselves. It is how thousands of Emma Curtis Hopkins's students healed themselves. It is how Mary Baker Eddy healed herself. It is how thousands of practitioners of New Thought and Christian Science have healed themselves. When we know the truth, believe the truth, think the truth, even breathe the truth, we can set ourselves free from illness, poverty, self-condemnation, regret, envy, and sadness. This is the truth that Jesus taught. It is the truth that Buddha taught. It is the truth.

It is because of our incorrect belief in separateness from the Divine that we suffer from sickness and depression. When we can say with Jesus that we are one with the Father, we can heal all errors. "Disease can no longer attack one whose feet are planted on this rock, who feels hourly, momently, the influx of the Deific Breath. If one with Omnipotence, how can weariness enter the consciousness, how can illness assail that indomitable spark? For how can a conscious part of Deity be sick?" (Anonymous, qtd. in James).

By the Laws of Mental Equivalents, Attraction and Correspondence, we draw into our lives the kinds of people, things and events that correspond to our thoughts, pictures and attitudes. What is true on the inside will be true on the outside. As within, so without. Our internal beliefs and thoughts are announced to the external world by the conditions of our lives. If we want a better life, we must think better thoughts. We must own the truth of our beings. We must turn to the divine source within and learn to rely on its guidance. We must go into the silence and commune with the One Who Knows until we too know. And then we must put into practice the truths we come to know.

We turn now to the perennial philosophy, the substance from which our many roads were constructed.

XIV.

TRUTH:
THE BALLAST OF THE ROADS

Truth is one, sages call it by various names.
Rig Veda

True religion is based on spiritual experience,
and dogmatic religion relies on authority.
Sarvepalli Radhakrishnan (1888–1975)

So far in our journey we have identified the main concepts of New Thought and have compared them to the teachings of Jesus, Buddha, the Taoists, the Hindus, and the many theologians, philosophers and psychologists we have encountered. In this chapter we explore the perennial philosophy, its basic components, its affiliates, and its connection to New Thought.

As mentioned in the introduction to this book, Gottfried Leibniz coined the term *philosophia perennis* in the seventeenth century to denote the eternal truth that underlies the various religious philosophies. Over time the perennial philosophy has come to be viewed as comprising the mystical elements of the various philosophies and is sometimes called *classical mysticism*, *mystical religion* or the *wisdom tradition*. The perennial philosophy, however, incorporates more than just religious philosophy. It actually includes many forms of philosophy, whether they are religious, psychological, cosmological or scientific. As the study of wisdom, philosophy embraces all of these various branches of thought, and each of these branches, even science, has specialities that are, or at least seem to be, mystical.

The teachings of the perennial philosophy can be found in the West in the Sufism of Islam and its descendent—the Baha'i Faith, in

Jewish Hasidism and the Kabbala, in Gnosticism, and in the Christian mystical tradition. In the East it is found in various Buddhist and Hindu traditions as well as in Taoism. These teachings appear in any philosophy that emphasizes personal experience and insight over revealed dogma and group ritual.

Traditionally, the perennial philosophy addresses four basic issues:

1. *The nature of God or Ultimate Reality.* Ultimate Reality is pure spirituality and pure perfection. As such, it is absolute, complete, unqualified, transcendent, eternal, indistinct, infinite, nameless, immaterial, autonomous, impersonal, unbounded, uncaused, unemotional, undivided, uncreated, and exists without reason.

2. *The universe and all created forms.* The phenomenal world is seen either as the illusion of reality or as an emanation or manifestation of Ultimate Reality.

3. *Human nature.* Humans consist of a finite body and an immortal soul containing a divine spark of Ultimate Reality. Most of us are unaware of this divine spark and we mistake the material body for reality. Our goal is to awaken to the truth of our being—that we descended from Ultimate Reality and are destined to return to It.

4. *The means by which humans gain knowledge of God or Ultimate Reality.* The philosophies have various means for attaining this knowledge; e.g., meditation, yoga, chanting, and prayer. The experience of attaining this knowledge is mystical, inexplicable and bestows a feeling of unification with the One.

From our visit to India and China in chapters ten and eleven it should be clear that the concepts of Hinduism, Buddhism and Taoism fall within the perennial philosophy. In fact, Hinduism is sometimes called *Sanathana Dharma*, Sanskrit for "Eternal or Perennial Truth." Because we have discussed these philosophies in depth, this chapter is focused mainly on the perennial philosophy's Western exponents.

Let's look at each of the four parts of the perennial philosophy from the perspective of these various exponents.

The nature of God or Ultimate Reality

Ultimate Reality is wholly spiritual and is complete and perfect. It is "the divine Ground of all existence, . . . a spiritual Absolute, . . . a God-without-form" (Huxley). In Eastern terms it is Suchness, Emptiness, the Void, the Tao, or Nirvana. It quite simply *Is*.

If it can be named, it is not Ultimate Reality. Thus all the many names we have for God—Elohim, Jehovah, Allah, Krishna, and Brahman—do not pertain to Ultimate Reality but are references to, or names for, aspects of Ultimate Reality.

Philosophers in the West have always sought to explain Ultimate Reality. The earliest Greek philosophers saw Ultimate Reality as the eternally-existing, unmoving and indescribable cause and totality of all things. It is always present and creates from within Itself all that exists. Thales (c. 650-560 B.C.E.), one of the Seven Wise Men of Ancient Greece and the first Greek philosopher for whom we have written records, said that everything is full of gods. This is interpreted to mean that God is everywhere, including inside all humanity. Anaximander of Miletus (610-540) thought that one neutral, infinite, eternal, and unknowable primordial substance exists from which all things are made. Pythagoras (c. 580-497) wrote that there is only one God, the Universal Spirit, who produces and gives life to all things and is within all things. Xenophanes (570-475) taught of a God that is uncreated, eternal, unchangeable and that contains within Itself the *Arche*, the first principle or primordial element, of all things. Parmenides (c. 540-470) declared the entire sensory world to be an illusion. He claimed but one permanent substance from which all things are made—The One. The One is the only reality and "is an uncreated, eternal, indestructible, unchangeable, unique, indivisible, homogeneous cosmic substance" (Sahakian). Heraclitus (c. 544-484) said that god is in everything, "From all, one; and from one, all." Anaxagorus (c. 500-428) viewed the physical and spiritual universe as flowing from the One, which consists of an immaterial substance called *Nous*, a purposeful rational mind that orders the universe so that all will be in harmony.

In the following centuries Melissus of Samos (c. 441) added the concept of the One or Being as the *Apeiron*, the boundless. Plato (c. 428-348) added the impersonal, absolute universals, and Aristotle

(384-342) posited an unmoved mover which exists eternally as pure thought, happiness and complete self-fulfillment.

For these early Greeks, Ultimate Reality is timeless, changeless, immaterial, impassive, and indivisible. As can be seen, the Hellenist view of God is impersonalistic—God is not a person.

As noted in chapter twelve, Origen synthesized Platonism with Christian theology. Origen saw God as pure spiritual essence, a unity, changeless, and the eternal creator of all things. God is, and has always been, continuously active.

Besides the fledgling philosophy of Christianity, the other philosophies of the second century C.E. were Neo-Platonism and Stoicism. Neo-Platonism attempted to blend Platonic, Aristotelian and Eastern ideas with Christian thought. It began in Alexandria with Plotinus as its principal protagonist. Stoicism had begun in the third century B.C.E. and accepted many Socratic ideas later absorbed into Christianity. All these philosophies accepted the Jewish doctrine of the immanence and transcendence of God and viewed God as universal intelligence expressing as nature and indwelling humanity.

The mystic Plotinus emphasized that everything emanates from an indescribable, ungendered One, for which nothing really can be said. With Parmenides, Plotinus notes that this One is most properly referred to simply as "It is." He does, however, equate God with *Nous*—Absolute Reason, Divine Mind or Intellectual Principle. With all the other mystics he asserts the oneness of everything that exists— the seer and the seen are one. But while God is All, It is more than All. It is all things, yet It transcends all things. It is nowhere, yet It is everywhere. As we have seen, this sort of paradox is common to mysticism and, therefore, to the perennial philosophy.

Also as noted in chapter twelve, the Gnostic gospels teach of Ultimate Reality. Codices found at Nag Hammadi, Egypt say God is invisible, eternal, complete, illimitable, unfathomable, immeasurable, imperishable, unobservable, unutterable, and unnameable. They also say that everything exists within God.

In Judaism can be found the concept of God as the mystical Nothing. Philo (c.20 B.C.E.-50 C.E.) taught a God that is far beyond the ability of human comprehension. God is infinite and nameless, but mostly what we can know of God is what he is not. Islam's great prophet Mohammed (570-632 C.E.) taught that God is closer than the veins in our neck, existed before all things, will exist after all things no longer exist, and is present everywhere.

During the scholastic period of medieval philosophy Erigena (c. 810-877) explained how immortality supports the concept of oneness. He states that God is the supreme unity and the original and universal Being, and created all things by particularizing the universal into the individual. He saw this process also working in reverse, for immortality is simply the particular reverting to its universal nature. All things eventually return to God, resulting in complete unity. St. Thomas Aquinas (1225-1275) taught that God is a single essence consisting of pure form, is complete, perfect and in need of nothing. And Meister Eckhart, the Christian mystic we discussed in chapter seven, said that God is "a sheer, pure absolute One, sundered from all twoness" (Huxley), a nonGod, a nonform, a nonperson, a nameless nothing, and is "as void as if he were not" (Stace). Nicolas of Cusa (1401-1464), a later mystic, saw God as a unity, the harmonious synthesis of all opposites.

In the seventeenth and eighteenth centuries, Berkeley, Fichte and Leibniz, referred to God as Spirit, and the originator of all that exists. Schelling and Spinoza equated Spirit with Nature. Kant said Ultimate Reality is a thing-in-itself. Hegel saw God as spirit, but he also saw God as pure thought. He declared that all the objects of creation are thoughts of God, that the Absolute is the Whole, and that there is nothing outside itself for it to know. And in the nineteenth century, Bahá'u'lláh, founder of the Baha'i faith, said God is One Source, One Light, and completely transcendent in its essence. Bradley said that the infinitely real cannot be a person, for personhood implies finiteness.

In the perennial philosophy, God is not a person. God is the Void or Emptiness, the Absolute, the Unmoved Mover, the Source and Maker of all things.

God is also equated with the Good. Socrates, Plato, Aristotle, and all those who followed Socratic philosophy thought of God as the good, as did many factions of the Eastern philosophies. This Socratic idea was later synthesized with the concept of God as the one permanent and immutable Being to form the notion of God as Mind or Intelligence. The theistic philosophy of the Platonists and Plotinus carried forward this concept of God, as did New Thought much later.

The universe and all created forms

All those who espouse the perennial philosophy see the phenomenal world as *maya*—an illusion of reality or as an emanation of the Divine Reality, the One manifesting as the Many.

The Hindu philosopher Shankara (788-822 C.E.) uses the example of a rope and snake in explaining maya as illusion. If while walking down a road at dusk we see what looks like a snake, we probably become nervous. As we get closer and discover that what we thought was a snake is really a piece of coiled rope, the illusion of a snake disappears along with our nervousness. This is often what happens in our lives. While operating in a state of ignorance, we see ourselves and our fellow beings as separate, mortal, suffering, and in bondage. We see this duality and limitation in the universe as well. However, as we move closer to reality through the various methods of "going into the silence," we realize that what we saw as separate and limited is actually Brahman. At this point the illusion evaporates along with all appearance of separation, limitation and duality. We now see Brahman everywhere, in everything.

The Buddha, too, saw physical phenomena as illusions, for "[t]hough the sentient beings thus to be delivered by me are innumerable and without limit yet, in reality, there are no sentient beings to be delivered" *(The Diamond Sutra*, qtd. in "The Perennial Philosophy"). Leibniz concurs: "There is, therefore, nothing uncultivated, or sterile or dead in the universe, no chaos, no confusion, save in appearance."

Another way of understanding maya as illusion is in comparing it to clouds that block the sun. The sun is shining as it always does, but because of the clouds we do not see it. But if we get above the clouds or if the clouds dissipate, we can see that the sun has been there all along. Maya can also be compared to a mirage. As the sun beats down on the earth, off in the distance we see a body of water. But as we approach it we discover that there is no water. It was an illusion. Reality is not at all what we had thought.

In the second way of viewing maya, the phenomenal world results from the One manifesting as the Many. This is a pantheistic view—seeing God in everything. According to this view, Ultimate Reality is not so much a creator as It is an organizer or thinker. There is only the One; therefore, all emanations or manifestations are *from* and *of* this One. Therefore, the substance from which the phenomenal world is made is the same substance which makes up Ultimate Reality. The *Tao Te Ching* says "The way begets one; one begets two; two begets three; three begets the myriad creatures." The way or Ultimate Reality is unity, but in manifesting as the phenomenal world, it is plurality.

The great Catholic saint and theologian Thomas Aquinas believed that God created the phenomenal world so that he could disclose himself in all possible ways. Therefore, the created world (the world of nature) embodies, and thus reveals, God's divine characteristics. Emerson and Thoreau, too, saw God in nature. Nature, then, is sacred. *Every* part of nature. And all parts are to be respected.

Plotinus taught that not only is God in nature, but all of nature can be found in each person. "All is everywhere, Each is All, and All is each" (Huxley). The Sufi and Baha'i sects have an almost identical concept: "Only God exists; He is in all things, and all things are in Him." The fourteenth century mystics Suso and Ruysbroeck wrote that all beings are intimately united, both during earthly life (since the image of God is found in all of us) and during life before creation (since we are the very essence of God). Leibniz thought that the world is made of fundamental substances called monads, each of which mirrored the whole universe. William Blake captured this concept in his poetry:

> To see a world in a grain of sand,
> And a heaven in a wild flower,
> Hold infinity in the palm of your hand,
> And eternity in an hour.

The very essence of nature, including humanity, is divine.

Human nature

We have seen that in the perennial philosophy Unity manifests as plurality. This is the duality of opposites spoken of by philosophers and theologians. In the One all opposites are unified. In the phenomenal world all opposites are seen as separate. Thus, while the One is motionless and changeless, the phenomenal world is active and ever-changing.

Humans begin existence in, or as part of, the One, are then manifest into the phenomenal world, and return, in their own time, once again to the One. The divine spark residing within each of us, sometimes thought of as the soul, is aware of this process and seeks to return to its source. Plotinus taught that it is the highest desire of the soul to commune once again with the One. The yearning for the One is "embedded in [its] ontological structure." Indeed, he believed that divine law requires both the descent of the soul as well as its return.

Bahá'u'lláh taught that the goal of the true seeker is "to drink of the honey of reunion with [God]." Jalaluddin Rumi, the thirteenth century Sufi poet, writes:

> I must pass on.
> All except God perishes.
> When I have sacrificed my angel soul,
> I shall become that which no mind ever conceived.
> O Let me not exist! for Non-Existence proclaims,
> To Him we shall return (qtd. in Huxley).

We saw in our discussion of Hinduism and Buddhism that the concept of the descent from and return to the One is a common one.

If we are part of the divine One, why do most of us see ourselves as separate and flawed? Numerous philosophers, mystics and theologians have addressed this issue. They all agree that imperfection flows from the material world and that by viewing ourselves as material rather than spiritual it is we who cut ourselves off from the knowledge of our true selves. It is the goal and purpose of life to attain this knowledge and return to God. This is achieved by "awakening" to the truth —that we contain a divine spark of God and are able to unify with the Divine. This is the mystical experience discussed in chapter seven. In this experience we understand that there is only God and we are part of It. We understand that all of humanity is part of It; therefore, as we are all various parts of the Whole, we are all connected. We all will come to understand this truth. It is just a matter of time.

Meister Eckhart said that the eye through which he saw God is the same eye through which God saw him. "[M]y eye and God's eye are one eye, one seeing, one knowing, one love." It is all in the seeing.

Most of us see our physical bodies and all the material world as real and separate. However, according to the perennial philosophy, the immortal soul is the only part of us that is real.

Esoteric Christianity teaches that the spark of divinity (the Christ) is available to all people all the time. In the New Testament we find St. Paul saying, "I live, yet not I, but Christ in me" (Gal. 2:20). Robert Barclay, one of the leading theologians of the Society of Friends movement (Quakers) in the seventeenth century, concurs in saying that the divine spark is Christ within.

So, the goal of life is to awaken to the truth of our being. The word *awaken* derives from the Old English *wacan* or *wacian* and is related to *watch* and *vigil*. Thus, when we awaken, we are watchful and vigilant as to the truth.

Chuang Tzu equates our earthly life with a dream and says that upon the Great Awakening we will realize that we have all been asleep:

> Once Chuang Chou dreamt he was a butterfly, a butterfly flitting and fluttering around, happy with himself and doing as he pleased. He didn't know he was Chuang Chou. Suddenly he woke up and there he was, solid and unmistakable Chuang Chou. But he didn't know if he was Chuang Chou who had dreamt he was a butterfly, or a butterfly dreaming he was Chuang Chou (Sec. 2).

This concept of awakening is sometimes written of as moving from the darkness into the light, as discussed in chapter twelve, or as becoming conscious, discussed in chapter seven.

We awaken when we learn the truth of whom we really are. Both Thales and Socrates are said to have urged, "Know thyself!" In response to the query as to his research into nature Heraclitus declared, "I am researching into myself."

Like awakening, learning of the self is known by many names. In Taoism it is wu wei, or creative quietude. Other Eastern philosophies refer to introspection as meditation. Plotinus called it intellectual contemplation. Psychologists such as Freud referred to it as self-awareness, and subjected his patients to introspection by means of free association and dream interpretation. The Gestaltists and the humanist Carl Rogers thought of it as insight.

Socrates believed that self-knowledge was necessary in order to live a better life, for he felt that knowing the self leads to happiness. All the mystics, as well as the Kabala, teach us to learn of ourselves. Juliana of Norwich, the fourteenth century English mystic, said that we cannot ever know God without first knowing our own soul. Eckhart concurs in saying, "To get at the core of God at his greatest, one must first get into the core of himself" (qtd. in "The Perennial Philosophy").

The writers of the Gnostic Gospels wrote that Jesus taught the importance of knowing ourselves. The Gospel of Thomas records Jesus as saying, "When You know Yourselves, then You will be known, and You will know that You are the children of the Living Father," and "He who believes to know the All but not himself falls completely short." The Secret Book of James says that Jesus taught his disciples to know themselves so, in using the analogy of harvesting corn, they would "be zealous to reap for [them]selves an ear of life, in order that [they] may be filled with the Kingdom."

The Kingdom Jesus speaks of is the spark of divinity that lies within. This, along with the concept of God forming all that is from within Itself, implies that Its creations embody the same nature as God. This is the reason for the belief in the inherent goodness and divinity of humanity propounded by the perennial philosophy.

We have seen that most of the cultures that existed prior to the advent of Christianity, both Eastern and Western, agreed as to the nature of God and affirmed that the universe and all its contents originated with God. However, during the centuries of Christianity's formation, not all agreed as to the nature of humans. Christianity and Neo-Platonism, the two dominant systems of religious thought in the West during this time, both viewed humanity as dual in nature, with the physical body of matter being evil, the soul being spirit and good, and both being real.

As shown in chapter four, this belief in duality posed the great mind/body problem. Huxley tells us that the Greek prefix *dys* (as in dysfunctional) and *dis* (as in disaster) both derive from *duo*, which means "two." Thus, our language confirms that separation is bad. He quotes Kabir, the fourteenth century Indian poet and mystic, as saying: "Behold but One in all things; it is the second that leads you astray." Indeed, Huxley says the exponents of the perennial philosophy insist that believing in separation "is the final and most formidable obstacle to the unitive knowledge of God."

The perennial philosophy holds the view of unity—Thou Art That, the Hindu concept discussed in chapter ten. In fact, we found this concept, though not necessarily in those exact words, along every road we followed in our journey to Truth.

The Christian mystics all spoke of this concept—The I and Thou, the knower and the known, the Maker and the made, the Soul of God and the soul of man. These are all the same. In the words of Eckhart, "God and I, we are one in knowledge." St. Bernard of Clairvaux said that God, "in his simple substance," is everywhere in equal proportions. Jesus said, "The Father and I are one."

Now, God is everywhere, but it is up to us to see and accept this truth, for we are made free. God will not, indeed *cannot*, force us to awaken to the truth of our being. We each choose the degree to which we experience God.

The Christian mystics all spoke of this truth, too. Ruysbroeck said we are as holy as we *will* to be. Eckhart declared that we must *let* God be God in us and that God will "pour Himself into thee as soon as He shall find thee ready." In the poetic words of St. Francois de Sales:

> Our free will can hinder the course of inspiration, and when the favourable gale of God's grace swells the sails of our soul, it is in our power to refuse consent and thereby hinder the effect of the wind's favour; but when our spirit sails along and makes its voyage prosperously, it is not we who make the gale of inspiration blow for us, nor we who make our sails swell with it, nor we who give motion to the ship of our heart; but we simply receive the gale, consent to its motion and let our ship sail under it, not hindering it by our resistance (qtd. in Huxley).

Our free will, then, is the cause of heaven and hell. William Law, the eighteenth century English mystic, tells us that we experience heaven when we work in conjunction with God and hell when we don't. The poet John Milton (1608-1674) writes that we "[c]an make a Heav'n of Hell, a Hell of Heav'n" (*Paradise Lost*). According to the early Christian Church Father Origen, misuse of our free will also is the cause of the Fall. Antisthenes of Athens (445-365 B.C.E.) says that we must control our inner world of desire, for desire holds us in bondage, making us slaves. The road to freedom begins in the fortress of our mind through our "own impregnable thoughts" (Sahakian). The Buddhist *Dhammapada* shows the importance of our thoughts by opening with the words, "All we are is the result of what we have thought."

The concept of sin, too, has been distorted over the centuries. Sin, or the lack thereof, has nothing to do with getting to heaven or going to hell. Sin, and evil as well, are simply errors. Socrates said good is whatever is of benefit and evil is whatever is of harm; thus evil is nothing more than a mistake or, as in Christian Science, a lie. Plato and Spinoza believe that all wrong action is due to intellectual error. William James said evil is *avidhya*, the Hindu word for ignorance, something "to be outgrown and left behind, transcended and forgotten."

Sin, evil, heaven, and hell, then, are found within, indeed are *created* within each person. Rumi says, "If thou has not seen the devil, look at thine own self." William Law explains it this way: Within each of us is our own Cain who murders our own Abel, if we allow it to do so. All evil, as well as all good, begins within the self in the mind and is externalized by our words and actions. In understanding the truth of our being and the oneness of all things, goodness is perpetuated, for God is the supreme good. In seeing the self and others as separate, evil, pain and suffering proliferate, for division is error and wrong thinking.

So, how does one attain this understanding?

The means by which humans gain knowledge of God or Ultimate Reality

The perennial philosophy teaches that while Ultimate Reality is unknowable or unspeakable, it can be known through experience. Thus, the paradox. This experience is mystical, emotional, intuitive and unifies the self and the One. It is wholly beyond rational words. Rumi said, "If you want to expound on love, take your intellect out and lie it down in the mud. It's no help." In the *Tao Te Ching* we find, "He who speaks does not know and he who knows does not speak." The language running around in our heads and out of our mouths is not the means in which knowledge of the One is obtained. The Gnostic Secret Book of John explains that God can be revealed to us in three ways: "*pronoia* (anticipatory awareness), *ennoia* (internal reflection), and *prognosis* (foreknowledge or intuition)" (Pagels).

Each of the perennial philosophies has various means for attaining this knowledge. The method used to reach the One in Vijnanavada and Yogacara Buddhism is yoga. For Zen practitioners it is *zazen* (sitting meditation) and *koans* (illogical statements or questions). In Hinduism it is also yoga and various forms of mediation and chanting. In Taoism it is *wu wei* (stilling the mind), becoming as the uncarved block, and T'ai Chi Ch'uan, a gentle but powerful martial art form often called moving mediation. In Western traditions it is meditation, prayer or practicing the presence. In all of these methods there is silence and there is nonattachment. The Gnostic book of Allogenes tells us that in the stillness of silence we may find the Blessedness from which we may know our true self.

The purpose of studying Buddhism is to learn of the self. From the *Dhammapada* we learn that one "who abides in loving-kindness [and] who is delighted in the Teaching of the Buddha, attains the State of Calm." The thirteenth century Japanese philosopher Dogen said that in learning of the self we forget the self. In forgetting the self we become enlightened by everything. "To start from the self and try to understand all things is delusion. To let the self be awakened by all things is enlightenment."

As discussed in chapter eleven, one must empty the mind of all thought in order to experience Ultimate Reality. This experience is actually one of *unknowing* and of simplicity. The eleventh century Greek theologian Symeon and the fifteenth century mystic Nicholas of Cusa both emphasized the importance of not knowing. At the time of unification the mind is pure and simple. This seems to be the same concept as the uncarved block of Taoism.

The not-knowing experience is one of letting go of the self and of attachment. St. John of the Cross said that attachment to anything prevents attaining divine union. Again we find paradox. In letting go of all things we gain everything—the All. This letting go has been taught for millennia. Jesus said we cannot serve two masters. He also said that we must lose our life in order to find it. The Sufis have a saying, "When the heart weeps for what it has lost, the spirit laughs for what it has found." In losing or letting go of the human self, we find the spiritual self. Sri Ramana Maharishi puts it this way, "By inquiring into the nature of the I, the I perishes. With it you and [the other] also perish. The resultant state, which shines as Absolute Being, is one's own natural state, the Self." In nonattachment, in simplicity and in silence we may enter the state of consciousness that allows an experience of divine unity and of our true selves. Evan Harris Walker describes such consciousness:

> Consciousness needs no word and needs no things. Those born blind or deaf and mute, they are as conscious as you or I. . . . Consciousness is the blue of the sky; it is C#, the taste of sweetness as it fills the mind, the smell of gardenia, the pain of love that is lost, the experienced murmuring brook as it is, the moon reflected in the pool.

So, the way to know Ultimate Reality is to experience it, whether it is by practicing yoga, sitting in the silence, chanting, or strolling through nature. God will not come to us unbidden, though. We must seek God.

The Golden Rule

While not falling specifically within any of the four basic elements, the concept of the Golden Rule is held by virtually all of the exponents of the perennial philosophy. We saw in chapter twelve that Jesus and the Eastern philosophies of Hinduism, Buddhism and Taoism teach this concept. So does Confucius, Mo Tzu and other Chinese philosophers. Writing during the Warring States period of Chinese history, Mo Tzu suggests that brotherly love—kindness and good will to all—is the solution to China's social problems. The Golden Rule also was taught in ancient Egypt and Greece, by the Baha'í Faith, and throughout the Middle East in the philosophies of Zoroastrianism, Islam, Judaism, and Jainism.

Along our journey we have discovered the perennial philosophy in various religions, philosophies and psychologies. It can also be found in science.

Science and the Perennial Philosophy

For hundreds, if not thousands, of years science and religion have been considered totally different disciplines. Though both seek to explain reality, their methodologies are vastly different. And while science looks for reality on the physical plane, religion searches the metaphysical realm. Traditionally, science has not spoken of the spiritual and has viewed the spiritual, if indeed it exists, as inferior to the material. However, since the advent of quantum physics almost a century ago, the manmade barrier between the two disciplines has been slowly dissolving. In fact, in 1982, the physicist Fritjof Capra wrote that the perennial philosophy provides "the most consistent philosophical background to our modern scientific theories."

Physicists have long sought the origin of the universe, the cause of the physical laws by which it works, and, for the past hundred years, a unified theory—a theory that explains everything. Such a theory quite possibly has been discovered. But first things first.

The term *physics* derives from the Greek word *physis*, which means "the endeavor of seeing the essential nature of all things." The Milesian philosopher/physicists Thales, Anaximander and Anaximenes first employed this term in explaining the essential nature of matter. The first physicists were hylozoists; they believed that matter is alive. Over a short period of time, however, live, active matter came to be seen as inert, and remained so in the eyes of science until quantum physics proved that not only is matter alive and active, but it is quite astounding stuff.

Until Albert Einstein put forth his first theory of relativity in 1905, Isaac Newton's classical laws of physics reigned supreme. Newton's laws accurately explain the everyday world we experience; however, Einstein discovered that Newton's laws do not explain the universe at large. In order to explain our universe, Einstein theorized that time is not absolute but is actually relative and simply another dimension, along with height, width and depth. These four dimensions he termed *space-time*. He also theorized that space-time is curved, a theory confirmed during an eclipse of the sun in 1919 when light was observed to be bent. This theory is now considered to be law and is the model used by today's physicists.

As with Newton's laws, Einstein's laws do not hold in all circumstances. When the subatomic world was discovered in the decades following relativity theory, it was also discovered that Einstein's laws break down in that quantum world. Physicists immediately set out to discover the laws of subatomics. And what they discovered was mind-boggling. The subatomic world is indeed a very strange world. Or is it?

Quantum physics is the study of the subatomic world, the world discovered when atoms are split into their constituent parts. Physicists discovered almost a century ago that atoms are made up of neutrons, protons and electrons. For many years these particles were thought to be the elementary particles, the building blocks of all physical matter. Further experiments, however, produced a whole slew of even more basic particles that physicists call *the particle zoo*.

It seems that in this very small world matter does not behave the way it does in our everyday world. In fact, matter is not solid and is not actually matter at all. It is energy. And what is energy? It is just a means for expressing observed effects, for measuring the positions of a substance at different times. In Einstein's famous equation $E = mc^2$, energy is equated with mass multiplied by speed squared, specifically the speed of light. What we think of as matter, then, is simply the observed movement of energy.

Atoms are incredibly small and consist mostly of empty space. To put this into perspective, think of the nucleus (the center) of an atom as four inches in diameter. The amount of empty space between the nucleus and the outer edge of the atom would be four miles wide. Most commercial airplanes fly between five and six miles above the earth's surface. Just as we don't consider the space between the Earth and the airplane as solid, neither is the space between the atom's nucleus and its outer edge solid. We experience solidity because of the strong *invisible*, *nonmaterial* forces that hold the protons and electrons inside the atom and hold atoms to other atoms. Thus, empty space plus immaterial force equals solid matter!

As time passed even stranger theories than Einstein's were advanced to explain the quantum world. In 1923 the French physicist Louis de Broglie introduced the idea that matter vibrates. Different types of matter vibrate at different frequencies (wave cycles per second). So according to Einstein and de Broglie matter is really energy vibrating at differing frequencies. These theories have since been proved correct.

The quantum world is a world of paradox. Matter is both continuous and discontinuous. Time either does not exist at all or it exists everywhere in the universe at once. The same is true for distance. Either the distance the subatomic particles travel does not exist at all or the particles "touch" everything in the Universe simultaneously. Particles either can be and not be at the same time or they can neither be nor not be. Particles are both destructible and indestructible and act simultaneously as both particles and waves.

Wave-particle duality was one of the first paradoxes discovered in the quantum world. From numerous experiments we know that light waves make rippling patterns just as does water in a pond when a rock is dropped into it. If two rocks are dropped into the pond, each of their circular ripple patterns spread out and interfere with each other causing overlap, an increase or decrease in size of the ripples, or depending upon their size, even annihilation. Light waves respond in a similar manner.

In the quantum experiments, called two-slit or two-hole experiments, photons (particles of light named by Gilbert Lewis in 1926 for *photos*, the Greek word for light) were fired one by one at a screen set behind a partition containing two holes. Experimenters expected that each photon would pass through one of the holes and then would be recorded on the screen as a white dot, and this is exactly what happened. However, after sending thousands of photons through the experiment one at a time, each white dot arranged itself on the screen so that typical wave interference patterns of alternating light and dark strips formed. This was an astounding result, for two or more objects are needed "in the pond" to created interference patterns. In these experiments, though, it seemed that each particle passed through both holes at once, somehow interfered with itself, and then placed itself on the screen exactly as needed to form an interference pattern.

These experiments brought up a number of curious questions. How does a single particle pass through two holes at once? Since the particles are all fired straight toward the partition, why don't they all take the same path? How does the particle know where to place itself on the screen so that the correct pattern emerges?

In order to explain these results, it was suggested that photons act as both particles and waves, somehow "talk" to each other, and seem to work together as a whole rather than as parts, no matter how far apart they are. Further experiments showed that individual electrons and entire atoms also have these characteristics. All these elements begin and end experiments as particles but in between travel as waves. Later two-slit experiments showed even stranger behaviors. It seems that a single atom can pass both ways through both holes at once and then interfere with itself. Thus, it can be in two places at the same time. These particles seem to be aware of all of the conditions throughout the entire experiment. This effect is known as nonlocality, but Einstein referred to it as "spooky action at a distance."

Many experiments have shown that it is impossible to say that these elements are either waves or particles. If the experiment is set up to measure waves, an interference pattern emerges. If it is set up to monitor particles passing through the holes, then that is what is seen. That seems rather commonsensical. However, the elements can be fired at the screen, and so are on their way to the partition, *before* the choice is made as to whether to set the test to measure particles or waves, and every single time the result is exactly what the test results should be. It's as if there is some sort of intelligence involved. The elements seem to "know" how they are expected to act.

Experiments with atoms have shown that atoms excited into unstable, high-energy states will continue in this state forever as long as they are being watched and will only jump down to stable, low-energy states when no one is looking. "A watched quantum pot" says physicist John Gribben, "never boils."

The standard interpretation explaining the effects of these experiments is known as the Copenhagen Interpretation. In 1930, a group of physicists working in Copenhagen, Denmark determined that the observer of the experiment determines the experiment's outcome. The act of observing a wave somehow causes it to collapse and to begin behaving like a particle at the critical moment when it passes through the hole. In fact, it only takes observance of *one* hole to determine the emergent pattern from *both* holes. Somehow the elements passing through the other hole know that we are looking at the first hole and also behave as particles. It doesn't matter how close or how far apart the holes are, these same results occur. Theoretically, the two holes could be on opposite sides of the galaxy and the result would be the same. Spooky action indeed!

The strangest phenomenon of all, at least from the physicists' perspectives, is that the activities of particles, indeed *even their existence*, seem to be dependent upon an observer. It appears that there is an intimate tie between physical reality and an observer. The quantum world does not seem to exist unless someone is observing it. Sound familiar? It should. Back in the 1700s Berkeley, whom we met in chapter four, surmised that the physical world only exists because it is being observed. Mahayana's Vijnanavada school, discussed in chapter eleven, also teaches the necessity of an observer or perceiver. Has modern science proved these philosophies correct?

The concept of reality being tied to an observer is also integral to the currently accepted model of how our universe began. The big bang theory describes a universe that started as a singularity, a point of infinitely dense energy, or something even more basic than energy, in zero volume and at zero time. This point of dense energy somehow exploded and has been expanding ever since. Physicists are unable to explain the point at the beginning of the universe because in a singularity all the known laws of physics break down. Thus, physicists are faced with trying to describe the indescribable.

The existence of an outside observer, a consciousness outside the universe, has been posited by a number of prominent physicists, including Stephen Hawking, probably the most well-known physicist today, to explain the big bang and other peculiarities of quantum physics. A universe with a beginning implies a Beginner. Many physicists are bothered by the idea of an outside observer, an observer which by necessity is beyond time and outside of space (because time and space are created in the big bang); that is, *an infinite and eternal observer.* This is metaphysics and the territory of philosophy and theology, not physics.

In order to get around the need for an observer, the many-worlds or parallel universes theory was proposed. In this theory, each time a choice is required at the quantum level, the entire universe splits into as many copies of itself as needed so that all possible outcomes occur. This splitting of the universe into parallel universes eliminates the need for an outside observer to collapse waves into particles and to make them real.

Another peculiarity of the quantum world is that there is no certainty. Everything works as probabilities. There is a probability that a certain particle may be here, or it may be there, in the next room, or on the other side of the galaxy. And if we can locate it, we cannot say how fast it is moving. If we know its movement, we cannot determine for certain its location.

Physicist Robert Oppenheimer, in his book *Science and the Common Understanding*, writes: "If we ask, for instance, whether the position of the electron remains the same, we must say 'no'; if we ask whether the electron's position changes with time, we must say 'no'; if we ask whether the electron is at rest, we must say 'no'; if we ask whether it is in motion, we must say 'no'" (qtd. in Capra). This reminds me of the passage from the *Upanishads* discussed in chapter eleven. The *Bhagavad Gita* also has a similar saying, "He is far and he is near. He moves and he moves not."

In 1967 physicists Abdus Salam and Steven Weinberg proposed a theory that unifies the weak and electromagnetic forces, two of the invisible, nonmaterial forces that hold particles and atoms together. It had been thought that these fields were carried by a variety of particles; however, Salam and Weinberg determined that what had been thought of as diverse particles are actually just differing aspects of photons manifesting at various energies and thus, various frequencies.

Physicist Gerald Schroeder suggests that the same thing is true of *all* particles. He says it is extremely likely that all particles are merely various manifestations of an underlying energy, an energy that just may be the manifestation of something even more ethereal. He calls this something wisdom, an idea, or information. If this is true, physics and metaphysics are not separate disciplines; instead they are parts of a continuum—physics leading smoothly into metaphysics, "from particle to wave to energy to idea." At bottom, the Beginner is an Idea. And where are ideas located? In the mind; in this case, the Supreme Mind.

In the related field of the psychology of the mind, the brain-mind model accepted by neurologists has come into question "because it fails to answer so many questions about our ordinary experiences, as well as evading our mystical and spiritual ones." This model asserts that our mind and our consciousness reside in the brain; however, neurophysiological research fails to conclusively show "that the higher levels of mind (intuition, insight, creativity, imagination, understanding, thought, reasoning, intent, decision, knowing, will, spirit, or soul) are located in brain tissue" ("Brain Waves"). Further, numerous studies support the phenomena of remote viewing (the ability to gather information about an object, place or person that is located out of sight, some distance from the viewer and sometimes also separated in time), ESP (the ability to sense the thoughts of others or things that cannot be physically seen), and precognition (the ability to see or know what will occur in the future) ("Who was JB Rhine?"). Mind and consciousness clearly are not local phenomena.

The mind again comes into play in a theorized model of the universe in which time is imaginary. This theory predicts effects we have actually observed and also effects that so far are unmeasurable but that are believed to exist. Hawking asks, "So what is real and what is imaginary?" and implies that the distinction may be solely in our minds.

The various quantum theories coupled with the observation that the subatomic world seems to work as a whole and "touches" everything at once, indicate unity within the diversity. There is no separation in the quantum world. According to Capra, the basic elements of matter are "interconnected, interrelated and interdependent" and "cannot be understood as isolated entities, but only as integrated parts of the whole." This implies that because all things are made of subatomic particles, all things that ever have been in contact will remain in contact forever. Unity has been shown to be basic to the universe.

An implication of all of these experiments and theories is that as conscious beings made up of conscious subatomic particles, the choices we make affect the physical world we see and experience. Physicist Fred Alan Wolf writes that because consciousness is able to change the actions of atoms, our thoughts can affect our bodies, indeed can heal them or make them sick (qtd. in Lemley).

It seems clear that the quantum world suggests that consciousness or an idea not only determines physical reality but that it also existed at the beginning of the universe or even prior to the beginning. Consciousness, then, is the Beginner, the eternal and infinite Outside Observer. Consciousness, too, is the stuff from which all things are made. From consciousness comes thoughts, and from thoughts come ideas. Ideas, as various forms of energy, produce waves and particles, and particles make up matter.

Interestingly, Maharishi Mahesh Yogi stated in the early 1970s that when scientists finally are able to break atoms into their fundamental particles what they will find is consciousness. Quantum physics seems to have proved him correct.

A number of prominent physicists support the conclusion linking the basic building blocks or basic reality with Consciousness or God. Stephen Hawking, one of the world's leading theoretical physicists, suggests that finding the theory of everything, the "principle of order and harmony," will be like seeing "into the mind of God." Similarly, Nobel laureate Leon Lederman says it will be like "looking into the face of God" ("Stephen Hawking's God"). Gerald Schroeder, former professor of nuclear physics at MIT, refers to it as encountering "the hidden face of God" or "the expression of wisdom." Physicist Evan Harris Walker simply calls it Consciousness or "the quantum mind." Freeman Dyson, Professor Emeritus at the Princeton Institute for Advanced Study, says it is "what mind becomes when it has passed beyond the scale of our comprehension," and John Archibald Wheeler, theoretical physicist and a later collaborator of Einstein's, likens it to an idea or information (qtd. in Schroeder). British scientist Sir James Jeans concurs in noting that the universe looks like a giant thought (Anderson and Whitehouse).

The current leading theory to explain the quantum world is also a unified theory that explains everything—a theory for which Einstein searched the last forty years of his life. This theory is known as M-theory. Its author, Edward Witten, a physicist at Princeton's Institute for Advanced Study, says "M" stands for magic, mystery or matrix.

Witten proposed in 1995 that the five string theories that previously had been presented to unify general relativity and quantum mechanics are not competing theories but rather explain different aspects of the same underlying theory—his M-theory.

In string theory, strings, not particles, are the fundamental constituents of matter. Strings require a space-time of 10 dimensions (degrees of freedom or movement) and are incredibly small. If the four-mile-wide atom we spoke of earlier in this chapter were expanded to the size of the universe, a string would be merely the size of a tree. The varying frequencies of the strings create the different particles in the zoo. Since these vibrating strings are the basic building blocks of matter, *all* things vibrate. Even the earth. (So, theoretically, the truck wavelength spoken of metaphorically in the last chapter actually could be reality, though because all vehicles are produced from essentially the same materials—metal, glass, plastic and fabric—the vibrations of trucks would be virtually the same as SUVs, sedans, and convertibles.) Strings are extremely versatile (in chapter eleven we discussed that this word is also used to describe the *I* of *I Ching* usually translated as "change"). Their many shapes create all the different forms we see in the world.

Witten's M-theory requires an eleventh dimension, which is a membrane, or "brane" for short. Theoretically, branes can be as large as the universe. Actually, a brane can *be* a universe, and there can be many of these universes—parallel universes. The universe in which we live could be a brane. Of these eleven dimensions the only ones we can sense are the spacial dimensions of length, width and height and the dimension of time. Though we cannot sense them, events that occur in the insensible dimensions affect us. A number of laboratory tests have been conducted in which the reactions that lead to the observable results cannot be followed. These reactions may exist in one of the seven insensible dimensions. Again, physicists have found themselves in the realm of the metaphysical; i.e., the unperceivable.

Even the questions quantum physicists ask are metaphysical: What is reality? Why is there existence? of the physical world? of empty space? of time? What caused existence? What caused the big bang? How did the big bang know to produce the relationships among elements that allows for stable chemistry? How do two atoms of hydrogen and one atom of oxygen know to combine to produce water? How do electrons and photons know when they are being observed? The questions are endless.

As strange as quantum physics seems and despite that fact that it has infringed upon the realm of metaphysics, it really is science. From quantum physics developed the technology that produced lasers, computer chips, magnetic resonance imaging and positron emission tomography scans (MRIs and PETs), the scanning tunneling microscope (STM), transistors, cellular phones, televisions, and microwave ovens. Quantum physics is even being used to design new medical drugs.

So, the field of quantum physics seems to be both scientific and metaphysical; seems to prove idealism, not materialism; and seems to contain much of the perennial philosophy. Hopefully, at this point in our journey, the reasons for this prolonged discussion are obvious.

We turn now to the parallels between New Thought and the various exponents of the perennial philosophy.

The Parallels

Before completing the last leg of our journey let's revisit one last time the sixteen common concepts of New Thought. These are:

- God is Spirit, Mind or Intelligence
- God is Good, Wise, Loving, etc.
- There is only God, and God is always present
- God is the Creator of all that exists and creates from within Itself
- God is a Triune Being
- God is impersonal and impartial
- There are spiritual or divine laws by which God works
- Jesus embodied the Christ consciousness, which consciousness is available to all humanity
- Jesus taught mental healing
- We are created in God's image and likeness; as such, our nature is good, and we are divine
- It is our birthright to partake of God's goodness
- We are given free agency or free will; thus, we are always at choice
- We are the means by which God expresses into the material world
- Our thoughts, attitudes and beliefs produce our experience
- Heaven and hell are states of mind or consciousness
- Evil and sin are simply mistakes resulting from ignorance and wrong thinking

Not all of these concepts are found in all the various exponents of the perennial philosophy. The concept of God as a triune being is common to some but not all of the exponents. The Trinity is not taught in the Bible and, therefore, is not found in Judaism. Neither is it found in Islam. Later forms of Buddhism and Hinduism teach a trinity. In Buddhism it is the Buddha, the Dharma and the Sañgha. In Hinduism, the Trimurti is Brahma, Vishnu and Shiva. In both of these cases, the trinity consists of three expressions of the one Absolute. New Thought follows these philosophies in viewing the Trinity as three aspects of the One: Mind, Idea and Consciousness; Spirit, Soul and Body; Mind,

Idea and Expression; or The Thing Itself, The Way It Works and What It Does. In this view the Trinity is actually a Unity. The only other exponents of the perennial philosophy known to me who taught the concept of a triune God are Eddy, Plotinus and Hegel. For Eddy the Trinity is "God the Father-Mother; Christ the spiritual idea of sonship; [and] divine Science or the Holy Comforter." Plotinus viewed the Absolute as consisting of The One, Spirit and Soul. Hegel's Absolute assumes three forms: the Idea-in-Itself—logic, the Idea-for-Itself or Idea-outside-itself—nature, and the Idea-in-and-for Itself—mind or spirit.

Another variance between New Thought and the exponents of the perennial philosophy is with the two concepts having to do with Jesus. While the concept of a divine spark inherent in humanity is taught in the perennial philosophy, it is not called the Christ nor is it specific to Jesus. Neither is the concept of mental healing specifically alluded to by the perennial philosophy, though it can be construed from its teachings, as it can from the theories of quantum physics.

It is interesting that the theories of quantum physics postulate an idea, wisdom, or consciousness lying beneath the energy from which matter is made. Throughout New Thought are found the concepts of God as Mind, Intelligence, Wisdom, and Consciousness, and the manifest world as Mind in form, Substance in action, and Being in manifestation. The physical world is quite literally an idea in the Mind of God. Holmes writes in *The Science of Mind* that the Thought of God is the Cause of all that exists, and since there are many existing things, there must be many thoughts in the Mind of God. Hence, unity becomes diversity.

The Bible clearly says that God created all things twice: "These are the generations of the heavens and the earth, when they were created in the day that the Lord God made the earth and the heavens, and every plant of the field, *before* it was in the earth, and every herb of the field *before* it grew" (Gen. 2:4-5, emphasis added). As with all creators, God made the universe first from the contents of Its mind and then fashioned it physically. Writes Emerson, "There seems to be a necessity in spirit to manifest itself in material forms; and day and night, river and storm, beast and bird, acid and alkali, preexist in necessary ideas in the mind of God." In speaking of the invention process, Thomas Edison comments that it is mostly imagination, that it is "conceiving what might be, before one has seen the way to realize it practically."

The God of New Thought and the perennial philosophy is the only Reality and creates from within. Therefore, everything in existence is made from God-stuff. As creations of the Divine, "ideas in the Mind of God," humanity is endowed with all the characteristics of divinity. It is our birthright to be free, to be whole, perfect and complete, as is God. Because God works by Law, It works the same always for everyone. Because we are born free, God can do for us only what we allow. So, while God is constantly manifesting abundance, health, and happiness, (because God is good), we only receive as much of that good as we permit. "God can only do for us what [God] can do through us." The rest of the basic principles common to New Thought flow from this concept of God and are found in the perennial philosophy.

I believe I have shown that for the most part New Thought and the many minds encountered along the roads to Truth taught the perennial philosophy. Indeed, the perennial philosophy and Truth are one and the same.

I have stated in the title to this chapter that the perennial philosophy is truth. In what sense is that so? Truth can mean 1) sincerity in action, character or word; 2) a fact or actuality; 3) a spiritual reality; or 4) being in accord with fact or actuality. It is truth in the last three senses. First, the perennial philosophy affirms the fact that God is, and secondly, is a spiritual reality—It is Ultimate Reality. Lastly, all the teachings of the perennial philosophy's exponents are in accord with that fact.

New Thought teaches the perennial philosophy. All of the minds we visited along the many roads of our journey taught the perennial philosophy. And the perennial philosophy is Truth.

BIBLIOGRAPHY

INTRODUCTION

Huxley, Aldous. *The Perennial Philosophy.* New York: Harper & Row Publishers, Inc., 1944.

CHAPTER ONE

Drewry, Henry N. and O'Connor, Thomas H. *America Is.* Ohio: Glencoe/ McGraw-Hill, 1995.

Leahey, Thomas Hardy. *A History of Psychology.* New Jersey: Prentice-Hall, 1987.

Miller, Marilyn and Faux, Marian, eds. *The New York Public Library American History Desk Reference.* New York: Macmillan, a Simon & Schuster Macmillan Company, 1997.

Nelson, Rebecca, ed. *The Handy History Answer Book.* Michigan: Visible Ink Press, 1999.

Norton, Anne-Lucie, ed . *QPB Dictionary of Ideas.* n.p.: Helicon Publishing Ltd., 1994. Orig. publ. as *The Hutchinson Dictionary of Ideas.* United Kingdom, n.d.

CHAPTER TWO

Allen, Abel Leighton. *The Message of New Thought.* New York: Thomas Y. Crowell Company, 1914. http://cornerstone.wwwhubs.com/ntbooks. htm. (Jan. 2004).

Atkinson, William Walker. *New Thought: Its History and Principles or The Message of the New Thought.* Holyoke, MA: The Elizabeth Towne Co. and London: L. N. Fowler and Co., 1915.

Braden, Charles S. *Spirits in Rebellion: The Rise and Development of New Thought.* Dallas: Southern Methodist University Press, 1963.

Dewey, John. "The New Psychology." *Andover Review,* 2, (1884) 278-289. http: //psychclassics.yorku.ca/Dewey/newpsych.htm. (Apr. 2004).

Doyle, Laurence. "Identity in an Infinite Expanding Universe." An interview with Reed Harris. *Christian Science Sentinel* (Jan 19, 2004).

Dresser, Horatio W. *The Quimby Manuscripts*: *Showing the Discovery of Spiritual Healing and the Origin of Christian Science.* New York: Thomas Y. Crowell Co., 1921. http://cornerstone.wwwhubs.com/ntbooks. htm. (Jan. 2004).

Drummond, Henry. *Natural Law in the Spiritual World.* London: Hodder and Stoughton, 1883, 1890.

Dyer, Wayne W. *Wisdom of the Ages*. New York: HarperCollins Publishers. Inc., 1998.

Fillmore, Charles. *Christian Healing*. http://webstyte.com/unity/crh.htm. (Jan. 2004).

—. *Metaphysical Bible Dictionary*. Unity Village, MO: Unity Books, 1931, 2000.

Holmes, Ernest. *New Thought Terms and Their Meanings*. New York: Dodd, Mead & Company, 1942.

—. *The Science of Mind*. New York: Dodd, Mead & Company, 1938 rev. ed.

Leahey, Thomas Hardy. *A History of Psychology*.

Mish, Frederick C., ed. in chief. *Merriam-Webster's Collegiate Dictionary*, Tenth Edition. Springfield, MA: Merriam-Webster Incorporated, 1994.

Murray, John. *New Thoughts on Old Doctrines*. N.p.: n.p., 1918.

Whipple, Leander Edmund. *Mental Healing*. N.p.: The Metaphysical Publishing Company, 1907.

Wood, Henry. *The New Thought Simplified*. N.p.: n.p., 1902. http://corner stone.wwwhubs.com/ntbooks.htm. (Feb. 2004).

CHAPTER THREE

"A Unity Chronology." Unity School of Christianity, n.d.

The Adventure Called Unity." Unity, n.d.

"Answers to Your Questions About Unity." Unity School of Christianity, n.d.

Awbrey, Scott. "Path of Discovery." United Church of Religious Science (1987).

Braden, Charles S. *Spirits in Rebellion*.

"Divine Science Founders." Divine Science School, 2004. http://www.ds school.org/founders/index.html. (Jan. 2004).

"History of Unity." http://www.firstchurchunity.org/html/history.html. (Aug. 2004).

"The History of Unity." http://www.unitymuskegon.org/inception.htm. (Aug. 2004).

Holmes, Ernest. *The Science of Mind*.

—. *Seminar Lectures*. Georgia C. Maxwell, ed. Los Angeles: Science of Mind Publications, 1955 rev. ed.

Institute for Sociology and the History of Ideas. "The Metaphysical Movement." May 16, 2003. http://www.sociologyesoscience.com/cbooks11. html. (Apr. 2004).

James, Fannie B. and Cramer, Malinda E. "Divine Science: Its Principle and Practice." *Truth and Health* and *Divine Science and Healing*. Denver: Divine Science Church and College, 1957.

Judah, J. Stillson. *The History and Philosophy of the Metaphysical Movements in America*. Philadelphia: The Westminster Press, 1967.

Murray, John. *The Murray Course in Divine Science*. New York, Society of the Healing Christ, 1927.

"Nona L. Brooks" and "Malinda E. Cramer." http://cornerstone.wwwhubs.com/ntbooks.htm. (Jan. 2004).

Radloff, David. "New Thought." http://religiousmovements.lib.virginia.edu/nms/newthough.html. (Jan. 2004).

"Twenty Questions and Answers About Unity." Association of Unity Churches (n.d.).

"Unity History." http://www.1spirit.net. (Feb. 2004).

Unity Movement Advisory Council. "A Unity View of New Age and New Thought." Association of Unity Churches and Unity School of Christianity, n.d.

"What is Divine Science?" http://www.angelfire.com/il/divinescience/. (Jan. 2004).

Witherspoon, Thomas E. *Myrtle Fillmore*. http://sociologyesoscience.com/cbooks11.html. (Mar. 2004).

Wood, Henry. *The New Old Healing*. Boston: Lothrop, Lee & Shepard Co., 1908.

CHAPTER FOUR

Anderson, C. Alan. "Contrasting Strains of Metaphysical Idealism Contributing to New Thought." http://www.websyte.com/alan/contrast.htm. (Jan. 2004).

—. "Excerpts from *The New Thought Movement: A Link Between East and West*." Delivered at the Parliament of the World's Religions, Chicago, September 3, 1993. http://www.websyte.com/alan/parl.htm. (Jan 2004).

Berkeley, George Bishop. "A Treatise Concerning the Principles of Human Knowledge." *The Empiricists*. New York: Anchor Press/Doubleday, 1974.

Brooks, Nona L. *Mysteries*. N.p.: Divine Science Federation Int'l, 1924. Third Printing, 1977.

Descartes, Rene. "Meditations on the First Philosophy." *The Rationalists*. John Veitch, trans. New York: Doubleday & Company, Inc., 1974.

Fillmore, Charles. *Metaphysical Bible Dictionary*.

Flew, Anthony. *A Dictionary of Philosophy*. New York: Laurence Urdang Associates Ltd, 1979. St. Martin's Press, 1984.

"Free Will." http://plato.stanford.edu/entries.freewill/. (Mar 2004).

"Free Will." http://www.newadvent.org/cathen/06259a.htm#anc. (Mar 2004).

Hansen, Roger P. "The Names of God in the Old Testament." *Heart & Mind* (1993). Gospel Truths Ministries, Grand Rapids, MI.

Holmes, Ernest. *New Thought Terms.*

—. *The Science of Mind.*

Hopkins, Emma Curtis. *Scientific Christian Mental Practice.* Cornwall Bridge, CT: High Watch Fellowship, 1958.

Laughlin, Paul A. "Re-Turning East: Watering the Withered Oriental Roots of New Thought." Paper delivered to the annual Conference of the Society for the Study of Metaphysical Religion in Ft. Lauderdale, Florida. Published in the *Journal of the Society for the Study of Metaphysical Religion* (Fall 1997). http://websyte.com/unity/westerville/wuf/food/pl-ntroots.htm. (Jun2 2004).

Lawson, Agnes M. *Hints to Bible Study.* n.p.: Colorado College of Divine Science, 1920.

von Leibniz, Gottfried Wilhelm Freiherr. "Discourse on Metaphysics." *The Rationalists.* George Montgomery, trans. with rev. by Albert R. Chandler. New York: Doubleday & Company, Inc., 1974.

—. "The Monadology." *The Rationalists.* George Montgomery, trans. with rev. by Albert R. Chandler. New York: Doubleday & Company, Inc., 1974.

McGreal, Ian P., ed. *Great Thinkers of the Eastern World.* New York: Harper Collins Publishers, Inc., 1995.

"Names of God Reveal Him." http://names-of-god.com. (Feb. 2004).

Nineteenth-Century Philosophy. Patrick K. Gardner, ed. New York: The Free Press, 1969.

Plato. *Plato's Republic.* Grube, G.H.A., trans. Indianapolis: Hackett Publishing Company, 1974.

Plotinus. *The Essential Plotinus: Representative Treatises From the Enneads.* Elmer O'Brien, trans. Indianapolis: Hackett Publishing Company, Inc., 1964.

Rausch, D.A. "Realism." http://mb-soft.com/believe/txc/realism.htm. (Apr. 2004).

Russell, Bertrand. *A History of Western Philosophy.* New York: Simon & Schuster, 1945.

Sahakian, William S. *History of Philosophy.* N.p.: Barnes & Noble, Inc., 1968.

Spalding, Baird T. *Life and Teaching of the Masters of the Far East.* Vol 4. California: DeVorss & Company, 1948.

Vedanta Society of Southern California. "What is Vedanta?" http://www.vedanta.org/wiv/overview.html. (Apr. 2004).

Wozniak, Robert H. "Mind and Body: René Descartes to William James." http://serendip.brynmawr.edu/Mind/19th.html. (Mar. 2004).

CHAPTER FIVE

Anderson, C. Alan. "Contrasting Strains."

—. "Excerpts from *The New Thought Movement.*

Braden, Charles S. *Spirits in Rebellion.*

Dresser, Annetta Gertrude. *The Philosophy of P. P. Quimby With Selections from his Manuscripts and a Sketch of his Life.* Boston: Geo. H. Ellis, 1899, Third Edition. http://cornerstone.wwwhubs.com/ntbooks.htm. (Jan. 2004).

Dresser, Julius A. "The True History of Mental Science." A Lecture Delivered at the Church of the Divine Unity, Boston, Massachusetts, 1887.

Dresser, Horatio W., ed. *The Quimby Manuscripts.*

Duckworth. Julian. *Presenting Swedenborg: A Roadmap for Readers.* http://www.geocities.com/suzakico/swedenborg.html. (Apr. 2004).

Eddy, Mary Baker. "Mind Healing History." *The Christian Science Journal.* (June, 1887).

—. *Miscellaneous Writings.* http://www.endtime.org/intro/mbe. (Apr. 2004).

—. *Science and Health With Key to the Scriptures.* Boston: The First Church of Christ, Scientist, 1875. http://www.spirituality.com/dt/toc_shj.html. (Apr. 2004).

"Emma Only." http://www.desert.xpressdesigns.com/pulseemma.htm. (Mar. 2004).

Evans, Warren Felt. *The Divine Law of Cure.* Boston: H. H. Carter & Co., 1881.

—. *Esoteric Christianity and Mental Therapeutics.* Boston: H. H. Carter & Co., 1886.

—. *The Mental Cure.* Boston: H. H. Carter & Co., 1869.

Hopkins, Emma Curtis. *Scientific Christian Mental Practice.*

—. "Twelve Powers of the Soul." Excerpt from a lesson given November 18, 1894. *Bible Interpretations Manuscript 2.* Chicago: The Ministry of Truth International.

Institute for Sociology and the History of Ideas. "The Metaphysical Movement."

McCrackan, William D. "Mary Baker Eddy." *Christian Science: Its Discovery and Development.* http://www.endtime.org/intro/mbe. (Apr. 2004).

"The Mysticism of Emma Curtis Hopkins." A compilation by PeaceRiver. http://www.highwatch.org/mysticism.htm. (Feb. 2004).

Peel, Robert. *Spiritual Healing in a Scientific Age.* New York: Harper & Row, 1987.

Radloff, David. "The Church of Christ Scientist (Christian Science)." http://religiousmovements.lib.virginia.edu/nrms/chrissci.html. (Jan. 2004).

Synnestvedt, S. "About Swedenborg." *The Essential Swedenborg*. The Academy of the New Church. http://www.theheavenlydoctrines.org/about swe.htm. (Mar. 2004).

"Tenets of Swedenborgianism." http://swedenborg.org/tenets/cfm. (Mar. 2004).

"Writings of Emanuel Swedenborg." http://www.swedenborg.net. (Mar. 2004).

CHAPTER SIX
Religious History

Barlow, Jonathan. "The Five Points of Calvinism." http://reformed.org/cal vinism/. (Mar. 2004).

Barry, William. "John Calvin." Tomas Hancil, trans. *The Catholic Encyclopedia, Volume III*. Robert Appleton Company, 1908. Online Edition K. Knight, 2003. http://www.newadvent.com/cathen/03195b.htm. (Mar. 2004).

Cable, Louis W. "Slavery and the Bible." http://home.inu.net/skeptic/ slavery/html. (Jul. 2004).

"Calvin." http://www.members.aol.com/ckbloomfld. Quoted in "Heretics and Heresies." *Ingersoll's Works*, Vol. 1. (Mar. 2004).

"Calvinism." http://reformeddocs.org. (Mar. 2004).

Corner, Daniel D. "His Ashes Cry Out Against John Calvin" http://www. evangelicaloutreach.org/ashes.htm. (May 2004).

Ganss, H. G. "Martin Luther." Marie Jutras, trans. *The Catholic Encyclopedia, Volume IX*. Robert Appleton Company, 1910. Online Edition K. Knight, 2003. http://www.newadvent.com/cathen/09438b.htm. (Mar. 2004).

Harris, Mark. "Unitarian Universalist Origins: Our Historic Faith." http:// uua.org/info/origins/html

Hines, Mike. "Did God choose black people to be slaves?" http://first christian.info/default,aspx?page_id=102200213345. (Mar. 2004).

Hodges, Miles H. "Luther Precipitates the Challenge." 2002. http://new genevacenter.org/west/reformation.htm. (Mar. 2004).

—. "The Protestant Reformation (Early 1500s to Mid 1600s)." http:/ /newgenevacenter.org/west/reformation.htm. (Mar. 2004).

Holder, R. Ward, Ph.D. "John Calvin Biography." *The Internet Encyclopedia of Philosophy*. http://www.utm.edu/research/iep/c/calvin. htm. (Mar. 2004).

Hooker, Richard. "John Calvin." http://www.wsu.edu/~dee/reform/calvin. htm. (Mar. 2004).

Loewen, James W. *Lies My Teacher Told Me.* New York: The New Press, 1995.

Mendelson, Jack. *Meet the Unitarian Universalists.* UUA Pamphlet Commission Publication, USA.

Rempel, Professor Gerhard. "Martin Luther and the Reformation." http://mars.acnet.wnec.edu/~grempel/courses/wc2/lectures/luther.htm. (Mar. 2004).

"What Started the Protestant Reformation?" http://reformeddocs.org. (Mar. 2004).

"Unitarian Universalist Association Principles and Purposes." http://uua.org/aboutuua/principles.html. (Mar. 2004).

"Unitarianism." http://www.newadvent.org/cathen/15154b.htm. (Mar. 2004).

Transcendentalism

"Divinity School Address" http://www.emersoncentral.com/divaddr.htm. (Mar. 2004).

Emerson, Ralph Waldo. *Emerson's Essays.* New York: Thomas Y. Crowell Company, 1926.

—. "The Transcendentalist." A lecture read at the Masonic Temple. Boston. January, 1842.

Finseth, Ian Frederick. "Liquid Fire Within Me: Language, Self and Society in Transcendentalism and Early Evangelicalism, 1820-1860." 1995. http://eserver.org/thoreau/amertran.html. (Mar. 2004).

Lewis, Jone Johnson. "What is Transcendentalism?" http://www.transcendentalists.com/what.htm. (Mar. 2004).

Miller, Marilyn and Faux, Marian, eds. *American History Desk Reference.*

Miller, Perry. *The Transcendentalists.* Boston: Harvard University Press, 1950.

Mish, Frederick C., ed. in chief. *Merriam-Webster's.*

Reuben, Paul P. *PAL: Perspectives in American Literature, A Research and Reference Guide - An Ongoing Project.* "Early Nineteenth Century - American Transcendentalism (AT): A Brief Introduction." http://www.csustan.edu/english/reuben/pal/chap4. (Mar. 2004).

Robinson, David. "George Ripley." http://www.uua.org/uuhs/duub/articles/georgeripley.html. (Mar. 2004).

"Thoreau: Genius Ignored." Excerpt from Lucius Furius. *Genius Ignored.* http://eserver.org/16080/thoreau/ignored.html. (Mar. 2004).

Thoreau, Henry David. *Walden and Other Writings.* New York: Nelson Doubleday, Inc., 1970.

"Transcendentalism." http://www.themystica.com/mystica/articles/t/transcendentalism.html. (Mar. 2004).

Trowbridge, John Townsend. "Reminiscences of Walt Whitman." *The Atlantic Monthly* (February 1902). http://www.theatlantic.com. (Mar. 2004).

Transcendental Influences

Braden, Charles S. *Spirits in Rebellion.*

Dresser, Julius A. "The True History of Mental Science."

Moyer, Annie. "19th Century Transcendentalism and The Yoga Sutras of Patanjali: Separate Paths, Same Destination." Teacher Training Paper, January 2, 2003. http://www.sunandmoonstudios.com/transcendental.html. (Mar. 2004).

Russell, Bertrand. *A History of Western Philosophy.*

Sahakian, William S. *History of Philosophy.*

"Selections from the New England Transcendentalists." http://www.theosophy-nw.org/theosnw/reincar/re-tran.htm. (Apr. 2004).

"Transcendental Forerunners." http://www.vcu.edu/engweb/transcendentalism/roots/rootsintro.html. (Mar. 2004).

Pantheism

Anderson, C. Alan. "Excerpts from *The New Thought Movement.*"

Anderson, C. Alan and Whitehouse, Deborah G. *New Thought: A Practical American Spirituality.* New York: The Crossroad Publishing Company, 1995. http://websyte.com/alan/ntlnapt.htm. (Mar. 2004).

Flew, Anthony. *A Dictionary of Philosophy.*

Harrison, Paul. "Natural Pantheism: a spiritual approach to nature and the cosmos." http://members.aol.com/heraklit1/index htm#history. (Mar. 2004).

CHAPTER SEVEN

Braden, Charles S. *Spirits in Rebellion.*

Institute for Sociology and the History of Ideas. "The Metaphysical Movement."

Mish, Frederick C., ed. in chief. *Merriam-Webster's.*

Spiritualism

"Andrew Jackson Davis." http://famousamericans.net/andrewjacksondavis/. (Mar. 2004).

Brodeur, Dr. Claude. "New Thought in America." Societas Rosicruciana in Canada. http://sric-canada.org/newthought.html. (Mar. 2004).

Fillmore, Charles. *The Revealing Word.* Missouri: Unity School of Christianity, 1959, 1981.

Leahey, Thomas Hardy. *A History of Psychology.*

Park, T. Peter. "The Poughkeepsie Seer." http://www.anomalist.com/features/seer.html. (Mar. 2004).

Stefanidakis, Rev. Simeon. "Forerunners to Modern Spiritualism: Andrew Jackson Davis (1826-1910)." http://www.fst.org/spirit3.htm. (Mar. 2004)

Troward, Thomas. *The Edinburgh Lectures on Mental Science.* New York: Dodd, Mead and Company, 1909.

Theosophy

"The Akashic Plane." Institute for Sociology and the History of Ideas (June 7, 2003). http://sociologyesoscience.com/cbooks13.html. (Mar. 2004).

Dresser, Horatio W., ed. *The Quimby Manuscripts.*

Fillmore, Charles. *Atom Smashing Power of Mind.* http://webstyte.com/ unityatm.htm. (Jan. 2004).

"H.P. Blavatsky." http://www.theosociety.org. (Mar. 2004).

Holmes, Ernest. *New Thought Terms.*

"Some Basic Concepts of Theosophy." http://www.theosociety. org. (Mar. 2004).

"The Subtle body." Institute for Sociology and the History of Ideas (June 7, 2003). http://sociologyesoscience.com/cbooks13.html. (Mar. 2004).

"Theosophy." Institute for Sociology and the History of Ideas (June 7, 2003). http://sociologyesoscience.com/cbooks13.html. (Mar. 2004).

Troward, Thomas. *The Edinburgh Lectures.*

Rosicrucians

Brodeur, Dr. Claude. "New Thought in America."

"Ella Wheeler Wilcox (1850-1919)." http://cornerstone.wwwhubs.com/nt books. htm. (Mar. 2004).

"Rosicrucianism [1]." http://crcsite.org/rosicrucianism. (Mar. 2004).

"Rosicrucianism [2]." http://meta-religion.com/Esoterism/Rosicrucianism/ Rosicrucianism/rosicrucianism.htm. (Mar. 2004).

Stewart, Gary L. Excerpt from "Introductory Monograph of the Confraternity of the Rose Cross." http://crcsite.org/symbolism. (Mar. 2004).

Troward, Thomas. *The Edinburgh Lectures.*

Mysticism

Ahmad, Sumayya. "Mysticism Transcends Religious Definitions." April 21, 2004. http://meta-religion.com/world_religions/articles/mysticism_tran scends.htm. Originally published at http://www.dailytrojan.com/news/ 2004/04/21/News/Mysticism.Transcends.Religious.Definitions-666465.shtml. (Jul. 2004).

The Bhagavad Gita. Juan Mascaro, trans. n.p.: Penguin Books, 1962, 1986.

Brooks, Nona L. *Mysteries.*

Dilworth, James. "Emanuel Swedenborg." http://www.themystica.com/mys tica/articles/s/swedenborg_emanuel.html. (Apr. 2004).

Eckhart, Meister. *Selected Writings*. http://www.members.aol.com/heraklit 1/history.htm. (Apr. 2004).

Fillmore, Charles. *The Revealing Word.*

Holmes, Ernest. *The Science of Mind.*

Hopkins, Emma Curtis. *High Mysticism*. California: DeVorss & Co. Inc., 1974.

"The Image of the Heavenly." http://sigler.org/boehm/. (June 2004).

"Immanence." http://www.themystica.com/mystica/articles/i/immanence. html. (Apr. 2004).

James, William. *The Varieties of Religious Experience: A Study in Human Nature*. New York: Longmans, Green, & Co., 1902.

Leahey, Thomas Hardy. *A History of Psychology.*

"Mysticism." http://www.themystica.com/mystica/articles/m/mysticism.html. (June 2004).

Sahakian, William S. *History of Philosophy.*

Stace, Walter T. "Mysticism and Human Reason." . . . *and more about God.* Lewis M. Rogers and Charles H. Monson, Jr., eds. Salt Lake City, UT: University of Utah Press, 1969.

"Writings of Emanuel Swedenborg."

Kabbala

"Kabbalah." http://en.wikipedia.org/wiki.kaballah. (Apr. 2004).

"Kabbalah." http://www.themystica.com/mystica/articles/k/kabbalah.html. (Apr. 2004).

Schroeder, Gerald L. *The Hidden Face of God*. New York: The Free Press, 2001.

"The Ten Sefirot." http://www.kheper.net/topics/kabbalah/sefirot.htm. (Apr. 2004).

Troward, Thomas. *The Edinburgh Lectures.*

Hermeticism

Fillmore, Charles. *The Revealing Word.*

Hermes Trismegistus. *The Corpus Hermeticum*. http://www.hermetics.org. (May 2004).

"Hermetica." http://www.themystica.com/mystica/articles/a/below_above. html. (May 2004).

"Hermeticism." http://meta-religion.com/Esoterism/Hermeticism/hermeti cism.htm. (May 2004).

"Hermetics." http://www.geocities.com/achreus/hermetic. (May 2004).

Three Initiates. *The Kybalion*. Chicago: Yoga Publication Society, 1936, 1988.

CHAPTER EIGHT

Anderson, A. Alan and Whitehouse, Deborah G. *A Practical American Spirituality*.

Atkinson, William Walker. *The Inner Teachings of the Philosophy and Religions of India*. Chicago: Yoga Publication Society, 1908.

Braden, Charles S. *Spirits in Rebellion*.

"Christian D. Larson, Influential early New Thought leader." http://corner stone.wwwhubs.com/ntbooks.htm. (Mar. 2004).

Dilworth, James. "Emanuel Swedenborg."

Drummond, Henry. *Natural Law in the Spiritual World*.

"Henry Drummond (1851-1897)." http://cornerstone.wwwhubs.com/ntbooks .htm. (Mar. 2004).

Holmes, Ernest. "Ernest Holmes Speaks . . . ." A talk given at the Wiltern Theatre, July 4, 1937. http://cornerstone.wwwhubs.com/ntbooks.htm. (Mar. 2004).

—. "The Final Sermon by the Sea." http://cornerstone.wwwhubs.com/nt books. htm. (Mar. 2004).

—. "Law of Our Lives: The Impersonal Face of God." *Creative Mind*. http://cornerstone.wwwhubs.com/ntbooks.htm. (Mar. 2004).

—. *The Science of Mind*.

—. *Seminar Lectures*.

—. *This Thing Called You*. New York: Jeremy P. Tarcher, 1948. Putnam edition, 1997.

James, William. *The Varieties of Religious Experience*.

Larson, Christian D. *Your Forces and How to Use Them*. 1912. http:// cornerstone.wwwhubs.com/ntbooks.htm. (Mar. 2004).

Leahey, Thomas Hardy. *A History of Psychology*.

Nicoll, W. Robertson. *A Memorial Sketch of Henry Drummond*. http://corner stone.wwwhubs.com/ntbooks.htm. (Mar. 2004).

Nineteenth-Century Philosophy. Patrick K. Gardner, ed.

"Ralph Waldo Trine." http://cornerstone.wwwhubs.com/ntbooks.htm. (Mar. 2004)

Russell, Bertrand. *A History of Western Philosophy*.

Sahakian, William S. *History of Philosophy*.

Suzuki, D.T., Fromm, Eric and DeMartino, R. *Zen Buddhism and Psychoanalysis*. New York: Grove Press, Inc., 1960.

Trine, Ralph Waldo. *Character-Building Thought Power*. http://cornerstone. wwwhubs.com/ntbooks.htm. (Mar. 2004).

—. *In Tune with the Infinite*. London: George Bell & Son, 1907. http:// cornerstone.wwwhubs.com/ntbooks.htm. (Mar. 2004).

—. *What All The World's A-Seeking.* http://cornerstone.wwwhubs.com/nt
books.htm. (Mar. 2004).

"Thomas Troward, Early Teacher of Mental Science." http://website.line
one.net/~thomastroward/. (Mar. 2004).

Troward, Thomas. *The Edinburgh Lectures.*

"William Walker Atkinson (1862-1932)." http://cornerstone.wwwhubs.com/
ntbooks.htm. (Apr. 2004).

CHAPTER NINE

Ayto, John. *Dictionary of Word Origins.* New York: Arcade Publishing,
Inc., 1990.

Brooks, Nona L. *Mysteries.*

Cady, Harriet Emilie. *How I Used Truth.* Kansas City: Unity School of
Christianity, 1916. http://cornerstone.wwwhubs.com/ntbooks.htm.
(Jan. 2004).

Dresser, Horatio W., ed. *The Quimby Manuscripts.*

Eddy, Mary Baker. *Science and Health With Key to the Scriptures.*

Evans, Warren Felt. *The Mental Cure.*

Fillmore, Charles. *Atom Smashing Power of Mind.*

—. *Christian Healing.*

—. *Metaphysical Bible Dictionary.*

—. *Teach Us to Pray.* http://tsmacademy.tsmj.org/library/. (Jan. 2004).

—. *Talks on Truth.* http://webstyte.com/unity/tot.htm. (Jan. 2004).

Holmes, Ernest. "The Final Sermon by the Sea."

—. *The Science of Mind.*

The Holy Order of Mans. "The Essenes." *Book of the Master Jesus Vol. I.*
Jesus of Nazareth. http://www.holyorderofmans.org/Jesus-of-Nazareth/
30-essenes. htm. (July 2004).

Hopkins, Emma Curtis. *Scientific Christian Mental Practice.*

James, Fannie. *Dawning Truth.* N.p.: Divine Science Federation International. Third Printing, 1968.

James, William. *The Varieties of Religious Experience.*

Lawson, Agnes M. *Hints to Bible Study.*

Leibniz, Gottfried von. "Discourse on Metaphysics."

McCrackan, William D. "Mary Baker Eddy."

Morrisson, James L. "Doing the Things Jesus Did." http://scriptureinsights.
com. (June 2004).

Murray, John. *New Thoughts on Old Doctrines.*

Trine, Ralph Waldo. *In Tune with the Infinite.*

Troward, Thomas. *The Edinburgh Lectures.*

Walker, Ethan III. *The Mystic Christ.* http://www.jesus-christ.ws. (July 2004).

Wood, Henry. *The New Thought Simplified.*

CHAPTER TEN
Ancient History
"Ancient China Timeline." http://www.bible-history.com. (Apr. 2004).

"Ancient Egypt Timeline." http://www.homepage.powerup.com. (Apr. 2004).

"Ancient India Timeline." http://www.eawc.evensville.edu. (Apr. 2004).

Elst, Koehraad. *Update on the Aryan Invasion Debate.* New Delhi: n.p., n.d. http://bharatvani.org/books/ait/ch22.htm. (July 2004).

Frawley, David. The Myth of the Aryan Invasion of India. http://www.hindu net.org/alt_hindu/1995_Jul_2/msg00087.html. (June 2004).

"The GBM Timeline of Western Civilization (Antiquity-1648)." http://www. a-ten.com. (Apr. 2004).

"Timelines of Buddhist History." http://www.buddhanet.net/e-learning/his tory/timelines.htm. (Apr. 2004).

"Time Line of Greek History and Literature." http://web.uvic.ca; http://www. yasou.org. (Apr. 2004).

"World Timeline." http://wwnorton.com. (Apr. 2004).

Hinduism
The Bhagavad Gita. Juan Mascaro, trans.

"Hinduism." http://meta-religion.com/Hinduism/hinduism.htm. (Apr. 2004).

Mueller, Max, ed. *The Upanishads, The Sacred Books of the East.* 50 vols. Oxford: Clarendon Press, 1879-1910. Reprinted in Alfred J. Andrea and James H. Overfield, eds., *The Human Record: Sources of Global History.* Third ed., Vol. 1. New York: Houghton Mifflin, 1998.

Pandurangi, Prof. K.T. "Essentials of the Upanishads." http://www.dvaita. org. (Apr. 2004).

"Vedanta." http://www.encarta.msn.com. (Apr. 2004).

Vedanta Society of Southern California. "What is Vedanta?"

Buddhism
Boere, Dr. C. George. "The Basics of Buddhist Wisdom." http://meta-reli gion.net/world_religions/Buddhism/basics_of_buddhist_wisdom.htm (Apr. 2004).

Burtt, Edwin A., ed. *The Teachings of the Compassionate Buddha.* New York: Mentor Books, 1955.

Conze, Edward. *Buddhism: Its Essence and Development.* New York: Philosophical Library, 1951.

de Bary, William Theodore, ed. *The Buddhist Tradition in India, China and Japan.* New York: Random House, 1969.

Moyer, Annie. "19th Century Transcendentalism and The Yoga Sutras of Patanjali: Separate Paths, Same Destination."

Smith, Huston. *The Religions of Man*. New York: Harper & Row, 1964, 1986.

Walpola, Sri Rahula. *What the Buddha Taught*. New York: Grove Weidenfeld, 1974.

Woodward, F.L. *Some Sayings of the Buddha*. London: Oxford University Press, 1939.

Reincarnation

Fillmore, Charles. *Dynamics For Living*. http://webstyte.com/unity/dtl.htm. (Jan. 2004).

"The Gospel of the Holy Twelve." Rev. Gideon Jasper Ouseley, trans. http://members.aol.com/esseneinfo/essenehome.html. (July 2004).

"The Gospel of (According To) Thomas." Wm van den Dungen, trans. Antwerp: 1997, 2002. http://sofiatopia.org. (June 2004).

Gruber, Elmar R. and Kersten, Holger. *The Original Jesus*. Rockport, MA: Element Books, 1995.

Holmes, Ernest. *The Science of Mind*.

"Selections from the New England Transcendentalists." http://www.theosophy-nw.org/theosnw/reincar/re-tran.htm. (Apr. 2004).

Yu-lan, Fung. *A Short History of Chinese Philosophy*. New York: The MacMillan Company, 1958.

SriAurobindo

McGreal, Ian P., ed. *Great Thinkers of the Eastern World*.

"Sri Aurobindo." http://meta-religion.com/Hinduism/sri_aurobindo.htm. (Jul. 2004)

CHAPTER ELEVEN

Taoism

Chuang Tzu. *Chuang Tzu Basic Writings*. Burton Watson, trans. New York: Columbia University Press, 1964.

Cleary, Thomas. *The Essential Tao*. New York: HarperCollins, 1991.

I Ching. Rudolf Ritsema and Stephen Karcher, trans. Rockport, MA: Element, Inc., 1994.

Lao Tzu. *Tao Te Ching*. Lau, D. C., ed. Harmondsworth, Middlesex, England: Penguin Classics, 1963.

Yu-lan, Fung. *A Short History of Chinese Philosophy*.

Zen Buddhism

Suzuki, D.T. *An Introduction to Zen Buddhism*. New York: Grove Press, Inc., 1964.

Suzuki, D.T., Fromm, Eric and DeMartino, R. *Zen Buddhism and Psycho-analysis*.

Walker, Evan Harris. *The Physics of Consciousness*. New York: Perseus Books, 2000.

Watts, Alan W. *The Way of Zen*. New York: Vintage Books, 1957.

Paradox

The Bhagavad Gita. Juan Mascaro, trans.

Huxley, Aldous. *The Perennial Philosophy*.

Lao Tzu. *Tao Te Ching*. Lau, D. C., ed.

Stace, Walter T. "Mysticism and Human Reason."

Yu-lan, Fung. *A Short History of Chinese Philosophy*.

CHAPTER TWELVE

Allen, Abel Leighton. *The Message of New Thought*.

Allogenes. *Allogenes*. John D Turner and Orval S. Wintermute, trans. The Nag Hammadi Library. http://www.gnosis.org/allogenes/got/html. (Aug. 2004).

Borg, Marcus ed. *Jesus and Buddha: The Parallel Sayings*. n.p.: Ulysses Press. http://www.beliefnet.com/story/10/story_1056_1.html. (June 2004).

Davies, Vicki. "Gnosticism." http://www.sd.com.au/db/gnostic.html. Quoted in http://religiousmovements.lib.virginia.edu/nms/gnosticism.html. (Aug. 2004)

"Dead Sea Scrolls." http://home.flash.net/~hoselton/deadsea/deadsea.htm. (July 2004).

Flew, Anthony. *A Dictionary of Philosophy*.

"The Gnostic Gospels." http://www.earlychristianwritings.com. (May 2004).

"Gnosticism." http://www.themystica.com/mystica/articles/g/gnosticism. html. (May 2004).

"Gnosticism description and history." http://meta-religion.com/Esoterism/ Gnosticism/gnosticism.htm. (May 2004).

"The Gospel of the Holy Twelve." Rev. Gideon Jasper Ouseley, trans.

"The Gospel of (According To) Thomas." Wm van den Dungen, trans.

"The Gospel of Thomas" and "The Gospel of Eve." http://www.members. aol.com/ heraklit1/history.htm. (May 2004).

"The Gospel of Truth." Robert M. Grant, trans. The Nag Hammadi Library. http://www.gnosis.org/naghamm/got/html. (Aug. 2004).

Hoeller, Stephan A. (Tau Stephanus, Gnostic Bishop). "The Gnostic World View: A Brief Summary of Gnosticism." http://www.gnosis.org/ gnintro.htm. (May 2004).

The Holy Order of Mans. "The Essenes."

Kiefert. William C. "Gnostic Christianity: The Secret Teachings of Jesus." February 2, 2001. http://www.gnosticchristianity.com. (May 2004).

Mizrach, Steve. "The Dead Sea Scrolls Controversy." http://www.dream scape.com/morgana/carme.htm. (July 2004).

The Lost Years of Jesus: The Life of Saint Issa. Nicolas Notovitch, trans. http://www.reluctant-messenger.com/issa.htm. (July 2004).

Pagels, Elaine. *Beyond Belief: The Secret Gospel of Thomas.* New York: Random House, 2003.

Sahakian, William S. *History of Philosophy.*

Walker, Ethan III. *The Mystic Christ.*

"World Scripture: A Comparative Anthology of Sacred Texts." Dr. Andrew Wilson, ed. International Religious Foundation, 1991. http://www. unification.net/ws/. (Aug,. 2004)

CHAPTER THIRTEEN

Allen, Abel Leighton. *The Message of New Thought.*

Atkinson, William Walker. *Practical Mental Influence.* Chicago: The Advanced Thought Publishing Co., 1908. http://cornerstone.wwwhubs. com/ntbooks. htm. (Feb. 2004).

—. *Thought Vibration or the Law of Attraction in the Thought World.* Chicago: The New Thought Publishing Co., 1906. http://cornerstone. wwwhubs.com/ntbooks.htm. (May 2004).

"Brain Waves and Consciousness." http://web-us.com/thescience.htm. (Sept. 2004).

Brooks, Nona L. *Mysteries.*

Capra, Fritjof. *The Tao of Physics* New York: Bantam Books, 1975, 1983, 1991.

Chopra, Deepak. *The Seven Spiritual Laws of Success.* Amber Allen/New World Library, 1994 (Audio tape).

Chuang Tzu. *Chuang Tzu Basic Writings.* Burton Watson, trans.

Dresser, Julius A. "The True History of Mental Science."

Drummond, Henry. *The Changed Life.* http://cornerstone.wwwhubs.com/nt books. htm. (Mar. 2004).

—. *Natural Law in the Spiritual World.*

Fillmore, Charles. *Jesus Christ Heals.* http://webstyte.com/unity/jch.htm. (Jan. 2004).

Fox, Emmet. *Make Your Life Worthwhile.* N.p.: Harper & Row, 1942, 1943, 1944, 1945, 1946.

—. *To Him That Hath.* http://www.absolute1.net/emmet_fox.html. (May 2004).

Hefner, Alan G. "The Laws of Magic." http://www.themystica.com/mystica/articles/l/laws_of_magic.html. (Apr. 2004).

Hill, Napoleon. *Think and Grow Rich*. New York: Ballantine Books, 1937, 1987.

Holmes, Ernest. *Science of Mind*.

James, William. *The Varieties of Religious Experience*.

Jones, Rev. Marie. "What is Metaphysics?" Jan 23 2001. http://suite101.com/article.clm/10213/58174. (Apr. 2004).

Judah, J. Stillson. *The History and Philosophy of the Metaphysical Movements in America*.

Murphy, Joseph. "The Miraculous Law of Healing." *The Amazing Laws of Cosmic Mind Power*. http://website.lineone.net/~cornerstone/murphy1.htm. (Apr. 2004).

Trine, Ralph Waldo. *In Tune with the Infinite*.

Troward, Thomas. *The Edinburgh Lectures*.

Wood, Henry. *The New Old Healing*.

CHAPTER FOURTEEN
The Perennial Philosophy

Ayto, John. *Dictionary of Word Origins*.

"Basic Teachings of Bahá'u'lláh." http://www.bahai.org/article-1-2-0-2.html. (Sept. 2004).

Chuang Tzu. *Chuang Tzu Basic Writings*.

"The Gospel of (According To) Thomas." Wm van den Dungen, trans.

G.S. Kirk, J.E. Raven, M. Schofield. *The Presocratic Philosophers*. Cambridge: Cambridge University Press, 1957, 1983.

Huxley, Aldous. *The Perennial Philosophy*.

James, William. *The Varieties of Religious Experience*.

Lao Tzu. *Tao Te Ching*. Lau, D. C., ed.

Leahey, Thomas Hardy. *A History of Psychology*.

von Leibniz, Gottfried. "Discourse on Metaphysics."

McMurrin, Sterling M. "Is God a Person?" . . . *and more about God*. Lewis M. Rogers and Charles H. Monson, Jr., eds. Salt Lake City: University of Utah Press, 1969.

Richard T. Nolan. "An Interpretation of Mystical Religion *or Perennial Philosophy*" and "Core Essentials of Perennial Philosophy." http://www.philosophy.religion.com/perennial/. (July 2004).

Pagels, Elaine. *Beyond Belief*.

"The Perennial Philosophy: the Evidence." http://www.livereal.com/spiritual_arena/perennial_philosophy_evidence./htm. (July 2004).

Plotinus. *The Essential Plotinus*.

Richardson, Robert D. "Emerson and the Perennial Philosophy." http://www.firstparish.org/richardson.html. (July 2004).

Russell, Bertrand. *A History of Western Philosophy.*

Sahakian, William S. *History of Philosophy.*

"The Secret Book of James." Ron Cameron, trans. http://www.earlychristianwritings.com/secretjames.html. (Aug. 2004).

"The Seven Valleys of Bahá'u'lláh." http://www.bahai.org/article-1-3-2-10.html. (Sept. 2004).

Smith, Huston. *The Religions of Man.*

Spinoza, Benedict de. "The Ethics." *The Rationalists.* R.H.M. Elwes, trans. New York: Doubleday & Company, Inc., 1974.

Stace, Walter T. "Mysticism and Human Reason."

Vedanta Society of Southern California. "What is Vedanta?"

Walker, Evan Harris. *The Physics of Consciousness.*

Science and the Perennial Philosophy

Anderson, A. Alan and Whitehouse, Deborah G. *A Practical American Spirituality.*

"Brain Waves and Consciousness." http://web-us.com/thescience.htm. (Sept. 2004).

Capra, Fritjof. *The Tao of Physics.*

Greene, Brian. *The Elegant Universe.* New York: W.W. Norton & Company, 1999.

Gribbin, John. *Schrodinger's Kittens and the Search for Reality.* New York: Little, Brown & Company, 1995.

Harrison, David M. "Elementary Particle Physics." http://www.upscale.utoronto.ca/. (July 2004).

Hawking, Stephen. *The Universe in a Nutshell.* New York: Bantam Books, 2001.

"Heisenberg Uncertainty Principle." http://www.aip.org/history/heisenberg. (July 2004).

Lemley, Brad. "The Wizard of Physics." An interview with Fred Alan Wolf. *New Age Journal* (May/June 97).

Schroeder, Gerald L. *The Hidden Face of God.*

Sharpe, Kevin J. "Mysticism in Physics." http://www.ksharpe.com. (July 2004).

"Stephen Hawking's God." http://www.pbs.org/faithandreason/intro/cosmo haw-frame.html. (July 2004).

"Superstrings." http://www.pbs.org/wnet/hawking/strange. (July 2004).

"The Elegant Universe." http://www.pbs.org/wgbh/nova. (July 2004).

Walker, Evan Harris. *The Physics of Consciousness.*

CHURCH HEADQUARTERS

Divine Science
Divine Science Federation International
3617 Wyoming Street
St. Louis, MO 63116
(800) 644-9680
http://www.divinesciencefederation.org

Religious Science
Religious Science International
P.O. Box 2152
Spokane, WA 99210-2152
(509) 624-7000
(800) 662-1348
http://www.rsintl.org

United Church of Religious Science
2600 W. Magnolia Blvd
Burbank, CA 91505
(818) 526-7757
http://www.religiousscience.org

Unity
Unity School of Christianity
1901 NW Blue Parkway
Unity Village, MO 64065-0001
(816) 524-3550
http://www.unityworldhq.org

INDEX

ABOUT THE AUTHOR

Sherry was born and raised in the Salt Lake Valley and has spent her adult years in various western states.

Returning to college after her divorce, she discovered an intrigue with Astronomy and earned an Associates Degree in General Science before pursuing a Bachelor's Degree in Physics for long enough to discover that her fascination with space was more philosophical than physical. And being in the midst of a quest for truth, she switched her major to Philosophy. Upon graduating with baccalaureate degrees in Philosophy and Psychology, and minors in Physics and Mathematics, she realized she had barely scratched the surface and so continued on with her studies. She received an M.S. in Philosophy for which she wrote a thesis entitled *The Psychology of the Tao*.

That was twelve years ago. Since then, she has broadened her quest to include forays into various metaphysical methodologies and spent almost five years immersed in the healing energies of Hawaii. She currently resides amidst the magnificent mountains in Park City, Utah.